"The Total Parish Manual by veteran pastor, Father William J. Bausch, is perhaps the finest pastoral manual of the decade. Grounded on a firm and clear theology of parish, the book offers practical advice on just about every aspect of pastoral work.

"It also offers, beside conclusions based on his experience, a great deal of flexibility to apply the material to the needs of different parish situations."

Msgr. Charles Dollen
The Priest Magazine

"None of Bausch's books could be written in an ivory tower but especially this one: his most practical. You will be impressed by the creative, imaginative and effective ministry being done by the pastor and people of St. Mary's. But take note of one sentence in the introduction: 'Do what you can, adapt what you may, and save what you will for a better day.' That will save you from drowning in a sea of brilliant ideas."

Rev. Frank J. McNulty, Pastor
Our Lady of the Blessed Sacrament Parish
Roseland, NJ

"Those in parish ministry are sometimes divided into the visionaries and the practical ministers. Father William Bausch regularly defies these categories. This book, like most of his books, is nothing if not practical, offering very specific ways to organize and carry out an enormous range of practices and programs. And the vision is obvious: a parish in which nothing of human concern is beyond its interest and in which anyone can take initiative and all should share responsibility.

"This book spells out the vision in terms that are easily understood and always suggestive. Father Bausch would be the first to acknowledge that the book reflects his experience as pastor of a large, middle-class parish and that its ideas will be most beneficial to similar situations elsewhere. But any parish, whatever the situation of its people, will find in it examples of pastoral imagination that they can adopt."

The Rev. Philip J. Murnion
National Pastoral Life Center

"Bausch provides a stunning array of ideas—programs, strategies, approaches, styles—all 'tested' in his own parish, St. Mary's in Colts Neck, New Jersey. The content is eminently concrete, right down to the actual texts of letters, announcements, and such. Lists of other resources, amazingly rich and diverse, also make this a valuable reference work. And all this wealth is presented in a candid and chatty style. Imagine sharing not only the ideas that worked, but also those that didn't, but might for you!

"More than a third of the volume is devoted to liturgical suggestions, often in great detail. At first this surprised me. Many ministers, including Bausch himself, would argue that parish is much more. But the fact that the majority of parishioners only encounter the parish at weekend liturgies, and Bausch's intentionally chosen focus on spirituality, justify the emphasis. In any case, other areas of parish life and organization also get helpful consideration.

"Not everyone will applaud every one of Bausch's initiatives. But his courage and his unwavering commitment to the people and their needs offer an inspiring model for pastoral leadership."

Timothy E. O'Connell
Institute of Pastoral Studies
Loyola University Chicago

"Ideas, ideas, and more ideas, that's what this book is all about. My suggestion to a parish would be to take each chapter, make a list of all the ideas contained in that chapter, pass the list around to the staff, council, and parish leaders and ask them, 'How many of these do you think we could try out in our parish?' That is how practical this book is and how useful it can be for a modern Catholic parish.

"These are not ideas that come out of someone's fanciful imagination, but ones that have been tried out, refined, adapted and applied to concrete needs and situations. There is even a chapter called 'Parish Potpourri' that includes ideas that worked for a while but have fallen by the wayside. Some of these, as the author mentions, may be resurrected at another time. They are still good ideas but the timing is off or the situation has changed.

"That's the beauty of this book. It provides a wealth of pastoral ideas. It's up to each parish to pick and choose which options or suggestions will work in this situation or at this time. Keep the rest on file. There may be a time when one of these ideas, which sounds farfetched or impossible at the moment, may be just the answer you are looking for in the future as issues and approaches change.

"Put this book to use, in other words. Underline, make lists, highlight and star, pass it around, try out a few of the ideas and see how people react. It's full of wise insights and practical applications just waiting to be tried."

Thomas Sweetser, SJ
Co-Director, Pastoral Consultants

WILLIAM J. BAUSCH

The TOTAL PARISH MANUAL

Everything You Need to Empower Your Faith Community

XXIII
TWENTY-THIRD PUBLICATIONS
Mystic, CT 06355

Acknowledgments

I wish to thank Sharon Sturchio for proofreading, and especially Kathy Mannix whose naturally sharp eye and sense of grammar and balance aided in keeping the manuscript within the realm of acceptability. I especially wish to thank my editor, John van Bemmel, who tackled with his customary care and diligence the tedious and difficult task of aligning the Parish Papers and text and guided the manuscript to its final form.

The art that appears on the following pages is by Steve Erspamer, S.M., and is re-printed by permission of the publisher, Liturgy Training Publications. It ap-peared originally in *Clip Art for Year A,* © 1992 Archdiocese of Chicago: 3, 13, 14, 16, 18, 19, 23, 28, 31, 42, 46, 49, 50, 52, 55, 58, 60, 62, 66, 74, 85, 86, 88, 97, 99, 100, 114, 118, 131, 137, 148, 152, 163, 170.

The art that appears on the following pages is printed from *ClickArt: Christian Illustrations* by permission of T/Maker Company, Mountain View, California, © 1993: 15, 17, 27, 35, 37, 38, 68, 77, 91, 107, 134, 146, 174, 186, 208, 210, 211, 214, 216, 221, 239, 243, 244, 246, 248, 291, 292, 309.

Twenty-Third Publications
185 Willow Street
P.O. Box 180
Mystic, CT 06355
(203) 536-2611
800-321-0411

ISBN 0-89622-607-7
Library of Congress Catalog Card Number 94-60340
Printed in the U.S.A.

Dedication

To the people of St. Mary's,
my family for the past twenty-two years,
especially the pioneers
who bravely grabbed the vision and ran with it.

Contents

Part IV: Planning

Part V: Sowing Seeds

Part VI: Rhythms & Reflections

Part VII: Parish Papers

Introduction

Two fellows, Murphy and Clancy, were walking past the church when Murphy said, "You know, I haven't been to confession for a while. I think I'll go in and get absolution." So Murphy went in to the confessional and acknowledged having his way with a woman.

"I know you by your voice, Murphy, and this is not the first time this has happened," said the priest. "I want to know the woman's name."

"It's not proper you should ask," said Murphy, "and I'll not be telling you!"

"If you want absolution, you'll be telling me. Was it O'Reilly's sister?" Murphy refused to answer.

"I'll ask again, was it the widow Harrington?" Again Murphy wouldn't reply.

"One more time I'll ask: Was it the Flannagan girl?"

"For the third time I'll not be telling you,"said Murphy.

"Then you'll get no absolution from me. Out with you!"

His friend Clancy was waiting outside. "Well, did you get absolution?" he asked.

"No, " said Murphy sadly, but then he brightened up and said with a smile, "but I got three good leads!"

Origin

And that about describes the gist of this book, or rather, this manual. It's a work of "three good leads," a work that is part recipe, part comment, part description, part resources. It need not be read from the first to the last page because, like any household guide, to plumbing for example, you can skip to your subject of interest in any of its seven parts.

The origin of this manual is threefold: 1) Over the years people from everywhere, prompted by my other books, would write asking about this or that ministry, this or that project. After so many requests we decided to put together a homemade booklet of standard 8 1/2" x 11" size, of various explanations. We had a printer run off 1500 copies and they were gone within two years. And we just put aside the thought of printing more. 2) Then, in 1989, my book *The Hands-On Parish: Reflections and Suggestions for Fostering Community* (Mystic, Conn.: Twenty-Third Publications) came out, and this prompted more inquiries about how do you do this or that. 3) For many years I have given workshops on the parish, but about a half dozen years ago, after a brief sabbatical, I resolved not to do this any more (except at the parish itself; I do hold a three-day workshop here every September), pleading—besides creeping old age—a matter of simple justice to be available to the people, since I have been and remain the only priest in the parish.

This publication, then, is a reaction to these three factors. For those who ask for information or workshops I can now refer them to this manual. Necessarily there are overlaps from previous books, but there is in this volume much more material, explanations, descriptions, and resources.

The usual format is to name the topic, give some theological and (opinionated) pastoral comments, describe what we do and how we approach the topic, provide some detailed procedures for implementation and list some resources. Thus, this really *is* a manual, a hands-on, how-to book. And it's a labor in that it requires a response, some work, and a fair amount of imagination.

A Mind Set

The best way to approach this manual is with pretense. Forget the finances, forget the lack of personnel or volunteers, forget the shortage of resources; yes, even forget the lack of progressive leadership. (We'll talk about these in the another chapter.) Just pretend that, if you had your wishes, what could you do to make the parish alive, creative, involved, and the very sign of Christ among us? How could all that evangelization effort to bring people back home be effective because "home" is a place worth coming to? Frustration or despair because your parish is dead or near dead, or envy because your parish doesn't have nearly half the things you'll read in this manual, is a waste of time. Do what you can, adopt what you may, and save what you will for a better day.

Of course, all this supposes that what you find here is acceptable, inviting, creative, perhaps daring. You may find that none of these descriptives apply. Or worse, you may find shallowness, mediocrity (reminds me of W. Somerset Maugham's quip: "Only the mediocre are always at their best."), self-serving pride, or a whiff of heterodoxy.

The truth is, you may be right. It's a fearful thing to share your activities, plans, and ministries. You're plunged into a deep humility when you realize how much more creative other parishes are, how much more basic and effective, how much you have to

learn from them. You're plunged into dumb-struck prayer and silence when you observe parishes and staff dealing with poverty, drugs, AIDS, and perhaps as many as 14 languages. There is no room to crow as you stand in awe of the heroism of the inner-city staff, the compassion of the ghetto church, and the fidelity of the minister who literally has nowhere to lay his or her head.

Still, there is room to share experience. So we share what we have found works and share it with the knowledge that if others have much to teach us, still others have much to learn. It is therefore with a sense of humility that we offer this manual. It is with a sense of the love of parish life that we offer these "three good leads."

It will be evident that I have used material primarily from my parish and therefore you will find St. Mary's and my name frequently in the examples. Rather than make up fictitious or generic names, I thought it best to use actual examples from actual places and events, but I apologize for the repetition and name-dropping. Nor did I make any distinctions, but throughout I used the term "pastor" without qualification, even though I am aware that nearly 12% of parishes among the 19,000-plus in the United States are "priestless." The term refers to any parish leader whoever he or she might be.

The table of contents tells it all. The first three chapters on the parish and getting collaborators have a little more theology in them, but that's because they more or less lay the groundwork for the rest that follows, although there is a good deal of everyday matters in them too. After these chapters, the rest qualify as material for practical assessment and implementation as befits a workbook called simply, *The Total Parish Manual*.

Beginning on page 187 is an assortment—called Parish Papers—of fliers, letters, and documents, which have been used at St. Mary's, that you are free to adapt or duplicate for your own use.

Be it noted also that this manual is particular; that is, I have not directly addressed the general issues and crises facing the church at large, but those larger issues—increasing lay participation and lay parish leadership, declining numbers of priests and seminarians, increasing ethnic and cultural diversity, the globalization of communications, the influence of the spirituality-seeking but organization-distrusting baby boomers—are having an enormous impact on our lives, on our parishes, and we would do well to attend to them.

See, in this regard, the four-part series "Searching Its Soul: The U.S. Catholic Church" in the *New York Times*, May 29 to June 1, 1994 issues; also Robert Schreiter's address to the National Federation of Priests Councils, "Influences on Future Ministry, *Origins*, May 26, 1994.

Note that each chapter begins and ends with a story, some of them, most of them, humorous. Life's too tough to be serious all the time, and it's good for Christ's disciples to lighten up a bit.

Finally, I dearly want to call attention to many excellent parishes in our country, parishes with gifts, with great leadership, with much to teach us all. Centers like the National Pastoral Life Center (299 Elizabeth St., New York City, NY 10012) can put us in touch with such parishes. Perhaps we could go visit them to observe and learn. There's the splendid document called *The Ten Essentials of Parish Life* (in English and Spanish) put out by the Diocesan Pastoral Council of the diocese of Oakland, California, that's worth looking at.

A few years ago the *National Catholic Reporter* asked subscribers to write in what's good about their parishes or parishes they knew. The response was overwhelming. Lots of letters, lots of positive words, lots of affection for this phenomenon we call the parish.

Parish Basics

Chapter 1

The Parish

"It must be said, although it is patent to anybody who lives a Catholic life, the parish is the Catholic Church and the neglect of parish and the parochial school both by our church leaders, and by our intellectuals, or would-be intellectuals, is blind folly."

—Andrew Greeley

Importance

For most people the parish is what they identify as "the church." Most people don't care what the Vatican does, or the pope (he's popular with an 89% approval rating, but not his teaching. In short, people love the messenger but not the message), or the bishop. They're important, make good copy, but they're remote. The average Catholic's and non-Catholic's experience of what they think the church is about is relayed through the local parish. Here the pastor is more significant than the pope, the sister than the cardinal, and the secretary than the bishop. I once wrote that the parish

is the first ecclesiastical hand that rocks the organized religious cradle. . . .the simple arithmetic is that before any human being gets to meet his or her chaplain, campus minister, retreat master, or tribunal official, that individual first has to pass through the influence of the local parish community. . . . [People] will enter into the mysterious rhythms of birth, marriage, sickness and death vis-à-vis the parish. The impression that the parish community makes at these archetypal

times will be lasting and often will be a critical factor in the subconscious appreciation of the church's mission. For all so involved, Catholic and non-Catholic alike, the parish will form a lasting impression of what they think 'the church' is all about (*The Christian Parish*).

These words are still true. The parish is important. Belatedly, the United States bishops agree. In their fine social justice pastoral, *Communities of Salt and Light* issued on November 17, 1993, the opening paragraph reads:

The parish is where the church lives. Parishes are communities of faith, of action, and of hope. They are where the gospel is proclaimed and celebrated, where believers are formed and sent to renew the earth. Parishes are the place where God's people meet Jesus in word and sacrament and come in touch with the source of the church's life.

That's high praise from the bishops who, in former days, took the parish for granted and often considered parishes as minor

7

distractions, whose philosophy was that any warm body could pastor a parish while the so-called gifted and promising clergy were saved for the "better" and "higher" administrative posts. Now they realize how vital and critical the parish is in the life of the church.

And, though modified, it's here to stay. I've read that the small base communities (more about this later) will eventually replace the large parish. I don't believe that for a moment. They will enrich the parish but not replace it. Besides, for the most part people really do love their parishes; and, if they don't, well, these days they can legally parish-hop until they find one they do like. The best way to discover a good parish is not to ask the pastor about it or read the parish mission statement, but to ask the everyday people who go there and let them relay the spirit of the place as it translates into everyday living.

The Corporation Model

Although parishes differ, they are surprisingly the same everywhere. Well, maybe it's not so surprising. Missionary Vincent Donovan gives us a clue to that sameness. He has remarked how much the church has copied the Industrial Revolution model. That model, he maintains, has four characteristics—and so has the church:

1. Maximization. The Industrial Revolution spawned large buildings and plants with the ability to manufacture interchangeable parts, all overseen by a president or founder or board of directors. We can see the church parallel in its large dioceses, the curia, and the ease with which the pope can appoint a man from Massachusetts as bishop of Mississippi

without any regard for the traditions, customs, and history of these places.

2. Standardization. Industry made standard parts, erected standard plants (note how all gas stations look alike) and produced standard personnel. In the church, notice sacramental preparation. All children all over the planet must make First Communion at the age of seven regardless of maturity, preparation, or background. Seminaries are the same throughout the globe. Ever notice how all priests, from whatever country, talk and act and even look alike? The seminaries soon discard anyone below the standard. And, of course, they also discard anyone above it.

3. Centralization. Industry has central headquarters that issues policies and decisions. The church has the Vatican, which does the same. In what is a very new, very recent twist, the pope now appoints all bishops all over the world. Historically, bishops at various times were appointed by the local community, princes, emperors, and so on.

4. Specialization. Industry has its specialists, trouble shooters, lawyers, and accountants. The church has its theologians, spiritual directors, curia, and chancery officials. The laity have accordingly learned to distrust their own spiritual and human experiences as revelatory of God in their lives without the scrutiny and approval of the expert.

There's a nice lesson regarding this last point from Ursula Le Guin. In her book *Dancing at the Edge of the World* (New York: HarperCollins, 1990), she hypothesizes a spaceship coming and the captain saying, "We have room for one passenger; will you spare us a single human being, so that we may converse at leisure during the long trip back . . . and learn from an exemplary person the nature of the race?" She says we would ship off a fine, bright, brave young man, highly educated, at his physical peak. But she would not. No, she would not even pick a young woman. She writes:

> I would . . . go down to the local Woolworth's, or the local village market-place, and pick an old woman, over sixty, from behind the costume jewelry counter or the betel-nut booth. . . . She has worked hard at small, unimportant jobs all her life, jobs like cooking, cleaning, bringing up kids, selling little objects of adornment or pleasure to other people. She was a virgin once, a long time ago, and then a sexually potent fertile female, and then went through menopause. She has given birth several times and faced death several times—the same times. She is facing the final birth/death a little more nearly and clearly every day now. Sometimes her feet hurt something terrible. She never was educated to anything like her capacity. . . .She has a stock of sense, wit, patience, and experiential shrewdness.

This is the one Le Guin would choose, even though she knows she would have a hard time convincing the old woman, "because only a person who has experienced, accepted and acted the entire human condition—the essential quality of which is Change—can fairly represent humanity. 'Me?' she'll say, just a trifle slyly. 'But I never did anything.'" Le Guin knows better. She says about the woman, "She knows, though she won't admit it, that Dr. Kissinger has not gone and will never go where she has gone, that the scientists and the shamans have not done what she has done. Into the spaceship, Granny."

Heavy Time Out

We get the point and we appreciate the validity of how much the church did become a kind of industrial complex with its clones all over the world. This concept has slipped very much into our subconscious in that the average Catholic, both clerical and lay, thinks of his or her parish as a subsidiary of the Vatican. The local parish is looked upon in relationship to Rome as the local Chevrolet dealer is in relationship to General Motors. The only reason we have parishes, we think, is that the pope, who is the pastor of the universal church, obviously can't handle the whole world, so he has deputies (bishops) who oversee the carved up smaller units (dioceses). But the bishop can't handle all his territory, so he in turn subdivides it into parishes. The parish is the last subdivision, with the implication that it can do nothing without the approval of the bishop who can do nothing without the approval of the pope. And it exists only at the behest of the next higher level. It has no innate justification. It is a franchise with all of its "products" bought from the parent company. Most people, as I said, subconsciously understand the local parish this way. It's what we call a vertical ecclesiology.

But the fact of the matter is that the church is experienced on many levels: the church as the Communion of Saints, the church as universal reality, the church as national entity, the church as diocese, and the church as parish. And current developing theology affirms that the parish is indeed a local church in its own right, not just an organizational, administrative subunit of the church universal. (See "The Ecclesiology of the Local Church" by Richard McBrien in *Thought*, December 1991.) The parish has its own justification, its own identity. Vatican II's doctrine of collegiality was very clear about this. It tells us that the local parish is fully church in its own right, though necessarily connected to the church universal. The "Dogmatic Constitution on the Church" (26) says:

> This church of Christ is truly present in all legitimate local congregations of the faithful which, united with their pastors, are themselves called churches in the New Testament. For in their own locality these are the new people called by God, in the Holy Spirit and in much fullness. In them the faithful are gathered together by the preaching of the gospel of Christ, and the mystery of the Lord's Supper is celebrated. . . .In these communities . . . Christ is present. By virtue of him, the one, holy, catholic and apostolic church gathers together, for the partaking of the Body and Blood of Christ does nothing other than transform us into that which we consume.

We should ponder these words as we rethink our parish life. The parish is not a mere subdivision of Rome or the diocese. It has its own integrity, shares a common mission, and is the church of Christ present in this place. Furthermore, it has its own identity because, contrary to popular belief, the local church did not begin as a subdivision of a universal church. In the New Testament it is clear that the church began as a local church in a particular place: Jerusalem. But it is equally clear in the New Testament that we do not have, say, a Corinthian subdivision of the Jerusalem church but, in the words of the Apostle Paul, "the church of God which is in Corinth" (1 Corinthians 1:2). As a matter of fact, the New Testament churches were remarkably diverse (See Raymond Brown's book, *The Churches the Apostles Left Behind*, Mahwah, N.J.: Paulist Press, 1984) and broadly united by several common elements such as: faith in Jesus as the Messiah, baptism, eucharist, apostolic preaching, the coming again of Christ, and mutual love.

So, as Cardinal Ratzinger says ("Some Aspects of the Church Understood As Communion," *Origins*, June 25, 1992):

> Among these manifold particular expressions of the saving presence of the one church of Christ, there are to be found from the time of the apostles on, those entities which are in themselves churches because, although they are particular, the universal church becomes present in them with all her essential elements. . . ."The universal church cannot be conceived of as the sum of the particular churches or as a federation of particular churches" [a quote from Pope John Paul II]. . . .Every member of the faithful, through faith and baptism, is inserted into the one, holy, catholic and apostolic church. He does not belong to the universal church in a mediate way, though belonging to a particular church, but in an immediate way, even though entry into and life within the universal

church are necessarily brought about in a particular church.

Well, this has been a little heavy, but it's worth sharing at the beginning of this manual so that we on the local scene can have a sense of truly being church here and now in this place we call our parish. Actually, all this should become clearer, because in practice we have all sensed and experienced what we might call a startling paradigm change that has indeed put an emphasis on the local church and its ministers. Let us see some of those changes.

Five Paradigm Changes

The shift from an exclusive preoccupation with central headquarters and its personnel to the local community and its ministers is happening every day. In fact, there are five such transitions:

1. Change of Ministers. Formerly, all ministry was in the hands of the clergy and religious with, at times, the laity helping out. The old Catholic Action model from the Vatican was, you recall, the laity *sharing* in the mission of the hierarchy. Now there is an increasing involvement of religious and laity in leadership at all levels, levels that used to be exclusively clerical.

2. Change of Focus. Formerly, ministry meant large gatherings for sacramental celebrations (the macro-church as we shall see in the chapter on small faith communities) so that a parish was identified as a community that gathers in large numbers for worship, for example, Sunday Mass. But now there are smaller groups meeting that put the accent not so much on the celebration of the sacraments and large groups but on the teaching, sharing,

praying, and witnessing functions of the church. We now often gather in small groups with or without clergy in a peer ministry. A new shape of ministry in the church.

3. Change of Place. Formerly, holiness was thought to be what took place in church or in the parish center. Now holiness is in the marketplace, in the home, in the school. Vatican II issued the call to universal holiness and proclaimed the centrality of baptism. Life experience along with tradition are valid avenues of sanctity. See, for example, my *Hands-On Parish,* Part I (Twenty-Third Publications) or Elizabeth Dreyer's book, *Earth Crammed With Heaven* (Mahwah, N.J.: Paulist Press).

4. Change of Authority. Authority is now more diffused from solo to collegial. We have synods, senates, and pastoral and parish councils—a major shift meshing clergy and laity.

5. Change of Dialogue. This means that formerly, monologue-like doctrine and spirituality came down from on high, funneled from the highest to the lowest level. Voices below, voices beside, voices different were not officially heard or at least validated. But now the various "theologies" force us to listen to how a woman reads the story of the Woman at the Well, how blacks read the Good Samaritan parable, how the peasant in the Brazilian barrio reads the story of Lazarus at the gate. In short, we have a new dialogue replacing the old monologue. Tradition and experience prosecute and challenge one another.

Styles

All these changes have impacted not only the church at large, but also the individual parish.

Parishes have responded, as you might expect, differently, and so you have a wide variety of them in style, emphasis, and mission. Here are some general styles that are found around the country—a quick thumbnail, but hardly exhaustive, sketch:

1. The Traditionalistic Parish. Here people are consumers. They come to get what they need from a parish which, though there's a large staff, is definitely run by the pastor. He may indeed be quite a nice man, but all power and decisions rest with him. He is the end spout of what has been poured down from the pope to the bishop to him. And he obediently pours it out on you. He gives the people a feeling of being in touch with "the good old days" before everything went haywire. That's a gift not to be despised, and many people appreciate that. There's not much shared, or collaborative, ministry in this parish.

2. The Charismatic Parish. Here I really mean the charismatic pastor. He is a gifted and exciting leader, open to new ideas while holding to the best of the old. The parish is alive with his leadership and gifts. The trouble is, of course, he doesn't build foundations, so that when he leaves, the whole enterprise collapses. A "chancy" kind of parish.

3. The Collaborative Parish. This style parish engages the talents and gifts of all the parishioners. The pastor resolutely declines to do others' jobs or look over their shoulders. You'll sense ownership, activity, prayerfulness, outreach, interdependency. One to prize.

4. The CFS Parish. The initials stand for the "Chronic Fatigue Syndrome." Here it's parish life on the edge. Overactive, frantic, many activities, but no "center." Everyone's exhausted from running and doing all day

long. Groups keep confronting each other because they all have the hall the same night at the same hour. An exciting place to be, but it will wear you down. Is anyone in charge?

5. The "Sherwin-Williams" Parish. A little of this and a little of that but not much of anything. There's not much enabling, no sense of mission. One thin coat covers all. Enough said.

6. The Factional Family Parish. The tone here is polarization. The pastor is Vatican I, the associate is Vatican II (or, just as likely, vice versa) and there is civil war which spills over to the parish at large, with hoards of people on either side writing to the bishop to denounce the other side. There's lots of energy all right, but it's all negative.

7. The "Nothin'-Honey" Parish. "What's going on at the parish this week?" You've got it: "Nothin', honey." Sacraments are offered but with bare-bones efforts and ceremony. Dysfunctional staff. That sort of thing.

Well, perhaps there's some stereotyping here, but the point is that parishes have charisms and styles. What's yours? A good rule of thumb is to play word association. Mention a parish (say, your own) and what word immediately comes to mind? Great bingos? Terrific basketball team? Paid off the debt, good money man (referring to the pastor)? Those accolades are all right as far as they go, but they don't go far enough. Do these phrases spring to mind: a "sense of Christ" or "There's a spirit (big S and little s) there," or "I get fed there," or "It's a good community, a caring one"?

Subliminal Messages

Whatever the style of parish, there are certain things a parish can do that make statements or give off vibrations that repel or attract. There is, in a word, such a thing as a theology of place: the architecture, the shape of the grounds, the indicators of life, community, and spirituality. We want to explore some of those indicators or suggestions that we have found helpful in creating an atmosphere of welcome and purpose.

1. The Church Vestibule. Besides a listing of the Mass and services schedule, near the entrance of the church we have:

a. a small rack that contains three items: copies of our *Parish Booklet*; a pamphlet which is a brief *history of the parish* from its origins to the present day; and a third pamphlet which is a *guided walking tour* of the buildings and grounds. The sign on the rack says simply: "Free. Take one. It tells you what we're all about."

b. Our vestibule contains the usual book and pamphlet rack, but since the vestibule is small, we have discarded the usual free-standing rack that takes up floor space and have substituted wall-hanging plastic units, the kind you see at travel agents' offices or in some libraries. These plastic modules are neat, attractive, and come in a variety of sizes to hold everything from magazines and paperbacks to pamphlets and flyers. I

 recommend them for small spaces—and for larger ones since they are so attractive. Your library or travel agent can suggest places to order them. In addition to this display, we have a *public bulletin board* for notices and a small *suggestion box* with a slot for suggestions. Whether it gets used often or not is not as important as the signal it sends that you're willing to listen. Finally, there is a

guest book placed on a small stand. There are always visitors of some kind, strangers, relatives of parishioners, etc. It's nice for them to have the opportunity to sign in (name and address) and nicer for you to have someone (we have this as a "ministry" for the elderly or shut-ins) who sends a letter to any legible signer. Our letter is as follows:

Dear Friends,
In our vestibule as you enter our church in Colts Neck, N.J., is a Guest Book. You were gracious enough to sign it and this correspondence is to thank you for doing so. We hope that you enjoyed your visit. We think, of course, that our buildings and grounds are beautiful and that our parish spirit is great. That you were able to share this for a while and even add to it is a cause for joy and gratitude. So we thought that we would write to tell you how appreciative we are.

Do drop by again and, once more, thanks for gracing us with your visit.

Sincerely yours in the Lord,
Ann Matier

If your buildings and grounds are not beautiful, you might say, "Our buildings and grounds need repair and are not the greatest but we make up for it in spirit and love. . .." The point is that the initial impression should be one of welcome and information.

2. Inside the Church. Here we have tried to convey a feeling of warmth, a sense that people live and worship here. We have done several things:

a. We have an open *Bible* (a very old one) at the entrance to the church, right in line with the baptismal font which is further down the center aisle. The notion is that before baptism one must hear and accept the Word.

b. On a blank wall we have placed our *Wailing Wall.* Our church wall is brick, so we had a carpenter put up wall board in front of it and then paste on cork, cut to simulate brick. Then we had the whole thing framed in a wood border that matched the church, and placed a permanent framed sign in the middle of it to explain what it's all about:

What you see here is an idea inspired by the Wailing Wall in Jerusalem (properly called the Western Wall, that is, the western wall of the Old Temple.)

Here generations of people have prayed and cried out their needs before God. Indeed, to this day, little pieces of paper with prayers and petitions are rolled up and inserted in the broken mortar between the bricks of the wall.

Our own Wailing Wall serves the same purpose. It is here in order that: 1) you might tack your needs, prayers, and petitions to it so that all who pause here may see, be moved, and pray, or 2) you might take the petition off the wall, keep it for a week and pray for the unknown writer whose heart is broken. Then you might initial it and put it back again so that the person who put it there originally may know that he or she is not alone; that someone gave comfort, sympathy, and concern.

In any case, the Wailing Wall stands here as a small shrine, a special place in our church where we stand with deep devotion and piety and raise our hearts and minds to God with longing, tears, and confidence.

Feel free to tack on your needs and look over others' needs. Most of all, stand here with a reverence and quiet that deep sympathy and charity always demand of us all.

Pins and paper pieces are tacked into the corner for use. The day after we put up our Wailing Wall it was nearly full of petitions. It's a great addition to any church, no matter what the style or architecture.

c. We have two follow-ups. Often people will mention the wall aloud at the *Prayers of the Faithful.* For example: "For all the petitions on the Wailing Wall, let us pray to the Lord." Once a year, since the wall is literally covered with petitions, we have *Compassion Sunday* as a way of clearing it off. At each Mass on the weekend we have a ritual where people gather a portion of the petitions and bring them forward in quiet procession to be placed in a container and burned. See Parish Papers, page 293, for suggested directions for the celebrant.

d. The *Plaque* and *Book of the Dead.* We have erected on a small portion of a wall in church an 18" x 20" wooden double-panel plaque with these words inscribed on it:

Beneath this plaque is the shelf on which lies the Book of the Dead, with the inscribed names of the deceased. Connecting names and faces helps parishioners to recognize the deceased.

In Memory of *(photo here; name under photo)* Recently deceased and buried from this parish community *(date)* Rejoice in the Lord always.	This week we pray for the following parishioners: *(list of 4 or 5 names)* May the Lord bless and guide them.

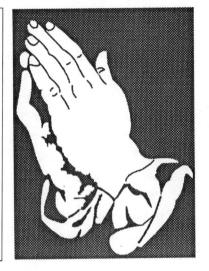

e. *The Responsorial Psalm Wall.* Another church wall also has a large bulletin board containing letters of gratitude and photos from people we have helped. A framed text in the middle of this board reads:

Responsorial Psalms

"What good is it, my brothers, if someone claims to have faith but has no deeds? Suppose a brother or a sister is without clothes and daily food. If one of you says to him, 'Go, I wish you well; keep warm and well fed' but does nothing about his physical needs, what good is it? In the same way, faith by itself, if it is not accompanied by action, is dead" (James 2:14–17).

St. Mary's has a long tradition of reaching out to others, within and beyond our boundaries. Almost daily, on behalf of those unable to do so, we take care of rent, food, heating, placements, clothing, etc. We give fully to Birthright, Interfaith Neighbors (housing), Martin House (house rebuilding in the inner city), Discovery House, Endeavor House, Mercy Center, Manna House, Emmanuel Center (cancer patients), and others.

Once a month we have a food collection for the poor. Our Sharing Shed is available for clothing, furniture, food and frozen meals—all of which you provide. Through our Samaritans we visit the sick and take them Communion, meals, and medicine. Through our Lazarus Ministry, we comfort the bereaved and provide for the wake and funeral. Through our organizations such as Martha/Mary and the Men's Guild, we raise money for many needs. We tithe our annual gross income to the international, national, and local poor, use the proceeds of the children's envelopes solely for the poor, have a summer garden of food for their needs, twin with

Sts. Peter and Paul, our poorer sister parish in Chile, and dedicate our former mortgage money to places of serious need.

We provide space in our buildings for meetings such as AA, Al-Anon, Gamblers' Anonymous, drug and rehabilitation counselor's group, Girl Scout leaders, Care-givers, Newcomers, mothers' groups, infant and adult massage, personal and family counseling, drug and alcohol counseling, spiritual direction, and other groups and services.

And all this is what we should do, what is expected of those who take the gospel of Jesus seriously.

Here then, on this board, you will find some "responsorial psalms," some letters of gratitude from those who have benefited from your kindness. Read them. Look at the faces in the photos. Their words are for you. And continue to pray for and give to those less fortunate and rejoice in our common connections.

We sincerely did not want to make this notice sound self-serving, and yet we wanted the people to be aware of all that goes on—and goes on as a "constitutive" part of our common ministry—because "familiarity breeds contempt" and they often take for granted the consistent effort that goes on to live the gospel.

A final and effective touch in this area: We supply random names of parishioners to the people we help so that, if they are in fact inclined to send a thank you letter, that letter will go to a specific individual or family, not

to the parish. They in turn will send us the letter to hang on our wall. The point is that parishioners get a chance to have a concrete, hands-on response that keeps them sensitized to actual needs and real people. We also hope that a bond will be forged between the sender and recipient.

f. *Bulletin Board.* Somewhere, inside the church, have a large bulletin board and every six weeks or so, have someone put up photographs of current activities. There's always someone snapping pictures at the religion classes, parish picnic, or Arts and

Crafts Show. By having a public *family album* you build up solidarity. Dress up the board with seasonal liturgical art and themes. People, young and old, like to see themselves. It makes them feel at home.

g. We have *permanent large photographs,* some fourteen of them, hanging around the church walls. They show the community in various stages of worship, celebration, and play. All is not liturgical. The message is that life within and without is grist for the Spirit.

3. The Parish Hall. This is a large hall connected to the church. Several things enhance its general usefulness.

a. We have taken a broad right angle cinder block wall space at one end and filled it, carefully measured and aligned, with as many photographs of all sizes as we could fit. Then we covered them with plexiglas (to keep poking fingers off) and put a three-dimensional sign over it all: " St. Mary's Community: Alive and Loving." It stands as an open family album and it's a real memory bank of people over the years. Attractive and appealing.

b. Large horizontal bulletin boards dot the walls for notices, decorations, and children's art work.

4. The Spiritual Center. In our spiritual center we have taken a cinder block wall in the corridor, pasted on wall boards, and then put in a history of the parish. We were founded as a mission in 1879 and became an independent parish in 1972. So we wrote up our history, got photographs and news clippings of former pastors and parishioners, and took the theme right up to the present time showing building and development over the years. We covered the whole thing with plexiglas. It's our permanent *historical wall,* a focused sense of rootedness for the natives and a pictorial history for the visitors.

5. Other Enhancing Items. These might include a banner or memento from a sister parish if a parish twins with another, a Bible placed in a prominent place, say, on the offertory table, a baptismal font with the lid off so that the water may shimmer; in short, whatever makes the church interesting, revelatory of its spirit, and inviting. Likewise, it is important that the symbols be strong: strong vestments, glass chalices and cruets that draw attention to the elements, real "bready" bread as opposed to a large wafer, and everything removed by the eucharistic ministers and brought to the sacristy for cleaning (public dishwashing before the People of God is as rude as washing dishes at the table before your dinner guests).

The point of all the above is not only to make your worship space reverent, but also inviting. Make it give off signals of aliveness, that people live here. They do things. They celebrate. They like it. They are church.

Summary of Chapter 1

1. The parish is important.

2. Formerly, it reflected a rather Industrial Revolution type of structure, with the notion of General Headquarters with its dependent franchises.

3. The parish is fully church in its own right and "the church of Christ is truly present in all legitimate local congregations of the faithful."

4. Parishes are more sensitive to this truth because the vast changes following Vatican II have put such emphasis on the local church and its ministers, clerical and lay.

5. Parishes, like people, take time to catch up and so you have parishes at various stages of renewal and of varying styles.

6. You can enhance your parish and make it "say" something. Suggestions are:

- welcoming and informative literature
- a Guest Book
- a Suggestion Box
- a public Bulletin Board
- a "Wailing Wall" or some such "shrine" for the heart
- notations of charity given and received gratefully
- a system to recognize the deceased through photographs
- a "Book of the Dead" in which to inscribe names
- photographs of "contemporary saints" in action
- signs of twinning or outreach
- strong liturgical symbols
- prominent display of the Bible and baptism font.

Catholic Tidbits

- Roman Catholics are the largest denomination in America with well over 58 million members.

- Catholic schools educate three million students annually and Catholic schools consistently rank highest in the nation for achievement.

- Catholic schools are among the largest servers of minority children.

- Catholic hospitals take care of some 54 million patients annually.

- Catholic social services are the largest caregivers of AIDS patients in the country.

- Catholics make up a majority of those serving in the Armed Forces.

- Catholic institutions offer homes to 78,000 orphans.

- Catholic Relief Services is the largest single private service in the world.

- Catholics assist some 12 million people annually through their social services programs.

A Bit of Trivia for Parish Life

Back when the West was being settled, the major means of transportation was the stagecoach. We all remember that from all those cowboy movies we saw. What we did not know is that the stagecoach had three different kinds of tickets: first, second, and third class. It's hard to imagine any distinctions. After all, how big is a stagecoach? It's just a box on wheels and everyone sits inside. But there was a difference and it was this:

If you had a first-class ticket, you could remain seated during the entire trip no matter what happened. If the stagecoach got stuck in the mud, or had trouble making it up a steep hill, or a wheel fell off, you could remain seated because you had a first-class ticket. If you had a second-class ticket, you could also remain seated—until there was a problem. In that case, you had to get out and stand to one side and watch while other people worked. You didn't have to get your hands dirty. You were just not allowed to stay on board. When the stagecoach was fixed you would get back on and take your seat.

If you had a third-class ticket, you would definitely have to get off if there was a problem. Why? Because you had to solve it. You had to get out and push or help lift or whatever was needed because you had only a third-class ticket.

Sounds just like some parishioners.

Chapter 2

Getting Co-Laborers

Collaboration: cooperation with the enemy!
Anybody can encourage. But permission to succeed comes only from an authority figure: parent, boss, or pastor.

Introduction

Let's start off with three quotations. The first is from a document of Vatican II, *Dogmatic Constitution on the Church,* 31.

> The laity are in their own way made sharers in the priestly, prophetic and kingly functions of Christ. They carry out their own part in the mission of the whole Christian people with respect to the church and the world. . . .the laity by their very vocation seek the kingdom of God by engaging in temporal affairs and by ordering them according to the plan of God.

The second is from Pope John Paul II, addressing a group of American bishops on their annual visit to Rome in July 1993:

> What you refer to as "collaborative ministry," when completely faithful to the church's sacramental doctrine, provides a sure foundation for building communities which are internally reconciled, and the spiritual energies of which are positively harnessed for the new evangelization.

The third is from Kenan Osborne's exhaustive study, *Ministry: Lay Ministry in the Roman Catholic Church* (Mahwah, N.J.: Paulist Press, 1993):

> As we know well, the bishops at Vatican II reworked the preliminary draft of the document of the church, *Lumen Gentium,* so that the fundamental importance of the entire people of God, the *Christifideles,* became paramount for all Christian ministry. Only on the basis of this fundamental significance of all baptized Christians (chapter two) did the bishops then discuss both the ordained and the non-ordained ministry (chapters three and four). Thus, we can speak of a mutual relationship between ordained and non-ordained ministry, but the linch pin must be seen in the baptismal-eucharistic sacrament of initiation. This integration of the sacraments of initiation (baptism-confirmation-eucharist) into the fundamental structure of church ministry is key to the understanding both of the church itself and of the various church ministries, which one finds throughout the Vatican II documents.

These quotations underscore the recovery of the basis of ministry from that of the exclusively ordained to that of all the initiated (baptized). There are no longer superior-inferior, active-passive, lay-clerical divisions and hierarchies. These have been replaced with the ancient scriptural paradigm of collaboration—and collaboration, or co-laboring, not by privilege or permission, but by baptismal right. The practical fallout of this is both the theoretical underpinning and practical explosion of involved lay Christians. [If you want to trace the evolution of such pristine shared and collaborative lay ministry to that of exclusively clerical ministry, read Osborne's long (718 pages) book or my shorter book (176 pages) *Ministry: Traditions, Tensions, Transitions* (Twenty-Third Publications).

For an excellent summary of a collaborative ideal, see Parish Papers, pages 189-192, *Called and Gifted*.

Of course, in the practical realm, the shortage of priests has done much to focus on the theology of lay ministries and emphasize the need of their existence. There was a 20% decline in diocesan priests between 1966 and 1984 and another 20% decline is projected to the year 2005. (An interesting statistic: Since 1981, 90 Episcopal priests have switched to the Roman Catholic church but 345 Catholic priests have switched to the Episcopal church). Also, by 2005, almost 46% of active diocesan clergy will be 55 or older and only 12% will be 34 or younger.

The next millennium will have even fewer priests coming up. Family life, the old cohesive bedrock supply of priestly vocations, has been severely fractured. Young priests who would model an attractive lifestyle are in short supply. Add other reasons such as scandal, materialism, dissatisfaction, individualism, and such, and you have those declining numbers. Father Eugene Hemrick,

Director of Research in the Office of Research for the U.S. Bishops Conference, predicts (in *The Priest*, August 1993):

> Instead of the priest being an ombudsman, he will become an orchestra leader encouraging lay ministries to take over roles priests once fulfilled. Out of necessity his ministry will be more focused on that which is in the nature of being a priest. His personal presence will be felt less, but he will compensate for this by utilizing the electronic world of the cellular and videophones, computers and the fax.

Ministry

We don't use the term "lay Christians"; we use the much more common term "ministers," although technically this is not quite accurate. Recent research (John Collins's provocative book, *Are All Ministers?* Collegeville, Minn.: Liturgical Press, 1993) indicates that in the New Testament the word "minister" was in fact confined to authoritative proclamation of the Word in order that those doing "activities" (what we casually call "ministries") could be educated and maintained in the truth. As Collins writes:

> A minister is one appointed to the task and in this instance the task is that of providing believers with the teaching which sustains them in faith and knowledge. . . .When we late twentieth-century Christians turn the word [ministry] into a nondescript service within the capacity of any believer, we gravely distort his [Paul's, writing in Ephesians 4:11–13] meaning.

In other words, a minister is an official appointee whose job or ministry it is to promote good order and the building up of the Body of Christ through sound instruction and the proclamation of the Word of God. The rest are collaborators, splendid and necessary doers of service. (Check also James Tunstead Burtchaell's book, *From Synagogue to Church: Public Services and Offices in the Earliest Christian Communities*, New York: Cambridge University Press, 1992.)

Be that as it may, the fact is that lay ministers—both in the strict, officially appointed sense and in the popular lay-volunteers sense—have increased enormously in the past twenty years. A survey taken in 1992 by the National Pastoral Life Center entitled *New Parish Ministers* (299 Elizabeth St., New York, N.Y. 10012, by Philip J. Murnion, David LeLambo, Rosemary Dilli, and Harry Fagan) indicates that "about 20,000 lay people and religious are employed at least twenty hours a week as parish ministers in half of the 19,000 Catholic parishes of the United States. This is in addition to those on staffs of the parochial schools and those in support and maintenance positions." What a difference from pre-Vatican II days!

Of these new parish ministers, 85% are women and slightly more than four out of ten are members of religious orders, who tend to be considerably older than the lay ministers. The average age of many members of religious congregations is 67 and the number of religious has decreased by approximately 45% for brothers and sisters and 27% for religious priests. And, of course, diocesan priests have decreased in number and have a mean age near 60. All this has accelerated the use of many lay ministers as sharers and collaborators. And, in so many instances, this has been a blessing both for the lay ministers themselves (though the paid ones generally receive a low salary) and the parish, because it has been shown that more ministers in fact increase the involvement of parishioners in parish life.

Because lay involvement is here to stay, more and more dioceses are looking ahead by providing solid, professional formation and training for such lay leaders for local parishes. They are seeking to "build a network of people across the diocese who form a supportive and challenging community of leaders." Such programs, usually two years in duration, revolve around the core aspects of theological, spiritual, and pastoral skills. Such dioceses have a screening process for candidates, ask for commitments, and share in the cost. Of course, it is easy to foresee that, down the road, well trained, dedicated, and theologically sophisticated lay leaders will surely put pressure on the current qualifications for ordination. In any case, your own diocese should have such a program, usually best connected with a university or seminary, rather than run by the diocese's own personnel whose resources and experience tend to be limited and parochial. For a fine resource, see the diocese of Burlington's (Vermont) Charter Document (from which the above quote is taken) for "Ministry Training Program" in *Origins*, (April 7, 1994, Vol. 23, No. 42).

Here in our manual we will be dealing almost exclusively with volunteers, people who generously give of their time and talent in the service of the gospel. By way of introduction, we should take note of a 1993 report (*Church and Community* by Thomas A. Van Eck, et al.) that churches are in fact the number one recruiter of volunteers with the second largest recruiter, youth organizations, only half as likely to get people involved in helping others. We should know that and take heart. The authors also listed three characteristics and policies of those churches most successful in drawing volunteers:

1. These churches gave volunteers adequate information about those whom they knew needed help. They didn't send them in blind or half-informed. They gave them a pretty good "job description."

2. They provided concrete ways for people to help. It was not just a vague "See what you can do" but rather "Here's what you can do."

3. They made prayer and scripture study important as ways for raising the volunteers' consciousness and sustaining their motivation.

To no one's surprise, the researchers also discovered that the pastor was the key to motivating people to help others. He (she) knew the volunteers' interests and appealed to them and helped match aid to need. An "I know mine and mine know me" application.

A Dozen Principles

In this chapter, therefore, I propose twelve principles for shared and collaborative ministry which, I suppose, amounts to the recruiting, care, and feeding of volunteers. In other words, these days, how do you get people involved and keep them involved? Or, as I am often asked, "How did you get started?" These principles are the answer. The first eight principles deal with policy and the last four directly with volunteers.

First Principle: Education. This first principle is a wide, long-term, remote process. It means that, although you may have a parish full of Ph.D.s, their theoretical and practical religious knowledge is almost nil. Every survey shows that the average Catholic has a minimal under-standing of the faith. The assumption is that you have a religiously preliterate congregation.

Furthermore, it is my experience that, when the changes of Vatican II came, no one bothered to explain them. Often as not, the pastor would get a notice from the bishop, say, to turn the altar around. He would read the directive (sometimes with ill-disguised disgust) from the bishop who himself might not be very happy with the directive. Period. No discussion, no background, no criteria to say whether this or that change is asinine (some were and are) or sensible (some were and are). People couldn't even critique the changes since they had no measurement with which to do so.

When I first came to my current parish, I therefore spent the first few years (yes, years) explaining and unfolding the changes of Vatican II. I did this in three areas:

1. Even though I knew I would offend the liturgical purists, I took advantage of the largest single captive group I would ever have: the Sunday congregation. I used homily time to explain and teach. As St. Paul reminded us, how can people be evangelized unless they hear the Word of God, and how can they hear unless someone preaches, and how

can someone preach unless he is sent? Sunday by Sunday I taught the spirit of Vatican II, including criticisms of it. But, mostly, I gave the *reasons* for the changes. Even those who didn't like the changes were at least mollified somewhat by knowing the reasons behind them. The "bottom line" of my teachings all came down to this: We are the church; we are co-responsible; we are a People of God.

2. I coordinated *bulletin inserts* with the talks. You can use those wonderful prepackaged ones (like the Franciscan "Updates") or write your own. We discovered a very high readership of these one-page, two-sided fillers. It follows that if you teach every Sunday of every week of every month of every year over a series of years, you have to have an impact on the consciousness of the people. You notice this when the vocabulary changes and the people's language reveals a familiarity with the concepts of being church.

3. I gave *courses*. In those early days when people turned out (alas, no more, as we shall see), between 100 to 150 people would come out for a series of lectures with the opportunity to learn and question, discuss and discover resources for further reading. Along with all of this was the actual doing, the participation, the invitations to lector, usher, visit the sick, and so on.

There is a subsidiary principle that gets tucked in with this first principle of education: the "either-or" syndrome. This means that through this long education process people *do* get a sense of being church, a sense of their baptismal dignity, and an awareness of their role in the congregational worship. In all of this, even though we all admit that something's been lost—a sense of mystery, respect, reverence, whatever—there has been a gain in

active participation, a sense of responsibility, an aliveness; untidy at times, but exciting. But not everyone is converted. And the "unconverted" should never be made to feel less Catholic, less a parishioner. It's a big church. It should not be either the novena to St. Jude or the guitar Mass; either the scapular or communion in the hand; either singing or silence; either Father or the eucharistic minister. We have room for all options even if the general thrust of the parish is toward shared and collaborative ministry, parish councils, and Vatican II. Those who don't or can't "buy" into it are valued members and should be included in all ways. I remember one gentleman who said the rosary all during Mass and at the consecration struck the rosary against the pew three times in place of the now absent bells. And why not? That's where he was. He was present in spite of his obvious pain and had gifts to offer us. No "either-or" in the family of God.

Second Principle: No-Strings Education.
Every year every parish gets tons of flyers and inserts announcing summer and winter workshops all around the country (National Catholic Reporter supplement, Crux, etc.). What we do is offer any parishioner a chance to attend those workshops within sensible distance (there are exceptions), with all expenses paid by the parish except their meals. Fortunately for us, not that many people go—usually around 15 to 20 a year. But add that up over the twenty years I've been in the parish and we have had some 400 people hear some gifted speakers, see some intriguing resources, and mix in the corridors with soul mates. They cannot come back untouched.

The "no-strings" part means that in all

truth they do not have to do anything. They have no accountability: They do not have to make a report, do a ministry, share ideas. Nothing. It is a totally free gift. But of course there is a difference. They've caught a fire and they've picked up a vocabulary and have seen a wider world. They've *got* to make a difference to the parish somehow. In the long run the parish benefits immensely.

Third Principle: Training Booklets. In order to reenforce the people's sense of community we put together a series of booklets. In these days of computers and clip art (such as seen in this manual), we easily and cheaply mass reproduced them so we did not mind if people stole them (and they did). We did give a nod to the many liturgical options offered, but at the start we did not want to overwhelm people. Nor did we want them to juggle several books, from missalettes to song books. So we put together one simple booklet that covered everything. This made it easy both to follow and participate.

They were booklets for occasional events. For example, on Good Friday we have outdoor stations of the cross. Some 1000 to 1200 people attend. It is easy to hand out a booklet we made containing striking reflections, responses, and songs. One booklet ties us all together. Another booklet is for Passion Sunday. We simply rewrote the passion narrative to give the people more speaking parts. Outside of a song book, this is the only booklet they need. We have produced a booklet we use at funerals containing songs, readings, prayers, and reflections. The family and visitors have this one booklet that guides them (especially the non-Catholics) and invites their participation. We have a "Now and Then" booklet that contains odds and ends such as: Benediction, Novenas, Soup 'n Song, the Easter gospel and proclamation redone for congregational participation, and some songs frequently used but scattered elsewhere. (Of course, we always get reproduction permissions.)

The point is that these occasional "training" booklets provide easy-to-follow directions and foster participation. They simplify special events; they are quite successful in getting the people to eagerly take part and they are thereby united.

Getting to Know You

Fourth Principle: "Getting to Know You." Research on why people leave their parishes and churches (see Robert W. Jeambey's *When the Ties That Bind Break*, Louisville: Presbyterian Publishing House) lists unacceptance and unrelatedness as high causes. People are lost in the crowd. They are not known to the "powers that be." Cliques freeze out everyone. The result is that a great deal of talent goes unused and people simply blend into the background as anonymous parishioners, especially in large parishes. We use seven immediate ways, besides the other principles that follow, to get people known, recognized, and involved.

1. A Parish-Wide Census. Several years ago we took up a census that was very successful and helpful. We broke the parish down into zones of contiguous neighborhoods and appointed a captain from that neighborhood for each zone. After much publicity (from the altar, bulletin, signs around town, etc.) we set a target date for a one-week census. The captains went to every house in their zone (Catholic or not), dropped off the census one Sunday and picked it up personally the following Sunday. That personal "neighborhood captain" touch accounted for a high return of 82%. The census had a front tear-off page that contained personal data: names, ages, sacraments received, marriage status, parish status (i.e., registered, not registered), drop out, etc., which was put in a sealed envelope before returning it to the captain. The rest of the census was a survey of opinions about everything from the Mass schedule to the quality of the homilies, music, religious education program, parish organizations, and the like. It also had a section where people could fill in a sentence such as: "Something I've always wanted to say to the pastor is _____." "I think the biggest problem we the people have to face today is _____." There was room for three respondents from each family and this section was entirely anonymous. There was also a section for time and talent on behalf of the parish and local community. (See Parish Papers, pages 193-209, for full census.)

2. *The Covenant.* Before anyone new joins the parish, they receive a Covenant to take home and look over. Then, if they feel they can sign it, they call the parish and one of us will go over to their house for the signing. The Covenant (see Parish Papers, pages 210-213) introduces the people to highly relational language and invites them to join the parish, not as a member of the Kiwanis Club, but as an organic member of a living faith community. Part of the Covenant pact is to sign up for a Christian service, no matter how brief. It may simply be a one-time commitment, for example, taking charge of the Advent communal confession or hosting our annual Christmas Concert, or carrying the food once a

year from the church to the Sharing Shed on food collection Sunday. A good source for volunteers.

The point is that, from the beginning, we have personal contact with new people and at the same time we get an ever-new cadre of helpers, people pulled into parish contact. Moreover, on the back of the Covenant form we have a place for their photo so we can recognize them again.

3. *Publicizing Newcomers' Names.* To help others know new people we take the photograph attached to the Covenant and 1) put it in our Sunday bulletin with the caption, "The Smith family has joined our faith community. When you see them, give them a gracious welcome." 2) include their photo in our quarterly newsletter, *The Mustard Seed;* and 3) put their photo and names on the public bulletin board in church.

4. *The Oliver Celebration.* This is a once-a-year (in the fall) welcoming party for all new members who have joined the parish. We have introductions and personal history. We have each family put together a puzzle made of jigsawed pieces of a large photograph of our church. We have refreshments and balloons, and each family leaves with the gift of a small green plant, a symbol of our anticipated growth together. For our purposes, I mention that as part of the Oliver Celebration program each parish ministry has a representative there who gives a quick sell to the newcomers with sign-up sheets to get them committed. Once more, we get to know the people through multiple contacts and invitations.

The name "Oliver Celebration," by the way, comes from the musical *Oliver!* where the words of one of the songs say, "Consider yourself at home, consider yourself one of the family"—a good description of what we're trying to do. The staff and other ministers sing this song at this event. In fact, some clever person rewrote the words to the song and I share them with you (just change the names—and try singing it out loud):

1. We welcome you to join
We welcome you to be a part of us.
We've taken to you so strong,
It's clear—we're going to get along.

2. Consider yourself at home,
Consider yourself part of our family.
We're a com-mun-ity of friends
Where prayer and commitments never
    end.

3. Our ministries and guilds are
    something to behold,
Father Bausch has told us all,
That love and kindness and Christian
    charity
Are found within St. Mary's walls.

4. Family Ed reaches out
The Samaritans visit parishioners.
They give to those in need
A worthwhile and wonderful thing
    indeed.

5. There are groups for one and all,
The Moppets care for the little ones,
Our senior members thrive

With companionship the Holy Spirit
    provides.

6. The Presbyters are those who gather
    every month
For fellowship and fun.
The Martha/Mary Guild provides our
    women with
Sociability surpassed by none.

7. Consider yourself our friends,
We're going to have no fuss.
For after some consideration we can
    state,
Consider yourself one of us.

5. Saturday Night Dinners. This may be unusual, but every Saturday evening, except for the summer and holidays, I invite two families (adults only) to dinner. Those families may include widows or singles, etc. In the course of many years you can give hospitality to hundreds and hundreds of families and in the process get to know them, what they do, and sooner or later how they can help.

6. Spreading the Word. As new people come into the parish, a further incentive to get involved is to pass on their names, addresses, and phone numbers to the already existing organizations with the plea to use such new talent. So I send a full listing of all newcomers to all parish ministries. Here is the enclosing letter:

Dear Friends:

One of the most important things we can do to insure our tradition of shared and collaborative ministry in our parish is to both invite and train others in our gifts. Nothing is so harmful as to always ask the same people, however generous and gifted they may be. We owe it to them to have others share in our many tasks.

Attached here, then, is a list of those parishioners who have joined the parish within the past year. Please feel free to call, write, or otherwise contact them—especially for a one-time affair—even if it means only baking a cake or pie or filling a Thanksgiving basket.

Don't worry if you think they are getting too many contacts. They can always say no. For newcomers, to be asked is to once again be made to feel known and welcomed and a part of our faith community. So introduce them to our many ministries.

So, once more, please use this list often and frequently. Line up a "veteran" with a newcomer. Expand our gifts, our people, our ministries.

I am grateful for what you do. The parish could not survive without your interest and dedication. We want to insure that what you are a part of, others may profit from and learn from—and ultimately pass on the tradition of service.

Thank you for all that you do. May this list be of assistance to you.

Sincerely yours,
Father Bausch

7. Acknowledgment. Acknowledge and work with the local leaders who are already there. Every neighborhood has its leaders and every ethnic and cultural group especially has its leaders and traditions. Those in multi-ethnic parishes should take note. We must respectfully work with them and draw them into partnership, all the while respecting their customs and our traditions. Our liturgy and their customs should cross-fertilize. Going to *their* homes for a dialogue is the best procedure. Timothy Matovina puts it well (*Worship*, July 1993):

A good first question for a pastoral minister upon coming to a parish or faith community is, "Who are the leaders of this people's life and worship?" This does not necessarily mean clergy, catechists, liturgical coordinators, or other designated ministers. Frequently those recognized as "pastors" by the local community do not have official titles. Often Hispanic communities will rely on *abuelitas* (grandmothers) or other elders for consolation, counsel, prayer, and community affirmation. Virgillio Elizondo has stated that, for Hispanics, the *abuelita* has served "as the priestess of the home religion." . . . In one parish I met a woman named Dina Licha who though not prominent in parish organizations, led the annual novena celebration of *las posadas* among her family and neighbors. These celebrations were the focal point of her neighborhood in the days preceding Christmas. Like Christ who recognized the ritual leadership of the woman who washed his feet, the first step in pastoral ministry is to recognize people like Dona Licha who are the natural leaders of life and worship in a local faith community.

This advice is made even more relevant as we realize that we now live in a highly multicultural nation, especially with the increase of Asians (an increase of 114% in the 1980s) and Hispanics. Formerly, minority groups were urged to give up their cultural practices and go American mainstream, thereby gaining the benefits of liberal social and economic prosperity. But soon it became apparent that the dominant culture did not deliver (often based on race discrimination), and the result was that groups began to resist assimilation and to maintain their distinctive features, asking the dominant culture to accommodate them. As the saying goes, America went from the melting pot to the salad bowl, and this has led to the language of multiculturalism. We therefore must tap into their language and their leadership and offer a parish that is large enough to be home to many. (See Robert J. Schreiter, C.PP.S., "Multicultural Ministry": Theory, Practice, Theology, in *New Theology Review*, August 1992. For the special needs of the African-American parish, see the same review whose entire February 1994 issue is devoted to this topic.)

Fifth Principle: RSVP. It is a truism for all groups, large and small, that if you ask for volunteers you can write down their names before they do. The parish is no exception. To ask for volunteers is to meet old friends. The plus side of this is that such people are loyal, willing, able, and generous, a very backbone. The minus side of this is that, precisely because the same people volunteer and do such a competent job, others back off. "I could never arrange flowers like Mary!" Perhaps not. Perhaps so. We'll never know if Mary has had a hammerlock on the job since 1947. This is why I seldom, if ever, call for volunteers. I always ask through a personal letter.

The personal letter lets people know that you both know them (not necessarily true; you picked a name from the census and asked "Who's this? Let's get them involved") and recognize them as being parish members. Besides, the mystique of the pastor's name still operates and people are reluctant to say no. The point is, with one eye on the census and the other on the Covenants, a personal letter of invitation to the home rather than a blanket call in the bulletin for volunteers is an excellent way of getting people, old and new, involved.

Sixth Principle: One-Shot Piggy-Back. This principle says that you ask someone to do something, say, coordinate the Senior Citizens day of recollection (with its conferences followed by entertainment and a free dinner served by the parish youth). After their initial dismay, you remind them that it's only this one time ("one-shot") and that usually sells them. After it's all over, they can disappear again. But what really clinches it is that the people who did it last year will piggy-back them, that is, work along with them and advise them and *their* only obligation is to do the same for next year's coordinators. In other words, the reality is that these days people seem to have less time. Usually both parents are working and commuting. Their lives are hectic. People simply cannot give long-term commitments or turn out for long-term courses or projects. But the one-time project is attractive, makes them feel useful and contributing, and respects their own schedules.

Seventh Principle: "The Glenmary Dance." This term comes from the Glenmary Fathers who move into no-priest territories, establish parishes, recruit natives, and then, when a native clergy is in place, move on. The principle here is that when someone has a job or learns a new concept or task, the teacher or leader should move away and let that person take ownership. A case in point is when we considered dropping Mass once a week and opting to choose another official liturgical way of worshiping, for instance, chanting the Divine Office. We got books and I trained the morning congregation in the ways of the office (hymns, psalms, scripture, homily) and then led it. After a while, when we got it down, I invited other people to lead it and I sat in the front pew. Then later I moved to the middle pew and still later to the back pew; and, finally, out the front door. I had done my "Glenmary Dance." The people now owned it and owned it well and movingly. They were empowered. The same with any ministry. After the people learn it well (the theology, the sources, and the practice) there is no need to hold on, much less to control. People are now in a position to make their own decisions.

Eighth Principle: "Happy Endings." There is nothing more dismaying than someone who wants a change but feels he or she will betray the pastor who, they feel, needs them; and all the while the pastor is in agony because he wants new blood and does not know how to graciously ask this volunteer to leave (and, remember, you can't fire volunteers). So, like the couple in O. Henry's *The Gift of the Magi*, they continue their lives at cross-purposes. That is why, beside the need to involve others, we have a principle that no one may serve in a leadership position in most ministries for more than two years. They must move on or "lateralize" into something else. I say "most" ministries because there are obviously some that require continuity because of specialization or because we do not have enough people to go around, such as organists and cantors. Otherwise, our organization presidents are in for two years as are lectors, eucharistic ministers, and parish council members (who may go to three years depending on the rotation cycle). This is generally a freeing principle. People have a sense of a beginning and an ending. Most, of course, return to membership or move easily and quickly into other ministries or allied ministries. Others become valued alumnae and alumni, such as the lectors and eucharistic ministers who fill in when there's a gap. All in all, this principle keeps the parish pot stirred and shares the responsibilities more widely.

Volunteers

Ninth Principle: Volunteer Respect. Behind this principle is a regard for volunteers as adults who should be treated as such. Often, however, pastors keep them children by asking them to do a task and then neglecting to give them the tools! And so the volunteers are left, Uriah Heep-like, to grovel to the secretary and apologize for interrupting as they beg envelopes and stamps, or ask to have things copied. We have solved that problem by taking it out of the (overworked) secretary's hands altogether and having a person whose sole job is to minister to volunteers. A few years ago we published this notice:

> Attention All Volunteers:
>
> Your scripture passage from now on is Genesis 41:55. Of course, you all know that that's the passage where the Pharaoh says to all who come to him for help, "Go to Joseph." So it is with you. From now on, if you need stamps, envelopes, phones, addresses, paper, things typed or copies run off—whatever you need—"Go to Joseph!"
>
> Joseph, in this case being Joe George, is in charge of volunteers and has his office in the Spiritual Center. He is there daily from 10:00 A.M. to 2:00 P.M.
>
> Be holy. Do not go to the parish office for your needs but to the Spiritual Center and so fulfill the Scriptures: Genesis 41:55.

This arrangement treats the volunteers with dignity. Furthermore, we have one office in our complex marked "Common Office." It's a free-standing office with desk, phone, and typewriter where people can go to work and get things done as volunteers. People are more likely to respond when they know their needs are respected.

Tenth Principle: Volunteer Gratitude. Quick and simple, each year we have a "Christmas in January" thank you party for all volunteers: live music, dancing, cocktails, and hors d'oeuvres. Little enough, but Erma Bombeck comes to mind:

Three years ago, I did a column on volunteers in an effort to point out that they don't contribute to our civilization. They *are* civilization—at least the only part worth talking about. They are the only human beings on the face of the earth who reflect this nation's compassion, unselfishness, caring, patience, need and just plain loving one another. . . .One has to wonder. Did we . . . remember to say to the volunteers, "Thank you for our symphony hall. Thank you for the six dialysis machines. Thank you for sitting up with a 16-year-old who overdosed and begged to die. Thank you for the hot chocolate at the Scout meeting. Thanks for reading to the blind. Thanks for using your station wagon to transport a group of strangers to a ballgame. Thanks for knocking on the doors in the rain. Thanks for hugging the winners of the Special Olympics. Thanks for pushing the wheelchair into the sun. Thanks for being. . . !

Eleventh Principle: Volunteer Training and Support. Training is critical not only for volunteers but also for the professional ministers. The training should include an expertise for the matter at hand, and the theology and the spirituality of why they're doing this in the first place. Obviously, some things like running a dance require no training, although it is wise (as we do) to *keep a log* of all events each time they happen and so build up an accumulated wisdom to pass on. Others, like the Lazarus, Bereavement, and the liturgical and social ministries, require training, theology, and spirituality. Often a parish can tap into a nearby university or seminary or religious house or simply budget workshops or speakers who will do the training. A poor parish might ask the chancery to underwrite a training session.

The type of support ministers and volunteers need comes in response to a National Association of Lay Ministries survey taken in 1990. Ministers across the country spelled out their needs in five categories: 1) Spiritual direction. Very few had the opportunity; many wanted it. We have a full-time, on-the-premises spiritual director. Others may make arrangements with other sources. 2) Retreats. We build these right into our yearly schedule. Every ministry is

required to make a day of recollection once a year. 3) Continuing education. This is an obvious need and should be addressed. 4) Support persons. The ministers needed a supportive staff and the larger support of diocesan groups. 5) Resources. They wanted available books, media, etc., to do their work and enlarge their experience.

In and Out

Twelfth Principle: The Swinging Door. This I have saved for last because it is a cautionary principle. The uncreative parish functions as a kind of service station. It's there to "save souls"; it is an island of grace. So people come to it not only to be serviced, but to find refuge from a wicked world. The sanctuary, as in medieval times, is salvation. Beyond it is danger. True, lay people are obliged to live in the world, but they must come to the fortress for refreshment and strength to resist the contamination involved in one's regrettable return to the world.

This is not the vision either of the gospel or Vatican II. True enough, there are more than sufficient daily horrors and indignities in the world but, in fact, the truth also is that the world is God-infested. The world of work and family and neighborhood is the proper arena of lay witness and spirituality. Remember the words we quoted previously from Vatican II? "The laity, by their very vocation, seek the kingdom of God by engaging in temporal affairs and by ordering them according to the plan of God."

My point is that we must be wary of fostering a sanctuary mentality by our successful recruiting of ministers and volunteers who necessarily help the parish. These people are invaluable, but they must in no way think that parish involvement is the extent of their mission or that they have satisfied their vocation. Far from it. They must understand that they are helping the parish to be not an "in *or* out" finality, but rather an "in *and* out" process. People come to the parish to worship, to focus on their proper calling beyond the parish as spouses, workers, and citizens. In a word, people assist in the parish not as an end in itself, but as a means for all to find courage and strength to go out and evangelize, to be leaven, to bear witness, to bring Christ to the marketplace, and to uncover and celebrate grace in life's everydayness. Lay ministry, no matter how we define it, should not be self-serving and in-house. It must face outward. To do otherwise is to ultimately foster a new brand of lay clericalism. The motto must be "in *and* out."

Allied with this caution is another: Church or parish ministry for the clergy and religious must not be the measurement for the laity. After all, for the former, it is full time; for the latter, it is part time, even for professional lay ministers, not to mention volunteers. What I am getting at is expressed by Dawne Fleri and Loughlan Sofield in *Today's Parish* (April 1989):

> Lay ministers who have a primary commitment to family, work, and community often experience guilt when comparing themselves to priests and religious. On contrast to these models, lay people may feel that they can never do enough ministry. This often drives them to take on the impossible task of maintaining a full-time ministry in the world, *and* a full-time ministry in the church. These lay ministers desperately need to understand that time spent with family, friends, co-workers, and in the community is true ministry. . . .And if these lay people do hold clergy and religious as their models, we need to help them see that the value of a model lies in the commitment and dedication of that person, not in the amount of time given to the ministry.

A man jumped into the river to save someone from drowning as the bystanders cheered him on. A little later he jumped into the river a second time to save another. More cheers. He did this three, five, ten times. After this, he turned his back on the bystanders and began walking upstream. Seeing another drowning person, the bystanders called out to their hero but he ignored them. They accused him of indifference, but he turned and said to them, "Save him yourselves. I'm going up-stream to find out who's throwing all these people in!" Thus the creative and the uncreative parish.

These, then, are our twelve principles for shared and collaborative ministry. In the next brief chapter we shall describe some of those ministries, how they are formed, and how they function. Meanwhile, this outline might help:

The Creative Parish	vs	The Uncreative Parish
1. Ministry=shared, collaborative, consultative		Solo performance by clergy and perhaps staff
2. Co-responsibility		Sole responsibility
3. Sacramental sign: points to…		Institution, self-contained
4. Collegial and *inter*-dependent		Hierarchical, *inde*-pendent
5. All baptized with a variety of gifts		Pastor, staff do it all
6. Vision, spirituality: in *and* out		Service station: in *or* out
7. Wide scope		Narrow (inherited) programs
8. Social justice		Local charity
9. Criterion: freedom		Criterion: obedience
10. Community of communities		Central headquarters

Summary of Chapter 2

1. Collaboration is rooted in our tradition and affirmed by Vatican II.
   2. Collaboration takes time and patience.
   3. Teaching and doing at the same time are a good combination.
   4. There are certain helpful principles in attracting collaborators. They are:
      a. Education of the parish.
      b. Education as a gift for individuals.
      c. Using training booklets to "prime the pump."
      d. Getting to know the people via census, covenants, celebrations, etc.
      e. Invite personally rather than seek anonymous volunteers.

f. Use the one-shot, piggy-back.

g. Turn over ministry to others as soon as possible. Let it go.

h. Have legitimizing endings.

i. Respect volunteers.

j. Show gratitude to volunteers.

k. Train and support volunteers.

l. The swinging door of being open to the world.

5. Respect the laity's tempo and commitments.

A chain letter:

If your pastor does not measure up, simply send this letter to six other parishes that are tired of their pastor too. Then bundle up your pastor and send him to the church at the bottom of the list.

In one week, you will receive 1643 pastors and one of them should be perfect. Have faith in this letter. One church broke the chain and got their old pastor back in less than three weeks!

Chapter 3

Organizations and Ministries

A fable. The hippo fell in love with a butterfly. He sought the advice of the wise old owl. "You must become a butterfly," the owl told the hippo, "and do it right now." The hippo was delighted. He plunged back into the jungle only to return shortly. "How do I become a butterfly?" he asked the owl. The bird of great wisdom responded, "That's up to you. I only set policy. I don't implement."

We have the usual ministries and organizations that require little explanation, for everyone else has them. A few special notes, however, might be interesting:

1. *The Samaritans* provide service for the sick and needy: driving people to clinics, bringing communion, visiting hospitals, nursing homes, boarding homes, and shut-ins, coordinating the clothing drives, etc. A nice addition is that, since the Sunday homilies are taped, the Samaritans bring a tape (and leave a recorder if necessary) to hospitalized or housebound parishioners so that they feel a part of the worshiping family. Plus they bring them the Sunday bulletin. As the Samaritans' self-description puts it:

> Samaritans are called to give service to the community in the name of Christ. Nourished by God's word and encouraged by shared prayer and retreat time together, the Samaritans, on behalf of the parish, bring organized and concerted efforts to those in need.

2. *The Presbyters* (sometimes called "The Emmaus Walk Group") is a loose grouping of retired men (not a retired group of loose men, as we like to kid) who meet for monthly lunch, informal socials and retreats, and offer various services to the parish. The name nicely connotes wisdom figures, but it's a wisdom that works. These experienced retirees advertise that they: 1) will fix small appliances, 2) help with tax returns, 3) do fix-up household work, 4) guide young businesses, 5) provide rides to shopping, airports, etc.

3. *The Holy Spirits.* Our code name for Senior Citizens who meet once a month, brown-bagging it for programs of aerobics, shared prayer, outings, bus rides, etc. The name change is worth noting.

4. *The Martha/Mary Guild* is others' Rosary-Altar Society. Worth noting: The name was changed to catch the nicer balance of action and contemplation; that is, they do not just run socials and raise money (which they do well) or take care of the usual and vital activities such as altar linens, church maintenance, flowers, socials, attic sales, Chinese auctions, etc., but they are obliged to make retreats and put an emphasis on the spiritual as well. And any money they raise must be put into liturgy-related activities or parish needs. They may never keep beyond a certain amount in their treasury.

5. *The "R- Team."* The initial stands for

"Retired, Rambunctious, and Ready." This is a group of men who each volunteer one full day's work a week to the parish. They are incredibly handy and knowledgeable. They give their talent to keeping the parish going by doing anything from handiwork to office work. A genuine asset to us and no mean gift to their wives!

Two other ministries need some more detailed explanation. They are:

I. The Singles' Journey

This is a group of people over age 35 who meet every Sunday, all during the year, after the 10:30 Mass, in our Spiritual Center. Its membership includes those never married and those widowed, but the great majority are divorced. Interestingly, the group does not divide but actually coalesces well. At this writing they have been meeting now continually for six years. Many original members are still there; others, as in the nature of the group, come and go as their needs demand—and are met. The most consistent and constant word I hear associated with the Singles' Journey group is "healing." Since they are adults, they are self-begun and self-run. Some of them, six years ago, decided to meet in our Spiritual Center just to explore the need for broken people (divorced) like themselves to get together. They were meeting for months before I, the pastor, knew about it, which thrilled me no end.

Their sense of being parish, being church, had caught on. They soon attracted others and as many as 75 can be present at a meeting. They welcome new members. No questions are asked. Their philosophy is not to cater to griping ("My ex hasn't sent alimony in nine months, the rat!") but to healing and growth (hence the "journey" in their title). They rotate leadership, invite speakers, have occasionally a special Singles' Mass, connect with other similar faith groups, and bond into support groups as well as social friends. Their official mission statement is lovely:

A Single Journey—Singles Over 35

Every Sunday at 11:30 A.M. friends gather here at St. Mary's for an hour or so of companionship, caring, and sharing. We are men and women who came as strangers and are now friends; we are separated, divorced, widowed, or never married, but find a strong, common bond in our struggles to live a committed Christian life as single persons. Our stories are unique and our paths are diverse, but we share as a common goal a desire to heal and to grow and to seek new directions in our lives. We understand that for each of us there is a time to speak and a time to listen, and we ask only that all respect the confidentiality of whatever is shared here.

Our purpose is our prayer . . .

Let us look objectively at the past—to learn from it, never to dwell on it. In each of our histories let us know which things are to be shared and which should be kept secret.

Let us look kindly at the present. May we be gentle with ourselves and each other for we are at different stages in our journey. We offer fellowship and support, never advice or judgment.

Let us look hopefully at the future. May we see the wonderful possibilities that are open to us as single travelers, and may we share both joy and sorrow, laughter and tears as we grow together.

Above all, let us be open to the wisdom of each others' words. May we learn to listen more than we speak, to give more than we gain.

We are here to be here for each other!

A truly important thing to note is that the Singles' Journey group is recognized by the parish as an entity, an authentic organization (regardless of whether such members are parishioners or not). This is realized in three ways: 1) They are called upon as a group to participate in all church activities. 2) Since so many of them are broken and feel alienated from themselves (being divorced) and often from the church, we offer them an opportunity to serve publicly at the weekend liturgies as ushers, lectors, and eucharistic ministers for a period of three months. This is a public symbol that they belong, a community gesture of embrace. (See the letter in Parish Papers, page 304.) 3) I draw on them as Saturday night hostesses. Which means: As I mentioned earlier, every Saturday evening (except for the summertime), for the past twenty years, I have invited parishioners to share dinner with me. There are usually two couples—and that includes widows, married, unmarried, any combination. Since I do the cooking, I need someone to help greet the people and make them feel at home and to work with me in getting out the food and cleaning up afterwards. I ask the single women from the parish and from the Singles' Journey to be hostess for a month at a time. They, like myself, get to meet people and

widen their circle of friends. It is a most happy arrangement all the way around.

To start a Singles' Journey, offer room and invite them in. Let the pioneers call other similar groups for guidance and encouragement. Or write to us.

Resources

Institute of Singles Dynamics, P.O. Box 11394, Kansas City, MO 64112 (Protestant), *Singles in the Church: New Ways to Minister with 52% of God's People* by Kay Collier-Stone from the Alban Institute, 4125 Nebraska Ave, N.W., Washington, D.C. 20016, and Father Greg Friedman's fine booklet for singles, *Why Bother With the Church?* (Cincinnati: St. Anthony Messenger Press, 1988).

II. The Lazarus Ministry
Commentary

As the name suggests, the Lazarus Ministry deals with funerals. This ministry, from its

In Memoriam

inception to the present, is the most praise-evoked and good will ministry we have. Understandably. Death and grieving are vulnerable times and people are susceptible to kindness. The whole impact of the Lazarus

Ministry at this time is a distinct *community* outreach as opposed to "Father" being the chief and often the sole actor.

Preparation

1. Years ago, sparked by reading Jessica Mitford's book, *The American Way of Death*, and having long noted how costly and how commercialized and, yes, even how pagan, some funerals were—how the faith dimension had almost drowned in the competitive trappings of American Bigger and Better—I consulted local funeral directors to see if we could make funerals more simple, more Christian, less expensive. They were quite cooperative.

2. In due time, I sent a *letter to all parishioners* discussing the Christian view of death and burial, and tentatively suggesting that they would have the option of having wakes in church (an ancient custom) and a place, if they so desired, to buy a wooden coffin at a reasonable price. And their own parishioners, the newly formed Lazarus Ministry, would be there to assist them.

The idea of a simple wooden coffin is not far-out. Recall the simple box in which Pope Paul VI was buried. Someone just has to start the trend. There have to be local carpenters who can make such a coffin. I just came across a news item from the *Washington Post* (September 22, 1993) telling how the children of a certain George Kramer, a building contractor, at his wish, built a simple pine box coffin for him. As his children said, "We're a family of carpenters. There's no reason we couldn't do this." Despite the sadness in doing the project, the children reported a certain peace and admitted that the work soothed them.

3. Meanwhile, I solicited some people of

the parish and began *training* them in the ways (and theology) of funerals and grief. We used Msgr. Joe Champlin's books and tapes (Ave Maria Press), the new rite of funerals (later when it came out), and other material. I also solicited help from some hospice people from a nearby hospital. By the time we heard tapes and speakers, discussed books and practicalities, we were ready to begin as a Lazarus Ministry.

4. *Policies* were spelled out in our annual parish booklet:

> With few extraordinary exceptions, everyone shall receive a Christian burial. No one—no matter how poor or in-different a Catholic, no matter how evil, or how the person died, whether natural-ly or by his or her own hand or by an-other's—will be denied Christian burial.
>
> The gospel imperative is that when a person is dead, all is over and the only final obligation that the Christian community has in charity is to pray for the deceased and to demonstrate by its liturgy that forgiveness, kindness, and reconciliation that Christ himself showed. For the Christian community to deny its ritual of prayer and worship, even to a public sinner, is not to imitate Our Master who prayed for those who crucified him and promised paradise to the Good Thief.

5. With few exceptions, funerals are held at the usual daily community Mass (9:00 A.M.). The advantages are: 1) As the only priest in the parish, I don't have to celebrate extra Masses, and 2) the consistent morning crowd provides strong body english and

directions to visitors and the occasional non-practicing Catholic who has no sense of church etiquette.

There is, by the way, no conflict with the current day's Mass intention. That intention is honored, even though there is a funeral.

6. Given the nature of our church, the only *flowers* permitted are one bouquet in front of the altar and a coffin spray. All other flowers are brought to the parish hall where hospitality will be held.

7. We have available at the wake service two cards: one, the usual *Mass card*, and the other is our *Social Concerns card*. This card, used for any occasion, has proven to be of great value. It gives the donors a great sense that something practical is being done with their offering and is a special boon to businesses and corporations, which are sometime less comfortable with the abstract and partisan Mass card, but always quite open to helping concrete social needs. (There is a copy of the card in Parish Papers, page 296. Copy it and then fold it two ways and you'll see how the card looks. Of course, modify it to suit your purposes.)

The Process

The best way to understand the process is, I think, to review what actually happens in the parish.

1. A *call* comes to the office from the family or, more likely, the funeral director, to arrange for a funeral.

2. As soon as the secretary gets the call, she immediately *contacts the captain* of one of the two Lazarus teams.

3. That captain swings into action by calling the funeral director to check a) the date of the funeral, b) where the wake will be held,

and c) the visiting hours.

4. Then the captain *gathers some members* and they go to the grieving family's house after having called first to make an appointment with them. They bring with them two booklets: 1) *Through Death to Life: Preparing to Celebrate the Funeral Rite* by Joe Champlin (Notre Dame, Ind.: Ave Maria Press, 1990) and 2) our own homemade booklet entitled "Prayers, Readings, Hymns for the Communal Celebration of the Christian Wake Service and Mass of Christian Burial." The title is an exact description of its contents with the addition of a section of "Some Private Prayers and Reflections," the Prayers at the Cemetery, and, on the inside back cover, the form found in Parish Papers, page 214.

5. Questions are asked. Had the deceased *any requests* concerning his or her funeral? Any special gift to be brought up at the offertory that is meaningful (a photo, tool, craft, etc.)? Who will bring up the gifts? Does anyone want to do the *reading*? Will there be a *eulogy*? If so, it will never preempt the homily at its proper place after the gospel, but will come at the end of Mass in place of the usual after-communion meditation time. What *readings* do they want? What *hymns* from the booklet?

The Lazarus ministers will offer practical helps such as babysitters, drivers, and pick-ups for those coming by plane, train, or bus.

This whole process and dialogue is very therapeutic and comforting.

6. If the wake is at the funeral parlor, the Lazarus ministers will conduct it there. They usually use *The Catholic Worship Book* (Baltimore: Helicon, 1975, p. 669), but sometimes they will use other services.

7. If the wake is in church, some members are on hand when the body is brought in.

They say:

> We welcome the body of our sister/
> brother,_____, into this church,
> this community of believers. We mourn
> the loss but rejoice in his (her) return to
> the Father.
>
> Let us join together in the prayer our
> brother Jesus left us:
>
> (All recite the Our Father.)
>
> May his (her) soul and all the souls of
> the faithful departed rest in peace. Amen.

8. The Lazarus Ministry has meanwhile contacted others to drop off cake and similar *light refreshments.* They put on the coffee in the connecting *parish hall* and stay all during the wake both in church and in the hall offering comfort, presence, and hospitality.

9. When the wake is over, the coffin is closed (if it had been open) and the body remains in the church all night. The funeral director comes early to re-open the coffin and make any other preparations before the family and friends arrive for Mass.

10. A description of how we conduct a funeral liturgy:

a. We ask the funeral director to assist the incoming people to *sit on both sides* of the center aisle rather than have everyone on one side, giving that lopsided feeling—especially if the pulpit is way over on the other side.

b. If the body is being accompanied by the pall bearers from the funeral parlor, they take the coffin all the way into church, directly touching the baptismal font, which is located at the front of the center aisle. This has two advantages: 1) The people are all inside and so can see the celebrant and hear the prayers. (It's unfair to have half of them standing on the steps outside, especially if the weather is bad.) 2) The proximity of the body to the font gives a great symbol and makes more meaningful the opening words (including those from St. Paul):

> I bless the body of N. with the holy
> water that recalls his (her) baptism of
> which Saint Paul writes, "All of us who
> were baptized into Christ Jesus were
> baptized into his death. By baptism into
> his death we were buried together with
> him, so that just as Christ was raised
> from the dead by the glory of the Father,
> we too might live a new life."

These words and the location of the coffin provide a great homiletic opportunity.

c. The celebrant enters in silence, goes to the other side of the font, and begins the prayers. The pall is near, ready to be used. When the celebrant is finished, the cantor introduces the first hymn. Our homemade booklets described above are distributed throughout the church.

d. At the end, before the body is removed, we invite the congregation to extend their right hand as we sing the Blessing of Aaron. Where the blessing of the body is called for, the celebrant uses the sprinkler resting in the water of the open baptismal font.

e. One verse of the closing hymn is sung while the body is brought to the church entrance. Then the celebrant says aloud the final prayer which is followed by a second verse of the hymn.

f. If needed, we provide luncheon in the hall after the cemetery services.

As I noted, the overall impression is one of the community being involved and concerned. The priest does not have to be there until Mass time—though, of course, he has touched base with the family all during the illness or been there if there was sudden death. He is part of a whole collaborative congregational ministry.

Follow Up

1. The *homily is taped* and later given to the survivors. It's a great comfort for family members and friends to gather at a later date and hear the words again at an emotionally slower pace.

2. The Lazarus ministers at their home visit have asked for a photo of the deceased, which is now attached to our public board in church along with the date of burial so that all parishioners have a chance to identify the deceased. (See Chapter 1.)

3. At Christmas I send a personal letter to the widow (widower) offering sympathy at this difficult time. Here is a sample:

Dear Bill,

The holiday times are probably the most difficult in dealing with the memories of your mother. I just wanted to let you know I am aware of this and that you have my sympathy and prayers.

Try to remember that Christmas means that God so loved the world that He sent His only-begotten Son so that those who believe may not perish but have everlasting life.

And everlasting life is the Christ Child's gift to your mother and a promise and comfort to you.

You have my prayers and that of the whole parish family.

Sincerely yours in Christ,
Father Bausch

4. Someone in charge sends a card on the anniversary of the death.

That card is as follows:

(On the front is this piece of clip art:)

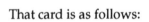

The inside text of the folded card reads:

With Sympathy and Love

It was a year ago that you lost someone near and dear to you. On this anniversary we, the people of St. Mary's parish, want to renew the promise of our prayers, the sympathy of hearts, and the fellowship of our common journey, united as we are with all of the Communion of Saints, past, present, and yet to come.

The People of St. Mary's, Colts Neck, N.J.

5. The name of the deceased is inscribed in the *Book of the Dead* beneath the notice board. This can be simply a three-ring binder with a nicely computerized script (and some appropriate clip art). For example:

1993
Eleanor Walsh, January 23
Robert Micelli, February 8
etc.

or you can get a formal book and have a calligrapher write in the names. This is what we have. The book then lies open on a shelf we have built in the church. This formal book, large and imposing with lovely scriptural quotations scattered on its pages, may be obtained from Liturgy Training Publications, 1800 North Heritage Ave, Chicago, IL 60622. It's called *The Book of the Names of the Dead.*

Another resource: *Blest Are They Who Mourn* edited by Diana Kodner (GIA, 7404 South Mason Ave., Chicago, IL 60638).

6. We have a fine Bereavement Ministry ready to help. (There is an excellent video called *Ministry to the Bereaved* with therapist Dr. Patrick Del Zoppo from St. Paul Center, 145 Clinton Ave., Staten Island, NY 10301).

7. Here is a worthwhile related topic. We have mailed every parishioner three items. One is a full text of the Catholic teaching on extraordinary means of survival, or a "Living Will," or what is properly called "Advanced Directive for Health Care" (which most hospitals demand before acceptance). Your diocese should have one, or else you may write to those dioceses that do, such as mine: The Diocese of Trenton, 701 Lawrenceville

Rd., P.O. Box 5309, Trenton, NJ 08638. We include also a sample of a living will in our mailing. See page 215 in Parish Papers.

A good resource is the pamphlet entitled *The Living Will* by Mary Senander (The Leaflet Missal Co., 976 W. Minnehaha Ave., St. Paul, MN 55104).

The third item is a very practical two-fold paper on "Instructions for My Funeral," which we obtained from Father Joe Nolan. People fill it out and give it to their lawyer or to the parish for safe keeping. The text is reproduced on pages 216-220 of Parish Papers.

Before you turn to that, I call your attention to one final note: The church, like official society, has no funeral services for the stillborn, no ritual, no community ceremony, although the *New England Journal of Medicine* estimates that some 31% of all pregnancies end in miscarriage. True, the Order of Christian Funerals has a "Rite of Final Commendation for an Infant" (no. 318), which can be used for a stillborn and a miscarriage, but there's no precise ritual as such. (See the prayer service on page 292 in Parish Papers.) As a result, the parents are left with no vocabulary, no means of expressing communal loss and grief, especially if a child was stillborn near gestation. Such a child is indeed real, very real to the parents. We have to provide for a ceremony. See the article "Meghan and Molly Deserved a Birth Announcement" in *U.S. Catholic* (February 1991). Note also three fine pamphlets: "Newborn Death," "Children Die, Too," and "Handling the Holidays" put out by Human Services Press, P.O. Box 2423, Springfield, IL 62705. A good resource for Christian funerals in general is Terrence Curley's book, *Console*

One Another: A Guide for Christian Funerals
(Kansas City: Sheed & Ward, 1993).

Pastoral Suggestions

As in so many other things, a lot of expectations have clustered around funerals, some valid, some invalid, and some no longer feasible. To make any changes in these expectations will take some persistent teaching (and considerable courage) since we are dealing with a highly emotional time. I have already proposed one change, namely, the expectation that the priest must be there from beginning to end. There was a period of tension for a while when I was not present at all phases of the funeral arrangements, for example, the house visit, the welcoming of the body into church, the wake service. But people soon learned to appreciate the efforts of the Lazarus Ministry, and their ministry is as much accepted and welcomed now as my absence is understood.

So, I suggest, we must make some movements now in other areas. Prompted by the continuing priest shortage, let me list two. First of all, it is not necessary that every person be buried with a Mass. That's a bombshell right there, since even the most nominal Catholic expects a Mass. But why? Only by habit and tradition. To bring this person to Mass when he (she) cannot choose, when all their life they chose otherwise, is kind of hitting them when they are down—or to satisfy the guilt of the family. Why can't we develop an acceptable and reverent service at the funeral home—and eventually, one led by a deacon or pastoral minister? This does not contradict our parish policy that no one will be denied Christian burial. The service *is* the community's burial service, but one held in the funeral home. It will take time to legitimize this, but it can be done. I think, for example, of the time when the mandatory pre-cana conferences were decreed for all engaged couples. For a while there was a hue and cry, but now, even the most distanced Catholic couple call in for the pre-cana schedule. That they must attend is simply a part of the taken-for-granted common consciousness now. So, in time, would the option of a reverent service in the funeral home rather than a Mass in church for anyone, practicing or not. We simply must begin to offer this option and make it acceptable. We must begin to publicize such opportunities out loud and consistently. It would help enormously, of course, if the bishops or the diocese would take such an official stand and legitimize the options.

Second—and again this goes against the grain—need we have only one body per one Mass of Christian Burial? If there are several deaths within the same period of time, why could we not have several bodies present at the one Mass? The answer is that we are individualist and consumerist even in our communal celebrations. I want *my* Mass for *my* husband with *my* people there—and only them! But in fact the presence of multiple bodies happens in time of plague or other tragedies. Moreover, as I indicated, since we at the parish normally have the Mass of Christian Burial at the regular morning community Mass, there are always "others" there, often more numerically than the family, friends, and relatives, and no one minds.

There is, in fact, a deeper sense when several bodies are present and, I think, there are marvelous opportunities for an extended and sensitive approach in the liturgy and homily that can underscore the whole community's common journey. After all, as we are fond of pointing out, we are a People of God, a community, those who celebrate multiple baptisms, confirmations, communal confessions, anointings and even, occasionally, weddings at the community Mass or public gatherings. Again, granted this process will take time to get into the public consciousness, but my point is that we must start now. Once more, it would be most helpful pastorally if the bishops began to promulgate this.

Summary of Chapter 3

1. A variety of ministries draws a variety of ministers.

2. Be mindful of the Singles in your parish, the largest growing segment in American society.

3. The Lazarus Ministry is very fruitful and fulfilling. To start one:

    a. Prepare the people by a letter; preach about it

    b. Have a written policy concerning those entitled to Christian burial

    c. If possible, celebrate the funeral at the daily community Mass

    d. Have a policy concerning flowers

    e. Offer an alternate card, socially based, to the Mass card.

4. The process is as follows:

    a. The Lazarus members visit the house on learning of a death

    b. They bring a booklet from which to choose music and readings

    c. They offer options for 1)preparation gifts, 2) readers, 3) eulogists

    d. They offer babysitting, drivers, and hospitality

    e. They contact the organist and funeral director to see where the wake is being held: at the funeral parlor or the church

    f. They welcome the body into church if the wake is there

    g. They do the wake service in either place

    h. They offer hospitality (refreshments, presence) if the wake is in church.

5. Follow-up consists of:

    a. A gift of the taped homily

    b. The exposition of a photo of the deceased in church

    c. A letter of sympathy at Christmas

    d. An anniversary card from the parish

    e. Inscription into the "Book of the Dead"

    f. The offerings of our Bereavement Ministry.

6. Consider the following:

    a. An alternate service in the funeral home in place of the Mass

    b. Several bodies at one Mass of Christian Burial

The parish uses voice mail. The message: "If you are calling from a touch-tone phone and would like to register in the parish, press one. If you're calling for the Mass schedule, press two. To complain to the pastor, press three. To complain *about* the pastor, press four, five, and six."

The Sacraments

Chapter 4

The Sacraments:
Baptism, Confirmation, Eucharist

> It would seem to me that as we talk sacraments, as we teach revisions, as we catechize, we must first of all look to the foundation on which all this rests: the believing community. If that is less than it should be, the sacraments will always be less than they should be. . . .I would say in practice that means the revival and support of the parish.
>
> —*A New Look at the Sacraments*

The celebration of the sacraments presumes communal exposure and involvement. That is why, like most parishes, we celebrate all the sacraments at either the community weekend Masses (baptisms, sacrament of the sick, and occasionally matrimony), the weekday community Masses (confirmation, First Communion, matrimony) or at a communal gathering (penance, or reconciliation).

It has long been our custom (not necessarily a good one) not to accept stipends for these celebrations on the premise that this is the people's church. They support it and are entitled to its services. There should not always be money connected with sacred events and it's nice for our people to report to others that no charge was involved to use *their* church. Besides, it's a way of nickel and dime-ing people to death. (Which is why, as I mention in my book, *The Hands-On Parish,* we never have more than one collection on Sunday and do not permit selling tickets before or after Mass.) Again, people come for one reason: to praise God—not to be a captive audience even for the most kindly and sensitive cause. Our experience is that people appreciate this and are more apt to be

generous where it counts: in the collection.

Baptism

Commentary
Theoretically, baptism has been restored as an integral part of the initiation triad of water, anointing (confirmation), and eucharist, and it has taken on a whole new focus as the primary and foundational sacrament of community insertion and ministry. Emotionally, of course, it runs far behind the sweet delights of the inverted order of First Communion and confirmation and the centuries-old tenure of the clergy as the only certified and lawful ministers. Still, in one way or another, most parishes try to make connections and to underscore the community centrality and commitment.

The Process

1. Like most parishes, we have a *prebaptism program*. (We'll save for another chapter the use and abuse of such programs.) We ask expectant parents to come for two evenings. Some parishes include godparents but, since they are often from out of town, we don't. We use the videotapes and booklets to open up discussion for parents and guide them.

2. When the prospective parents call in, they are referred to the couple in charge of the prebaptismal program and are also *assigned a couple* who will help them at the actual ceremony.

3. Also, the parents are sent a *newsletter* before the birth of their child, and at birth: a) a growth calendar, b) an audiocassette (one side "lively" and the other side "quiet-time" nursery songs), and c) a baptismal information sheet and tract.

4. Our policy is to have baptisms on the second Sunday of the month at the noon *community Mass*. This is standard, known to the congregation, so that they may come or attend another Mass.

5. At the beginning of Mass, relatives and friends are shown to reserved seats while the parents and godparents remain in the back of church. When all is ready, before Mass starts, the host couple announces to the congregation that we will celebrate at this Mass the baptism of Susie Smith (let's call her), the child of Mary and John Smith. Then the parents, carrying the baby, and the godparents process in with the celebrant and other ministers. They file into the front pew reserved for them.

6. After the homily, the parents, child, and godparents are called to the sanctuary and stand there facing the congregation.

7. The celebrant, standing before them and facing them, proceeds with a modified rite (the scriptures, for example, are omitted since they have already been proclaimed). At the proper place he turns to the congregation and asks them the usual questions, but adds an *additional charge:*

"Do you, the Christian family gathered here for worship, promise to provide the living context of faith, hope, and love so that this child can grow up naturally and easily knowing and loving God?"

"We do."

"Do you promise to be a support to these parents who cannot raise their child alone in the faith, but will always need your prayers and encouragement?"

"We do."

"Since, then, it is your will that Susie Smith should be baptized in this holy, Catholic faith, I ask her parents and godparents to approach the baptismal font."

BAPTIZED INTO CHRIST'S DEATH

8. Toward the end of the ceremony, we add three things:

First, we ask for the oldest member of the congregation to step forward. After some hesitation some wonderful and venerable person raises his or her hand. We then ask that person to come up and lay his or her hands silently on the infant's head as a sign of the transmission of the heritage and a blessing from an elder. It's quite a moving gesture.

Second, we ask the parents to share briefly with the congregation what they wish for this new infant, what they would like this child to be, to become. (This is optional.)

Third, we ask the whole congregation to stand, raise their hands over the child, and sing one verse of what has become our parish signature, "The Blessing of Aaron" (Jack Miffleton, World Library). It's a precious moment.

9. We then announce that we have a new family member and the entire congregation *applauds* and the parents and godparents return to the pew.

10. At the *prayers of the faithful,* as we do at all Masses that weekend, we pray for those to be (or who have been) baptized.

11. At the end of Mass, in place of the usual meditation time after communion, the celebrant reads a *letter* we have prepared, a letter to be given to the child just before his or her confirmation. Then the letter is handed to one of the parents. It goes like this:

Dear Susie,

When you were born, your parents thought so much of you that they wanted to share the most precious gift they had: their faith.

So they approached the Christian community at St. Mary's, Colts Neck, New Jersey, and asked the people if they would be willing to have a new member, and would they be willing to create the climate within which you could and would grow to know and love Jesus Christ.

The community said yes, and so on Sunday, February 14, 1994, you and your parents and godparents, family and friends, came to St. Mary's. There at the twelve o'clock Mass, in full view of the congregation, you were inserted into the Christian family.

The people were happy and they applauded you afterwards. And then your parents brought you home and had a celebration there too because of this joyful event.

That was many years ago. Now you are ready to complete your initiation into the Christian faith through the sacrament of confirmation. You are now ready to speak for yourself and declare yourself a Catholic and your desire to bear witness to the gospel in your life.

We hope this letter finds you ready and willing to do so—as we hope that the years past have given you comfort and joy in the Lord.

Signing this letter are your pastor at that time, Father Bausch, Sister Stella, and some people from the congregation who were present when you were baptized and who first welcomed you into our midst.

Today, as you read this letter before you are confirmed, remember this: We still welcome you, pray for you, hope for you, and, through the years and distance, love you.

Sincerely yours in Christ,

12. At the end of Mass the parents, infant, and godparents recess with the celebrant and ministers and stand at the exit to receive the well wishes of the congregation.

Follow Up

There are several follow ups after the baptism:

1. The family is sent a *series of newsletters*, which are single sheets in a three-way fold. They are sent 2, 4, 6, 8, and 12 months after the baptism.

2. They also receive an *anniversary card* from the parish. It has some clip art on the front and the inside text reads as follows:

front panel

(inside text)

Happy First Anniversary!

One year ago this week, your baby was welcomed into the Christian community of St. Mary's. The event was, you recall, a lovely rite of entrance into the People of God who, overjoyed with a new member, applauded and rejoiced. We just want to wish you a Happy First Anniversary of this baptism along with the promise of our prayers. We know that your parenting, by word and example, continues to connect your child with this community and continues to draw your little one closer to the Source of all life.

The People of St. Mary's, Colts Neck

3. The parents receive *more newsletters* at 18 months, two years, and three years.

4. They also receive, courtesy of the parish, a copy of the magazine *Catholic Parent*.

5. Every Thursday the M.O.P.I.T.S. (Mothers of Preschool, Infants, and Toddlers) meet. Mothers are invited to meet for group discussion, parenting skills, and the chance to hear any adult vocabulary beyond mommy, daddy, and potty. Babysitting is provided.

6. Parents are also invited to become a part of the Family Education program that meets once a month on Sundays. (Some respond, some don't.) In this program, planned by the parents themselves, a common topic is explored as the parents and older children learn in one room and the smaller children are farmed out according to age to other rooms. Then they all return to gather for a common sharing and celebration.

7. Finally, in our New Year's Sunday bulletin we have a section entitled "Pilgrimage of Faith: The Beginning and the End." See a sample of this on page 221 of Parish Papers.

Practicalities

1. The white cloth given at the ceremony opens to function as a small pillow with a baptismal motif sewn on it. It is made by the senior women of the parish as part of their ministry.

2. We've hardly ever had a crying child to shout over, but if that occurs we have a nearby Cry Room to which to hustle the child.

3. The host couple informs all those proud, camera-carrying relatives that no pictures are allowed during the ceremony. However, afterwards they may take all they want and the priest will be happy to re-pose any scene.

4. The signatures on the letter read at the end of Mass are taken by the host couple from people who are there waiting for Mass to begin.

5. Yes, we make exceptions to the standard communal baptism at Mass and, for good reasons, allow other times for the ceremony. But this is rare. Most people expect and look forward to the communal ceremony during Mass.

Resources

1. For those newsletters, our source is the Concordia Publishing House, 3558 Jefferson Ave., Saint Louis, MO 63118. Ask for their "Nursery Roll Packet." It includes the newsletter, logos, growth chart, the audiocassette, a book, *Read Me a Bible Story*, and a book of devotions. Altogether a pleasing packet to work with. Get someone to take this on as a ministry. Read "Infant Baptism: Making the Most of the Rite" by Paul Covino (*Today's Parish*, March and April 1992).

2. The *Catholic Parent* magazine is from Our Sunday Visitor, 200 Noll Plaza, Huntington, IN 46750. There are others, of course.

3. Don Bosco Multimedia, 475 North Avenue, P.O. Box T, New Rochelle, NY 10802 has a fine series of short books under the general title *Families Nurturing Faith*, covering such topics as: A Parents' Guide to Preschool Years, to the Grade School Years, the Young Adolescent Years, and so on. Note also the book, *Holy Families: Christian Families in a Changing World* by Robert J. Hater, Tabor Publishing, 25115 Ave., Stanford, Suite 130, Valencia, CA 91355. See especially the article, "An Infant Baptism Program that Works," *Today's Parish*, April/May, 1993.

4. There are many excellent prebaptism programs. We use the three-part videocassettes put out by the Franciscans called *Baby's Baptism: Sacrament of Welcome*, Franciscan Communications, 1229 So. Santee St., Los Angeles, CA 90015. Another is *Your Baby's Baptism* published by Liguori Publications, One Liguori Drive, Liguori, MO 63057.

5. General background for baptism: William J. Bausch, *A New Look at the Sacraments* (Mystic, Conn.: Twenty-Third Publications, 1983) and Joseph Martos, *Doors to the Sacred* (Old Brookville, N.Y.: Triumph Books, 1991) and Regina Kuehn, *A Place for Baptism* (Chicago: Liturgy Training Publications, 1992).

6. Note: Almost every group has had a lobby in Washington to press their agendas—except parents. Now at last such a lobby exists. It is called Parent Action and its aims are to increase public awareness of the role of the parent, to highlight and pass family-friendly legislation in the areas of health care, child care, education, employment and income security, connections among parents through Public Action Network and corporate partnerships that help employers implement policies that do not force parents to choose between family and job. Join! Membership is a suggested $25 a year. Get your parish to join. Write: Parent Action, B & O Building, 2 North Charles St., Baltimore, MD 21201, phone: 1-301-752-1790.

Confirmation
Commentary
We will forever argue over the age for celebrating confirmation, as we will always despair of its tendency to be a "graduation ceremony" for the young people who statistically leave the church in great numbers after they are confirmed. But whatever age we choose, or whatever the diocesan policy, most parishes try to personalize the experience for the young people and to include the whole community. We celebrate confirmation every two years for students in grades 8 and 9 and here's how we try to accomplish both.

The Process
1. The students or candidates are given a homemade booklet for themselves and their parents that acquaints them with all they need to know and prepare for.

2. Each time we have confirmation (every two years), we get a special team to run the confirmation program. We do not use the regular teachers. We recruit others who will simply devote their time and energies to this project.

3. The outline of preparation is as follows:

a. The Public Pledge and the Signing of the Scroll. The students have turned in wallet-size photographs of themselves which in turn are pasted on a large scroll (like a window shade). The candidates then attend all the weekend Masses on a given date where they, their parents, and the congregation make a mutual pledge, which goes as follows (the text is printed beneath the pictures and a copy of it is in all the pews):

I pledge to try, with all my ability, to prepare in a meaningful way for the sacrament of confirmation.

I will participate in all the meetings, instructions, and activities.

I will place my talents at the service of others, so that I may come to give freely of the gifts God has given me.

I pray for growth, and a greater maturity in faith, hope, and love.

I pledge to try to accept more responsibility in my family, in my church, and in my community, not as a child but as a young adult Christian.

I ask the help of the the Father, the Son, and the Holy Spirit.

Then the parents add their pledge:

I pledge to you, my son (daughter), that I will do all I can to help you prepare for the sacrament of confirmation.

I will give you my support, my encouragement, and my prayers; and in all this, I ask the help of the Father, the Son, and the Holy Spirit.

Finally the community adds its pledge:

I pledge to you, the confirmation candidates, my support in your special projects, my encouragement in your experiences of Christian service, and my prayers in the days ahead.

I ask the help of the Father, the Son, and the Holy Spirit.

This ceremony takes place at Mass after the homily. The candidates then come up and sign the scroll. Afterwards the scroll is hung over the main door for all to see until after confirmation.

b. A Christian Service Project. The candidates must do about 15 hours of community service and write an account of it. A detailed list of places of service are suggested (nursing homes, elderly in need of help, hospital, helping at the Bible Vacation School, etc.). There should be resource people available to contact if they have questions.

c. Personal Interview. This should be arranged with the members of the confirmation team, including the pastor, deacons, the Director of Religious Education, and the Spiritual Director.

d. *Prayer Partners.* This is designed to help the candidate better realize the parish community dimension of confirmation. So that each candidate will have a Prayer Partner, parishioners already confirmed (including teens and adults) promise to write to the candidate several times during the preparation period to let them know that they are being prayed for and to share insights about their own faith journey. We attract such prayer partners by putting a notice in the parish bulletin. The response is always there. It's a kind of faith pen pal and very effective. Here's a copy of the Sunday bulletin insert:

Would You Like to Be a Confirmation PRAYER PARTNER?

Our parish eighth and ninth graders are preparing for confirmation in the fall. In order to increase awareness of the parish community dimension of confirmation, we would like each confirmation candidate to have a Prayer Partner. This already confirmed Catholic (including teens and young adults) would write to an assigned candidate at least five times between April and September, letting the teen know that he (she) is being remembered and prayed for. Prayer Partners will receive a set of five prayer cards, one of which can be included in each note.

Please return the form below to the R.E. Office or the parish office, to the ushers, or place it in the offertory basket, by February 24.

A listing of all those in this year's confirmation class is on the reverse side of this notice.

Any questions? Call Lucille Castro (DRE) at the Religious Education Office.

☐ Yes, I would like to be a Prayer Partner for confirmation.
☐ No, not at this time.

I would like to be a Prayer Partner for (indicate choices of any specific candidate). We will try to give you one of your choices.

1._____
2._____
3._____

☐ I do not have a preference and will be happy to be a Prayer Partner for any candidate you assign me.

Name _____
Phone _____
Address_____

All Prayer Partners receive a letter of acknowledgment and thanks from the parish.

e. Retreat. All candidates are expected to make a common retreat sometime before the sacrament is celebrated.

f. Letter of Intent. The candidate is required to write a formal letter of intent to the pastor stating—in his or her own words—what they have done during the preparation time, what they plan to do in the future to live out their commitment, and a formal request for the sacrament.

g. Offertory Bearers. All during the preparation time, the candidates are assigned to be offertory bearers at the various Masses; their names are in the bulletin as such on that particular Sunday.

h. Prayer Booklet. Each candidate is given the gift of a small booklet called "Tracks," a compilation of prayers written by teens themselves. They like this.

i. Dress Code. We ask them to wear suitable clothing for the occasion, which excludes jeans and sneakers (some may have to rent shoes!). To avoid unseemly competition, we always use confirmation robes.

j. The Liturgy. The candidates, of course, take part in the confirmation liturgy itself as lectors, etc. And for the confirmation we prepare a complete booklet with a confirmation cover (from one of the professional houses). The booklet includes the entire script, from music to dialogue with the bishop, to the necessary congregational prayers and responses.

4. Sponsors. These are not what they once were in the early church. Now they are often chosen for reasons of social and family courtesy or obligations. For these reasons, theologian Joseph Martos has suggested abandoning sponsors and godparents altogether, but his suggestion has not been well received. Some parishes do have meetings with the sponsors but we do not. Instead we reach out to them (some of whom live far away) with a letter and a suggestion as follows:

Dear Sponsor:

Congratulations! A teenager has asked you to be a sponsor for confirmation and you have accepted.

Here at St. Mary's our confirmation candidates sign a covenant in which each person agrees "to prepare in a meaningful way" for confirmation. One of our hopes is that each confirmation candidate develops some awareness of personally accepting the decision made at baptism to follow our Lord Jesus in the Christian community of the Roman Catholic tradition.

Many years ago the sponsor and candidate shared a strong bond of faith as the neophyte sought to grow in the Christian life, and the sponsor walked the path of growth and faith-deepening as a fellow pilgrim in the faith journey.

In order to help develop some sense of faith sharing in this process, we would like you to take the time to give the teen you are sponsoring the gift of your personal perspective by writing a brief letter. We would like this letter sent to your teenager in care of St. Mary's Church. Your letter will be presented to him (her) and read privately as part of the confirmation retreat in early May. In order to be sure that your letter is completed and that your teen will have such

letter of affirmation, please be sure the letter is here by Easter Sunday, April 19. As you can imagine, your teen will really miss a meaningful time at the retreat if your letter is not here.

In writing to this special teenager who has chosen you, you may wish to touch on the following points:

•Fond memories of this teen as a child

•Special qualities you see in him (her)

•Prayers or religious songs that have meaning for you

•People who have influenced you in trying to lead a good life

•Ways that being a Christian has helped you

•Memories of your own preparation for confirmation

•What helps you to keep believing in God

•A promise to pray for this teen

•Some of your hopes or dreams for him (her).

We hope that you like this idea and that, even if you find it difficult or challenging, you will realize that this can be something very special for the teen who has chosen you as sponsor.

Sincerely yours in the Lord,
Lucille Castro

5. Presenting the Letter. Long-time parishioners at this time give the baptismal letter to their children. (See the section on baptism, pages 49-54.)

6. Seating. At the confirmation Mass, the candidates sit in *alternate rows*: that is, one row of girls followed by a row of boys, etc. This fulfills the requirement of our bishop that candidates be segregated, while at the same time it mixes them. In other words, you don't have all boys on one side and all girls on the other.

7. Uniting the Sacraments. Also, to once again show the union between baptism and confirmation, instead of that part in the liturgy where the bishop sprinkles them with holy water, we have them come out of the pews and dip their hands in the *baptismal font* and bless themselves.

8. Closing. At the end of the liturgy all the

candidates gather in the sanctuary around the altar, and one of them speaks for the group in giving thanks to all, inviting all to the hall for refreshments. Then the congregation is invited to raise its hands over the candidates to sing the Blessing of Aaron.

Resources

Any of the usual resources are helpful from the religious trade companies. For the theological view, see William J. Bausch, *A New Look at the Sacraments* (Mystic, Conn.: Twenty-Third Publications, 1983) and Joseph Martos, *Doors to the Sacred* (Old Brookville, N.Y.: Triumph Books, 1991). For a short book—fewer than 100 pages—on the sources of development of this sacrament, see *Sources of Confirmation from the Fathers Through the Reformers* (Collegeville, Minn.: Liturgical Press, 1992) and especially, *Confirmation: The Baby in Solomon's Court* by Paul Turner (Mahwah, N.J.: Paulist Press).

First Communion

First Communions, of course, bring out fond relatives, grandparents, and friends. The spiritual hoopla far exceeds that of the definitive baptism, for the children are at a most attractive age. We try, like most parishes, to make it a joyous and an instructive occasion.

Process

1. *Options.* Children can make First Communion with the group, on a special family day at the family's choice of time and date, or they may have a combination of the two.

2. *Gowns.* Again, to prevent the junior clothes competition, the children rent *gowns*

for the occasion.

3. *Preparation.* Classes and parents meetings are routine, but we have some special twists.

4. *Prayer.* The children are exposed to an exercise in *prayer time.* Our spiritual director takes them for a class and helps them in prayer.

5. *Tour.* They get a special tour of the church by the pastor.

6. *Bread Baking.* There is a special evening of baking bread. Here the children themselves mix, roll, and shape the bread. We supply all the ingredients and our version of Julia Child to guide them, while the parents bring a 9" metal (not aluminum foil) cake pan, an apron, and, of course, a camera. See the recipe in Parish Papers, page 222.

7. *Photo.* Each child brings a wallet size *picture* of himself (herself). These pictures will be pasted on a cut-out felt chalice pattern which in turn is pasted to an altar hanging (antependium).

8. *Banner.* Each family makes a special family banner that will hang on the pew in which the child and his (her) family will sit. See the design in Parish Papers, on page 223.

9. *Seating.* At the liturgy *each family has a row* with the child processing in and sitting in the aisle seat with them.

10. *Booklet.* The usual complete booklet containing all the necessary songs, prayers, and responses is given to all. The First Communion children do the readings and the prayers of the faithful. Our children's choir (dubbed "The Moppets") sings and their teachers are the offertory bearers.

11. *Dialogue.* Of course, there is the usual *opening dialogue* with the parents:

Celebrant:	Parents, what do you ask of the church?
Parents:	I ask that my child receive the Lord in the eucharist, and by this, grow as an active member of God's family.
Celebrant:	Do you feel that you, as a parent, have done your best to teach your child about Jesus, his love, his teachings, and his presence in the eucharist?
Parents:	I do.
Celebrant:	And, as a witnessing parent, have you taught your child to pray?
Parents:	I have.
Celebrant (to children):	Boys and girls, your parents have said that you are ready to receive Jesus in the eucharist. On behalf of our parish family, I welcome you today to the Holy Table.

12. Renewing Vows. After the homily there is the usual renewal of the baptismal vows and at the end the celebrant gives the instruction: "To show you are ready to join us at God's table, we ask you now to come to the *baptismal font* and renew your baptism by signing yourself as God's child with the Sign of the Cross."

13. Song. At the end of the liturgy we call the First Communion children up around the altar where the pastor leads them in a final old campfire song: "Let us break bread together.

We are one . . . drink wine together . . . thank God together . . ." and, finally, the last verse, "Let us hold hands together, we are one . . ." which is what we do.

14. Photos. At that time parents can take pictures. *Picture taking is not allowed at the ceremony itself.* If parents wish, we will have a videotape (you hardly know the videographer is there: no lights and no moving around), which they can purchase.

15. Fellowship. As usual, the ceremony is followed by refreshments in the parish hall.

Summary of Chapter 4

Baptism

1. Prebaptismal program
    2. Assigned couples to assist parents
    3. Newsletters
    4. Community Mass celebration
    5. Passing on of the tradition by a senior member
    6. Parental wish-sharing
    7. The Blessing of Aaron by the congregation
    8. Letter to be opened at confirmation
    9. Anniversary card
    10. Complimentary copy of the magazine, *The Catholic Parent*
    11. Mothers' groups offerings
    12. New Year's listing of the newly arrived and newly departed

Confirmation

1. Homemade booklet to students and parents outlining full process
    2. Public signing of scroll
    3. Christian service project
    4. Personal interview
    5. Prayer Partners
    6. Retreat
    7. Letter of intent to pastor
    8. Preparation gift bearers
    9. Gift booklet
    10. Confirmation robes
    11. Sponsor letter sharing

First Eucharist

1. Options: individually, group, or combination
    2. Teaching in prayer
    3. Bread baking evening
    4. Altar antependium with children's pictures
    5. Individual pew banner
    6. Each child with a full family pew
    7. Dipping into font
    8. Communal song with the kids

Resources for Parenting

Family Wellness Associates, P.O. Box 7869, Santa Cruz, CA 95061
Practical Parent Association, 5505 W. Piano Parkway, Plano,TX 75093
The Parenting Connection, 1010 N. Alvernon Way, Tucson, AZ 85711

There is historical evidence that the earliest Christians had seen baptismal initiation as commitment to active discipleship, but by the middle of the third century this view began to be transformed into the belief that one became a Christian in order to be saved.

—Camilla Burns, S.N.D. and Mary Elsbernd, O.S.F.

Chapter 5

The Sacraments: Reconciliation, Anointing

In a poll taken in 1993, in preparation for the Pope John Paul's visit to Colorado for World Youth Day, the Catholic Church Extension Society took a poll and found these three items to be the areas of greatest concern to teenagers: 1) sex, 2) drug and alcohol abuse, and 3) AIDS.

Reconciliation

It's a fact of current Catholic life that those old, long-line confessions are gone. If you want a head count, try this: The National Opinion Research Center reported that in the ten years from 1964 to 1974 there was a fall in monthly confessions from 38% to 17% (although weekly communions in that same period rose from less than 20% to more than 59%). In 1982 the Federation of Diocesan Liturgical Commissions found that only 8% of Catholics went to confession every few weeks, 30% every few months, 23% twice a year, 15% once a year, and 11% every few years. By the late 1980s a Notre Dame study found that 27% of Catholics never go to confession at all; 35% once a year, and only 6% go monthly or more often. And all this fall-off has taken place in spite of a newly revised rite that was supposed to make confession easier and more attractive. Of course, we should note that this survey is talking about confession as we knew it: the one-on-one, spiritual direction, Saturday encounter. As we shall see, perhaps confession, or reconciliation (to use the now appropriate term), is quite alive in another form. At any rate, this is why most parishes,

even at Christmas and Easter, have sharply curtailed the hours for confession.

Many theories have been put forth for this decline of the old Saturday confession, ranging from the sense of the loss of sin to indifference to a reaction against the old "grocery list" approach and guilt trips. Or perhaps people have learned the interesting history of penance and the many other ways the early church forgave sins. Whatever the reason, it seems very few Catholics go to private confession any more. Nor, obviously, has the revised rite brought them back. What *does* seem to bring them out in numbers is the communal confession.

Indeed, the communal confession powerfully emphasizes the community aspect of sin and repentance. So let's talk about that "second rite" (not the third, which is general absolution to a large crowd).

Commentary

1. There are three rites to the new order of reconciliation:

Form A deals with the reconciliation of individual penitents; that is, the procedure for a one-on-one encounter between penitent and priest.

Form B deals with the reconciliation of several penitents with individual confession and absolution. This is the communal confession where a large number of people gather for a common service of song, scripture, examination of conscience, and prayer and have individual reconciliations as part of the service.

Form C deals with the reconciliation of penitents with general confession and absolution. This last one is an extraordinary measure where there are many penitents and a small number of confessors, and within a reasonable time, the individual reconciliations of Form A would be impossible.

We are not dealing in this manual with Form A, an obvious and common procedure. Nor do we deal with Form C, which is reserved for unusual circumstances. Rather, as we indicated, we want to concentrate on Form B, and perhaps offer a surprising solution to handling large crowds by a small number of priests or even by a single priest.

2. Let me first describe a typical Form B communal confession whose theme plays on that of light and darkness. Several priests are available, perhaps a dozen or more.

3. When the people arrive, the church is in darkness except for our dome light in the center of the ceiling. An opening hymn is sung and the opening prayer is given. A lector reads the opening scripture, which is followed by a sung responsorial psalm. The celebrant then reads a gospel passage and gives a homily. All remain seated while two narrators alternate in reading a challenge to conscience, pausing after each challenge to give the people ample time to reflect on their words, and then there is the recitation of the confiteor.

4. After that, the clergy step forward and the people in the front pew hand them their stoles. The clergy then sit on chairs which have been placed all around the sanctuary.

5. Next, the people are invited to come forward for individual reconciliations. The single dome light is put out and all is in darkness. There are congregational candles beside each priest. As the priest is finished with each penitent, he hands that person a candle. That person goes to one of the two standing candlesticks in the side aisles and lights his (her) candle. Meanwhile, during all the time of these reconciliations, background music is being played and pertinent meditation slides are being shown. (We have the screen and automatic projector already set up.)

6. The symbolism is strong: Soon the totally dark church is alight with some 450 to 550 candles (our usual crowd).

7. When all are finished, the dome light and other lights go on and candles are extinguished. A communal penance is suggested and common absolution is given, followed by the kiss of peace, a closing prayer of thanksgiving, and a hymn. And, of course, refreshments follow in the hall.

Solving a Problem

The goal is to keep the communal ceremony within a reasonable time frame, say, an hour. However, sometimes (most often) we have only a few priests. We used to be able, in early days, to get about 15 or 20. But as other parishes picked up on the communal confessions and the number of priests declined or were spread out elsewhere, we were lucky to get four or five. Sometimes I could get no one. One way to solve this dilemma is to have the communal confession at times other than the seasonal Advent and Lent. Have them in the off seasons, perhaps once a month at different parishes. Still, the liturgical seasons are ripe for people to come to the communal confession. So, what do we do when you have, say, one priest and a church of 450-550 (our usual overcrowding)? What you do is to have Form B, the reconciliation of many penitents, with one priest. How is this possible? How can one confessor reasonably hear that many individuals?

The key is in the word "hear." What we have to recall theologically is that the actual physical verbalizing of one's sins is not the only way of expressing individual sorrow. The truth is that *any gesture* that expresses sorrow and repentance is a sufficient sign to warrant forgiveness and reconciliation. Think of scripture. Think of the parable of the Prodigal Son. He sinned, repented, and rushed back home to say his rehearsed litany of sins to his father. He didn't get a chance. He was silenced by hugs and kisses. His very gesture of returning home was enough for the father. Obviously, what the father was forgiving was not a verbal confession of sins—there was none—but the very physical sign of his son being there in the first place. The son kneeling before the father's feet told it all.

We're suspicious. After all, the Council of Trent taught that Catholics are obliged to confess their mortal sins according to species and number. Therefore, one has to talk out loud. But the key phrase in this directive is "mortal sin." How prevalent is it? Mortal sin, teaches St. Thomas Aquinas and many other theologians, is a rare item. That leaves venial sins, and venial sins are the stuff of Form A (individual reconciliation) and Form B (the

reconciliation of many penitents in a communal setting). This means that a simple generic confession and sign of repentance are sufficient. "O God, be merciful to me, a sinner!" is sufficient. Striking one's breast in humility and sorrow is sufficient. (Sound familiar? It's the Lukan story of the Publican and Pharisee in the Temple.) This is why *any individual action or movement* that acknowledges a state of general sinfulness and sorrow is adequate. And that is why the single absolution to a large crowd who have individually expressed to that sole confessor some gesture of sin and sorrow is sufficient.

It's as if each of the 500 people in church came up to the single priest and made a verbal confession. Only in this case, the case of Form B (many penitents in a communal assembly), the people did not come up and speak, but they came up and made some gesture. What gestures do we use? We have people come up (as they normally do at communion time) to be anointed with oil on the forehead; or to dip their hand in the baptismal font as a sign of their desire for renewal; or to bring a piece of paper with their sins written on it to be dropped into a container and burned; or to come up for a simple laying on of hands; or to touch or kiss the crucifix. The critical point is that each person makes that Prodigal Son gesture of repentance and sorrow. Then absolution can be given to all. This is not a general absolution. It is in reality individual reconciliation of several or many penitents.

Resources
The best article I can recommend that gives a fuller explanation is Timothy O'Connell's. See *Chicago Studies* (August 1993), "Reconciliation Renewal: Healing for Today's Church." Also

see Ladislas Orsy's article in the 1984 *Theological Studies* and Gerald Kelly's in the same journal (1945).

Of course, another response to the many people vs few priests situation is to have one-on-one reconciliation within the communal ceremony up to a certain time limit (say, an hour). Complete the service, let the people depart, but have the priests stay afterwards in the church to finish hearing the confession of those who were not able to earlier.

See the sample Communal Confession for Advent, put together by Grace Collins, a member of our liturgy committee, in Parish Papers, pages 288-291.

6. Finally, there should be an occasional evening, open to the public, for reconciliation and healing for those who have suffered the loss of a child due to stillborn, miscarriage, illness, accident, or abortion. During this open-ended service, at no time will it be necessary for the participants to identify the experience. For those who wish, priests will be available for the sacrament of reconciliation. This is a moving and consoling prayer service. See section 22 in the Order of Christian Funerals.

Resources

Many fine reconciliation programs are available both in booklet and magazine form for children and adults. See, for example, Gwen Costello, *Reconciliation Services for Children* (Mystic, Conn.: Twenty-Third Publications, 1992). See also Bausch and Martos (cited earlier).

Anointing

Commentary

There has been a general movement away from seeing the old "extreme unction" in terms of a deathbed sacrament in preparation for the next life. And the communal aspects of this sacrament are underscored not only in the small group anointing, such as at a home or hospital with relatives and friends present, but also in the larger parish gatherings.

Process

1. *Healing.* Several times a year we have Healing Masses. We bring in priests who are in this ministry and they celebrate such Masses in the evening—usually to a full church.

2. *Group Anointing.* Otherwise, as a parish, once a year we have a general group anointing at the last public Mass on Sunday (during good weather!).

3. *Caretakers.* Not only are the physically, emotionally, and mentally ill invited, but also the caretakers: doctors, nurses, first aid squads (it gives us a chance to publicly acknowledge them)—and a representative number of them come in uniform—plus, of course, members of our Samaritan Ministry who arrange the entire liturgy and provide for the practicalities such as transportation for those who need it and refreshments afterwards.

4. *Handicapped.* Front pews are saved for those who are the handicapped and we do have "handicapped" sidewalks and entrances at our church for easy access.

5. *Booklet.* As always, we provide the congregation with a complete booklet of text, song, and directions (following the norms of the decree from Pope Paul VI, nos. 80–85).

6. *Samaritans.* One variation we make is that when the priest extends his hands over the sick, the Samaritans (representing the congregation) join him. At the actual anointing, one of the Samaritans also lays his (her) hand on the shoulder of the recipient.

7. *Enough Priests.* It is wise to have at least three priests, since the number of people to be anointed is considerable.

8. *Anointing of Celebrant.* At the end, we do two things: 1) The congregation extends its hands over the sick and sings our traditional Blessing of Aaron. 2) The main celebrant asks for prayers and the laying on of hands from one of the sick. This was inspired by a story that Father John Haegle relates.

He tells of a small halfway house down the street from the parish in which he worked. The place was a home for emotionally or mentally disadvantaged young adult males. Some of them were Catholic and would come to church on Sunday. One of them, Adam, would speak out loud in church, asking questions about the homily or scriptures. Well, one Sunday afternoon, Father Haegle got a phone call from the hospital. The nurse told him that there was a young man who wanted to see him right away. So he took himself to the hospital with the sacred oils and the Blessed Sacrament and his ritual book to find Adam with his leg up in a cast.

"What happened, Adam?"

"Adam fall down and got hurt. Father, pray for him."

So Father Haegle did precisely that: He prayed for him, anointed him, gave him communion and the final blessing, chatted a while, and then prepared to leave. But Adam suddenly said,

"Not finished yet."

"Oh, I'm sorry," replied Fr. Haegle. "Did I forget something?"

To which Adam responded, "Adam pray for Father." So Adam sat him down on the edge of the bed and laid his hands on him. All of a sudden, relates Father Haegle, he realized how much *he* needed healing, how good it felt for someone else to lay hands on him. Reflecting on this, he realized that, in the long run, ministry is not something we do to people or even do for people, but rather it is an experience we share together. Ministry is mutual celebration of the sacred presence. The experience also reminded him and all of us of Adam's truism about ourselves: "Not finished yet."

That's why we add the blessing and laying on of hands for the main celebrant at our public anointing at Mass.

Summary of Chapter 5

Reconciliation

1. Celebrate a communal confession with individual, one-on-one confessions, playing with strong symbols such as darkness and light.

2. The same, but within a time limit; the rest can return after the ceremony.

3. Have creative individual "gestures" that signal repentance along with absolution.

4. Prepare your own communal confession.

Anointing

1. Once or twice a year, have a communal anointing at Mass.
    2. Involve the community's caregivers.
    3. Use an easy-to-follow booklet.
    4. Have the main celebrant also prayed over.
    5. Provide for "Healing Masses" at other times.

A few years ago at the Seattle Special Olympics, nine contestants, all physically or mentally disabled, assembled at the starting line for the 100-yard dash. At the gun they all started out, not exactly in a dash, but with a relish to run the race to the finish and win.

All, that is, except one boy who stumbled on the asphalt, tumbled over a couple of times, and began to cry. The other eight heard the boy cry. They slowed down and paused. Then they all turned around and went back. Every one of them. One girl with Down's syndrome bent down and kissed him and said, "This will make it better." Then all nine linked arms and walked together to the finish line.

Everyone in the stadium stood and the cheering went on for ten minutes. People who were there are still telling the story. Why? Because deep down we know this one thing: What matters in this life is more than winning for yourself. What truly matters in this life is helping others win, even if it means slowing yourself down and changing your course.

Chapter 6

The Sacraments: Marriage

A young woman protested to her mother that *she* was the one being married and should be allowed to make her own decisions. "After all, mother," said the bride-to-be, "you had your wedding 23 years ago." "No, dear," came the reply, "That was *my* mother's wedding."

Commentary

In this chapter I want to focus on the preparation for marriage as well as on the actual ceremony. Let me start by saying that to try to make the whole wedding day sacred is futile, and we might as well come to terms with that. The pressures of the day, the preparation, and the family hassles keep the focus elsewhere.

Anyway, a serious preparation is in order if for no other reason than the astonishing divorce rate, with its well documented consequences of across-the-board scarring of the children. Most dioceses require some 9-12 months notice—allowing for reasonable exceptions. But most of that time, vis-à-vis the church, is taken up with getting the proper documents and going to the Pre-Cana or the Engaged Encounter weekend. Likewise, we have to face the fact that as the number of priests dwindle, get older, and are overburdened, they have less time and sometimes considerably less sympathy for dealing with young couples, especially those living together, entering a second marriage, or coming to church for the fourth time since they have been on planet Earth (the first three, of course, being baptism, First Communion, and confirmation). They'll come, of course, "because they're Catholic and always dreamed of being married in church."

Some priests are quite conscientious, while others contribute to the horror stories of "Get out of here! Go get married by the mayor!" Add to this the all too frequent instances where the backgrounds are poor (youth, addictions, immaturity, broken homes, etc.) or where the couple's mentality is quite secular.

Like the young man who just got engaged exclaiming to his buddy, "You know, it's odd, but now that I'm engaged I'm beginning to feel nervous about getting married." His friend replies, "I know what you're thinking. It's only natural to be nervous. Marriage means a big commitment. Seven or eight years can be a long time!"

We may smile or be aghast at the cynicism, but young people are raised on impermanence and change. Anyway, we know that the average parish priest can't do justice to a decent preparation.

It has always boggled my mind that dioceses do not invest more money in this whole area of marriage preparation; they don't spend nearly as much as they spend on therapies, counseling, tribunals, and annulments. I would think any bishop would do well to foot the bill for well-balanced people to go to school to get their expertise in marriage and family counseling and marriage preparation, and then dot them all around the diocese—with the taken-for-granted understanding that they will give major time and counseling to engaged couples, with the priest as adjunct for those spiritual and liturgical matters closer to him.

Since most bishops do not foot the bill, years ago, as a parish, we did precisely that on our own: got our own on-the-premises counselor. Here's how it happened. Briefly, about a dozen years ago Ralph Imholte came to me from another parish asking if he could be a deacon—his own pastor didn't believe in them. I said yes, but I had a condition. I knew that in fact, while the deacon is technically the bishop's right-hand man, in practice he stands or falls with the local pastor. If the pastor uses him, fine; if not, he sits in the pew like an overgrown ordained altar boy, twiddling his thumbs. So I insisted that he must attach himself to a ministry so that if I ever moved, he would have his own field of ministerial work, his own expertise—and his own identity.

He said that he was happily married (still is) and would like to share that with others. So I agreed to send him to Iona College in New York where he got his background. Later he got his certificate in counseling from Seton Hall University. The point is that he has turned out to be an excellent counselor and, in addition to all kinds of counseling, he does all the pre-marriage work with the engaged couples. I want to share that process.

You may, of course, skip this next section and go on to the way we celebrate a church wedding, but I include it in order 1) to show you what is involved and 2) to give any professionals a process and resource in case they may want to look into it. In any case, you should know that there *are* resources and people (if you'll invite and support them) to do this most critical work of laying the first foundation for the family. No guarantees, of course, but our track record of sustained marriages is pretty good.

The Process
Session I
1. *Getting Details.* The initial meetings begin with the usual housekeeping matters: tentative date for their wedding, whether they're having a Mass or a ceremony without Mass, etc.

2. *Learning about the Couple.* Then time is spent in getting to know them, especially the male, who is usually there under silent protest. Ralph usually can get to them through sports, etc. He manages to hook them.

3. *Parish Booklet.* Then he gives them the instruments of their time together. He gives them, first, our own homemade parish booklet to be taken home and read at their leisure. It's basically a handy information tool, and saves them a lot of questions. Here's a summary of that booklet.

a. *Homily and Data.* The first pages give a short homily on marriage and it has a place for information: names, date of wedding, time, etc. and tells them of the basic laws of church and state (must be 18, free to marry, etc) and our policy on Nuptial Masses or other ceremony.

b. *Program.* The next pages unfold our seven-step program. In summary:

Step I: The initial contact with the priest.

Step II: Contact our deacon-counselor to begin the series of sessions.

Step III: Twice a year we have a public betrothal ceremony at the community Mass and invite them to attend one of them. (See pages 74-75.)

Step IV: We send them a series of flyers and thought provokers throughout their engagement.

Step V: We give them the directory so they can choose either the Engaged Encounter weekend or a Pre-Cana.

Step VI: We meet again, now that all is over, for final plans.

Step VII: Follow up. About six months to a year after the wedding, we contact them to see how they're doing. That's why we're careful to get their new address.

c. Certificates. Next is a checklist of needed certificates: baptism, First Communion, confirmation, Precana or Engaged Encounter, blood test, marriage license, letter of freedom (if required) and, if necessary, proof of the completion of any counseling requirements, date and time of rehearsal.

d. Practicalities. Then, we deal with the practical matters: flowers, bridal runner (yes, if you wish), music (contact one in charge; you can have anyone, any tune that's permitted), rice throwing (yes, but the birds like seed better), other ministers (by all means), where to get license and blood test, and, finally, that sensitive issue, the photographer and videographer.

Actually, we have a paper that we give the couple to hand to their photographer or videographer and I always have extra ones at rehearsal time to hand out personally. Almost all are agreeable and it works out fine. The paper we hand out—which is in this booklet—is as follows:

Photographer

You may take pictures, flash or otherwise, when people and the bridal party are coming in and going out, before and after the wedding. You may also take *one* picture during the actual ceremony. Otherwise you must *stay in the back and not move around* and take time shots (no flash). Actually, with the natural light in the church, these shots are most effective. Of course, after all is over, you may re-pose the wedding as you wish.

Video

You may videotape as much as you wish when the people are coming in and going out before and after the wedding. After that, you must not move around, but stay against any one of the three back walls. With your zoom lens this is both comfortable and effective. (We presume there will be no camera lights.)

The reason for these rules is that in a round church such as ours, walking around is very distracting and noticeable and we want both the dignity and religious aspect of the celebration to take precedence. Thank you for your cooperation.

Likewise, to jump ahead a bit to the day of the ceremony, as the actual wedding starts, and as I eye all those multitudinous camcorders and cameras being carried in, I always put words into the bride and groom's mouth. To wit (said smilingly): "Mary and John have requested that, since they have their own professional photographer and videotaper or videographer, as they like to be called, you do not take pictures during the ceremony. Afterwards, they will be most happy to pose and re-pose for you to their—and your—heart's content."

People are very cooperative and it works out well. The ideal is to have printed rules beforehand. It saves a lot of trouble. And of course, over the years, the photographers get to know you and your rules and are fine about it.

e. Cohabiting. Then, in our booklet, there is our policy on cohabiting couples.

f. Memo. Finally, our booklet ends with this plea on the back page:

A Memo to Brides and Grooms

Just a concern that we wish to raise (without being a spoilsport). Can Christians justify spending hundreds, perhaps thousands, of dollars on a single day's celebration (caterers, photographers, gowns, etc.) in view of the large numbers of people today who are unemployed, homeless, and hungry?

Is this consistent with the gospel and your own personal values?

A suggestion: If you spend a lot, donate a little to charity. To our parish Social Concerns Fund. To Mother Teresa's Soup Kitchen in Newark. To whatever good work you feel will represent the concern and kindness you would like to see in your own marriage.

It's a thought, a way to thank God for your bounty of love and friends. God bless your marriage. May you never know want.

4. Directory. The second booklet the engaged couple receives is a directory for the year's Pre-Cana and Engaged Encounter weekends.

5. Workbook. Finally, they are given *Only Love Can Make It Easy* by Bill and Patty Coleman (Mystic, Conn.: Twenty-Third Publications, tenth printing, 1990). That will be their general workbook.

6. Lifestyle. With the opening session moving along (these booklets, along with our homemade booklet, you recall, are simply given to be taken home), Ralph moves into a quick activity with the couple. He gives them the small, single page "Lifestyle Scale" developed by Roy M. Kern (Published by CMTI Press. Box 8268, Coral Springs, FL 33075), which is a quick instrument to give some insight into the couple's individual personalities.

7. Interactions. Then he gives them the "Prepare Inventory," an excellent tool used with over 350,000 couples. It has 125 statements covering 13 different categories of marital interactions that primarily reflect the patterns of their family of origin: Family Cohesion, Family Adaptability, Equalitarian Roles, Sexual Relationship, Children and

Parenting, Religious Orientation, Family and Friends, Leisure Activities, Conflict Resolution, Financial Management, Realistic Expectations, Personality Issues, and Communication. (*Source:* Prepare-Enrich, Inc. P.O. Box 190, Minneapolis, MN 55458). Ralph has the couple separate and fill out the inventory, which he will mail to the company for a printout.

8. After this, he gathers information for the parish record, talks with them about the history of their relationship, and closes by making the next appointment.

Session II

1. This session is devoted to going over the Kern "Lifestyle Scale" to adjust or revise and acknowledge the personality of themselves as a couple and each other individually and the possible impact on their relationship.

2. The couple does the CCE (Couples' Communication Exercise) which is part of the "Prepare-Enrich" process regarding 11 categories that attempt to identify strengths and growth areas in their relationship. Then this is compared to the inventory results.

3. Now Ralph begins processing the computerized printout of the Prepare Inventory (remember, he sent it back to the company in Minnesota which then returns a printout of the couple's responses) by going over with the couple each category thoroughly, especially those areas where they show different views.

Sessions III & IV

Ralph continues to go through the entire computer printout of the Prepare Inventory. He attempts to get the couple to speak openly with one another rather than with him, and he

helps facilitate some methods of communication, fair fighting, and conflict resolution.

Session V

1. Here Ralph introduces the Genogram (family of origin and family history starting with their grandparents), looking for behavior patterns in each partner's family and for possible patterns (unconsciously) repeated in their own relationships.

2. Then he reviews the data found in the workbook, *Only Love Can Make It Easy*.

Session VI

1. Here Ralph looks at the overall picture of their relationship, comparing it to the Locke-Wallace study of 150,000 couples who have been followed up (and still are) for seven years: those whose marriages succeeded and those whose marriages failed.

2. He then discusses with them the pros and cons of their relationship.

3. At this time, all documents (and dispensations, if required) are checked to see if all is in order.

Session VII

1. The liturgy is planned.

2. The prenuptial (diocesan) form is completed.

Whether all the above is mystifying to you or not, the point is that a thorough premarriage preparation is a great gift to the couples. (And Ralph will add many more hours where needed.) The strength of the various tools is that it puts on the table subjects the couple either deny or are unwilling to face up to. Ralph, with the aid of the tools, simply won't allow them to ignore what should be brought out in the open. He confronts them until they're forced to face potential marital hazards. We've had couples call off their marriage, discovering they were not ready to be married or at least not to each other; others, once the valuable contact is made with a caring counselor, feel free to contact him when the marriage runs into some snags.

The Betrothal Ceremony

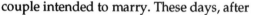

Originally the betrothal ceremony was a public announcement that a couple intended to marry. These days, after the family, friends, and grapevine, the newspapers get the official word. So we're not breaking any news in our betrothal ceremony, but rather putting a focus on 1) the holiness sign of marriage and 2) the need for the community's acknowledgment and prayers. We send out invitations to all engaged couples (see sample letter in Parish Papers, page 297). Most of them, remember, we have been dealing with in our premarriage counseling program. We invite them to the main Mass where we have seats reserved for them.

After communion, at the meditation time, we call them into the sanctuary facing the congregation:

Celebrant: My dear friends, I would like you to meet (here he calls out the names of the engaged). These are all engaged couples and are members of our community of St. Mary's. They are concrete, living examples of the new commandment Jesus spoke of in this morning's gospel reading: Love one another. (Note: Whatever the reading is, we can bend it to the occasion.)

We have invited them here for just that one reason. The love that burns inside them for each other, Jesus says, is a signal, a symbol, a sacramental sign of his love for us. Their love is also a living example of how we all are to love one another (celebrant turns here to couples). We, your community here at St. Mary's, need to see this love of yours and to be strengthened by it, as you need to be strengthened by our prayers and support.

Therefore, we ask you publicly to pledge your love as a sign for all of us to see. Accordingly, I ask you:

Do you believe that God is calling you to be husband and wife? (We do.)

Do you believe that you are being called to love God by loving one another? (We do.)

Do you believe that your love for one another, now and in the future, is to be a sign, a sacrament, for all people, of how God loves them? (We do.)

Therefore, having seen evidence of your love and your intent (addressing the congregation), we ask you gathered here this morning to rise and call out your Amen to these intercessions for these couples:

That the Lord would grant them his loving protection from the strong tides of daily troubles that could pull them apart from one another, let us pray to the Lord . . .

That you would shield these couples from that terrible social sickness of no commitment, let us pray to the Lord . . .

That you would show them how to rechannel the hidden streams of selfishness that might separate them, let us pray to the Lord . . .

Almighty God, fountain of all love, bless these couples. We pray that what you have joined in promise may be brought to fulfillment. We ask this through Christ Our Lord. Amen.

Now I ask the men to take the left hand of their future spouse, the hand with the promised engagement ring, and I ask the congregation to raise its right hand in blessing over these couples as we sing our traditional Blessing of Aaron.

After the communal blessing, there is applause and the couples return to their pews.

The Marriage Ceremony

1. I would like to share with you some variations we have introduced into the marriage ceremony. We always have the bride and groom and best man and maid of honor sit in the sanctuary *facing the congregation.* We have a set of chairs on each side of the altar, and the bride and maid of honor and the groom and the best man, having processed in, move to those chairs. Everyone gets a view. The focus is on them. They face the people at all times.

2. The ushers and bridesmaids enter the front or side front pews.

3. At the actual exchange of vows, we call down the bride and groom and best man and maid of honor and then signal the ushers and bridesmaids to join them. The result is the entire bridal party standing on the sanctuary step *facing the congregation* (like a chorus line). The celebrant is the only one at certain times with his back to the congregation.

4. After the vows and rings are exchanged, the ushers and bridesmaids return to their places and the bride and groom and best man and maid of honor split up, the bride and groom going around one side and the best man and maid of honor the other side until they wind up like concelebrants on *either side of the celebrant* behind the altar. They stay there for the entire Mass—except for the sign of peace. At communion they return to their sanctuary chairs.

5. The usual variations are honored: own lectors, Prayers of the Faithful composers and readers, musicians (following our diocesan guidelines), lighting the wedding candle (sometimes with the parents taking part), roses to the parents at the Sign of Peace, the pre-recessional Blessing of Aaron, etc.

6. On the way out, the bride and groom (as they did when they entered) have to split up to walk around the *baptismal font,* which is in the center of the aisle. As they pass it, they

dip their hands in it and sign themselves as a symbol of new life, new beginnings, new blessings.

On pages 224-243 of Parish Papers is a photocopy of the homemade parish marriage booklet that we give the couple when we first meet them. We go over it and try to clarify where we stand. You will also notice that there is a statement on living together before marriage. We do not expect everyone to agree with this policy and we ourselves are open to revision and dialogue, but at least it starts the conversation.

Resources

Your Wedding by Greg Friedman, for engaged and interfaith couples; *Before You Say 'I Do'* by Tom Richstatter; and *Marriage: Sacrament of Hope and Challenge* by William Roberts, all from St. Anthony Messenger Press, Cincinnati.

An excellent book is *Perspectives on Marriage: A Reader*, eds. Kieran Scott and Michael Warren (New York: Oxford University Press, 1993). Also see *Making Your Marriage Work: Growing in Love After Falling in Love* (Mystic, Conn.: Twenty-Third Publications, 1989); Gerald Foley's book for marriages in trouble, *Courage to Love . . . When Your Marriage Hurts* (Notre Dame, Ind.: Ave Maria Press, 1992); and, finally, *Marriage Savers: Helping Your Friends and Family Stay Married* by Michael McManus (Grand Rapids, Mich.: Zondervan). Note: Second marriages for older adults are increasing as are second marriages in general. A different design is in order, and a different preparation. A good resource is *To Trust Again: Remarriage Preparation Program* by William Urbine (ACTA, 1990) with a couples' workbook and leader's guide.

Summary of Chapter 6

1. Be convinced of the necessity of trained premarriage counselors.

2. Have a workbook for the couple that displays expectations and needs.

3. Offer a public betrothal ceremony at Mass.

4. Have a printed policy on photographers and videographers. It saves a lot of hassle and eventually sets the ground rules.

5. Have the couple always face the congregation. Wean them away from the kneelers, with their backs to the people.

6. After the vows, invite them to join the celebrant at the altar.

7. Encourage participation and personal moments in the ceremony.

The Pastor's Dilemma

If a priest preaches over ten minutes, he's long-winded.
If his homily is short, he didn't prepare it.

If the parish funds are high, he's a businessman.
If he mentions money, he's money mad.

If he visits his parishioners, he's nosy.
If he doesn't, he's snobbish.

If he has fairs and bazaars, he's bleeding the people.
If he doesn't, there's no life in the parish.

If he takes time in confession to help and advise sinners, he takes too long.
If he doesn't, he doesn't care.

If he celebrates the liturgy in a quiet voice, he's a bore.
If he puts feeling into it, he's an actor.

If he starts Mass on time, his watch is fast.
If he starts late, he's holding the people up.

If he tries to lead the people in music, he's showing off.
If he doesn't, he doesn't care what the Mass is like.

If he decorates the church, he's wasting money.
If he doesn't, he's letting it run down.

If he's young, he's inexperienced.
If he's old, he ought to retire.
If he dies, there was nobody like him and there will never be his like again.

The Liturgical Year

Chapter 7

Seasonal Time

Father Smith, who felt he lived a pretty good life, was dismayed to get to heaven and find himself shackled to an ugly and foul-mouthed woman. Then he spotted his bishop chained to a charming beauty. Father Smith went straight to St. Peter to complain. "It's none of your business," snapped St. Peter. "You get on with your penance and let her get on with hers!"

Under this heading are described those liturgical times of the year in the life of a parish when special emphasis and events are the order of the day.

1. Advent. We gather all of the materials sent by publishers, scatter them on a table, and ask three families what, among all this, they would like to receive to help them celebrate a better Advent. Their choices are then purchased and soon every parish family receives an *Advent Packet.*

The *Advent communal confession* takes place at this season. And, of course, we have the Advent wreath.

2. Christmas. A practical as well as highly symbolic gesture is to have a *different neighborhood* decorate the church each year. This is in contrast to most parishes where an unofficial committee of a handful of people do this each year—and have done it since the first Christmas—and don't anyone dare move a poinsettia! Our way spreads both the creativity and the ownership as parents, grandparents, teens, children, etc., all take part. You take your chances of course (it may wind up looking like Woolworth's), but the gamble is worth it.

Before Christmas we have a raffle among the children. Ten cents a ticket with the proceeds going to the poor. The prize? The privilege of decorating Father's tree! Yes, I have an (artificial) tree, and among the fifth and sixth graders the race is on for five people from each class to decorate it. The winners arrive, make happy chaos, somehow get the tree done, and are treated to games, refreshments, and a video: Disney's *Christmas Carol* (yes, big as they are and as often as they see it, they love it). They're after fun; I'm after contact and community building. Then I send each one a thank you letter. To wit:

Dear Erica,

I want to thank you for trimming my tree last Wednesday afternoon. You and the others did a great job and everyone who sees it admires it.

Thanks for your kindness and generosity. You are a good friend.

I hope you and your family have a very blessed and happy Christmas.

Sincerely yours,
Father Bausch

At the Christmas vigils (four Masses: 5:00, the children's Mass at 7:00, 8:30, and 10:00; we've never had a midnight Mass) we have a candlelight communion line. (See Holy Thursday, page 83.) At all Masses we have a tableau: Little children precede the entrance rite, bring up the infant, and lay him in the crib in front of the altar. (This is a concession to sentimentality and even misplaced theology. It puts the emphasis on the sweet baby whereas the emphasis should be on God's passionate desire to be with us at all costs. See my homily, "Christmas Passion" in *More Telling Stories, Compelling Stories*, Mystic, Conn.: Twenty-Third Publications, 1993.)

3. *Epiphany*. For this day we have people stationed at the church door to commandeer three or four unsuspecting children who are willing to be dressed in royal robes and headdress and join in the entrance procession, stay up on the altar, and become the offertory gift-bearers. A tad coy, but it's still the season of good will and high feelings.

4. *Lent*. Lent, as you suspect, is multifaceted. We usually offer a variety of opportunities for lectures and devotions. The idea is to have something three times a day for maximum opportunity.

As a prelude to Lent, we have "Fat Tuesday," which entails a pancake breakfast in the parish hall after the morning Mass (9:00 A.M.) for all who wish to come. Volunteers do the work, of course, and it's a fun time that all enjoy. Lent involves the following:

a. We remove our central statue of the Risen Christ from the sanctuary and replace it with a bare cross as the main focus.

b. We remove all flowers (we have only one bouquet in front of the altar) and replace them with a Crown of Thorns, a plant cultivated to make a circle of thorns.

c. We send out a lenten packet similar to the Advent one. We have a lenten communal confession.

d. We offer a one-and-a-half-hour lecture series on the *Passion Narratives* every Monday evening in church.

e. We have a *Holy Hour* every Tuesday evening from 8:00 to 9:00. This holy hour has become traditional. It always draws a full church, mostly, I think, because of the dynamics. The format is simple. The church is darkened except for a small light on the lectern and an overhead light for singing the entrance hymn. The overhead light is immediately extinguished after the hymn. The ambiance is appealing. People have been subjected to stress and unbelievable noise and unending advertising all day long. Here is one time they can come and sit in the darkness and relax. It's private time, meditative time—and most welcome time.

There is an opening prayer and then, for about forty minutes, a kind of stream of consciousness as the celebrant preaches on a single theme and lets the quiet, the words, and the darkness soothe and work on the people's spirits. This talk always ends in an action, such as the communal confessions. People are invited to move in procession for various gestures: They may come down the center aisle and dip their hands in the baptismal font, or bring up a piece of paper to be burned in the burner provided, or bring up pieces of wood (coffee stirrers) to be inserted into a prominent styrofoam cross, or come up to receive an anointing on the forehead or hands, or touch a picture of the wounded head of Christ, or kiss a crucifix. This procession takes place in the dark with soft music playing in the background.

When the procession is finished, there is a litany, a closing prayer, and final benediction.

f. On the Tuesdays of Lent we also have *Soup 'n Song*. This is a short service at noon consisting of an opening hymn, prayer, scripture reading, brief homily, and Benediction. It lasts about 20 minutes. It is designed for the working people who can come at their lunch hour. Following the service in church, all proceed back to the parish hall where volunteers have prepared homemade soup and bread. The hope is that, whatever the people would have paid outside for a normal lunch, they put into a box for the unemployed.

g. We have *extra Masses* on Wednesday and Thursday evenings and Stations of the Cross, led by the people, on Friday evenings. Morning office is celebrated on Thursday and Friday mornings at 6:30 to catch the commuting crowd.

5. *Holy Week.* This is the best week of the year. The people who come to these non-obligatory services *want* to be there and that makes a difference.

1. *Passion, or Palm, Sunday.* As we mentioned elsewhere, we have our own homemade booklet containing the Passion. We rewrote it ourselves to give the people more speaking parts. (There is a professional booklet called *The Passion of Our Lord Jesus Christ According to John* arranged for Readers Theatre, by Ronald E. Brassard, Pastoral Press, 225 Sheridan St., N.W., Washington, D.C. 20011. There are other publications that arrange scripture in dialogue form for three readers for regular Sundays and major feasts. See, for example, *This Is the Word of the Lord,*

Notre Dame, Ind.: Ave Maria Press, 1974.)

We have a procession at each Mass. The palms are given out by the ushers and greeters as the people enter church. For logistics sake, the procession includes only those people on either side of the center aisle.

2. *Tuesday of Holy Week* is always our *lenten communal confession* (standing room only), which was described in Chapter 5.

3. *Holy Thursday.* My personal favorite liturgy. We do, I admit, have something of a different liturgy. It begins with the church in total darkness and a silent procession of 12 white-robed, sandaled apostles (six males and six females ranging from 8 to 80) leading in the celebrant, who is barefoot and dressed in a simple white garment girded with a towel. He joins two lectors, and a three-part narration begins. When it comes to the part where the washing of the feet is narrated, the celebrant leaves the altar and goes to the platform to pick up the bowl and basin that are prominently featured and begins washing the feet of the 12 representative apostles. The choir meanwhile sings the haunting "In Remembrance" (Nashville: Broadman Press).

After the washing is over, the celebrant returns to complete the narrative with the other two lectors and then goes to the lectern for the homily.

After the homily, the church lights are put on so people can sing the hymns. The canon is punctuated here and there with a refrain by the celebrant, "And so we sing," which brings a harmonized short refrain from the choir.

Before the celebrant receives communion, he pauses while the parish council president (called the speaker here) stands up in his (her) pew in the congregation to begin a dialogue with him. Here is the exchange:

Speaker: Since this evening marks not only the institution of the Most Blessed Sacrament, but also the beginning of the priesthood that presides over the Christian community and the eucharist, I, on behalf of the people of St. Mary's, Colts Neck, respectfully request a statement of rededication from our pastor, Father Bausch.

Father Bausch, do you reaffirm your presidency of this community and its eucharistic celebrations—in short, your priesthood—before your people?

Father: I do.

Speaker: Do you as pastor promise to serve your people and, to the best of your ability, under the Spirit, to lead them to salvation?

Father: I do.

Speaker: Do you renew your vow of celibacy which urges you to the service of all; that being no one's father, you are father to all; that being no one's spouse, you are a spouse to all; that having no family of your own, everyone has a claim on you?

Father: I do.

Speaker: Do you repledge yourself to the community of St. Mary's, Colts Neck, and renew your commitment to this parish and your fidelity to its spiritual welfare?

Father: I do.

Speaker: Do you wish to make your own statement of rededication both to your priesthood and to this community?

Father. I do. Before God in heaven and before you, this Christian community of St. Mary's, I reaffirm my priesthood.

It is something that means more to me than life itself.
It is a source of profound happiness and fulfillment.

It is a precious and, at times, difficult pilgrimage, but one that is supported by the Spirit and by my fellow travelers.

I recognize that my priesthood must be in harmony with the gifts of all of you who have been given the Spirit in baptism; that my priesthood has meaning only in terms of all the people: in terms of "washing the feet" of all.

Therefore, I willingly and happily restate my intention of commitment to God's work. I once more humbly give myself over to the Spirit who alone can absorb my weaknesses and bring goodness out of human frailty.

I renew my vows of celibacy and obedience. I renew my public love for the priesthood and God's fragile church. I renew my dedication for another year to the people of St. Mary's.

I pray, as always, that my sins will not hinder God's work nor my human limitations frustrate God's designs. And I continue my deep and abiding gratitude to the people here who have been, and continue to be, a never-failing source of encouragement and strength—indeed a true and beautiful family to me.

I proclaim my words tonight in the Spirit and with the Son in the unity of the everlasting and ever-loving Father. Amen.

All proceeds normally. At communion time there are many stations for receiving under both species. As the people come up, they carry unlighted candles (which they found in the pew when they came in). As they return from communion, they light their candles from two candlestands within the body of the church. The church lights are extinguished and soon we have a candlelight procession of communicants.

Following communion and the meditation time, the procession with the Apostles takes place as the congregation sings.

After the reposition of the Blessed Sacrament, the Apostles go in front of the altar to receive in silence the articles stripped from the altar. When all is done, the baritone cantor says, "Having sung a hymn, they went out to the Garden of Olives." The celebrant and Apostles leave in silence.

The Apostles quickly go to the church doors, handing to everyone as they exit a small round loaf of bread to be shared in fellowship. (Some of these loaves in small baskets were prominent on the altar.)

Resource

A short work (79 pages), *A New Commandment: Toward a Renewed Rite for the Washing of the Feet* by Peter Jeffrey (Collegeville, Minn.: Liturgical Press).

The letter sent to the Apostles:

Dear Friend,

As you know, each year we have the Holy Thursday evening Mass at 8:00 P.M. At this moving Mass we have the traditional Washing of the Feet of the "Twelve Apostles." This year, Holy Thursday is March 23.

I would be very much pleased if you would consider being one of the Apostles this year. Your presence and participation would mean so much.

The process is very easy, and on the evening before Holy Thursday, which is Wednesday March 22, at 7:30 we will have a practice.

Please consider this invitation. I understand, of course, that you may not be able to make it, but if you could, I and the community would be grateful.

Please call the parish office as soon as possible (780-2666) and leave your reply.

Thanking you for your attention and for being a part of our parish family, I am

Sincerely yours,
Father Bausch

4. Good Friday. For years the Mass of the Presanctified was pretty much a hodge-podge with no special focus. Revisions have improved it, but meanwhile, we have developed an alternative. On Good Friday at 3:00 P.M. we make the outdoor stations. Years ago we had a carpenter send out plans for a man-size cross to fifteen families. These families made the crosses and we have used them ever since, erecting them at Passiontide all across our vast twenty-five acres. Rain, shine, hail, sleet, sub-freezing weather—we're out in all weather, some 1000-1200 of us, from all faiths and walks of life. It's a very moving spectacle and very witnessing to the cars going by on the highway in front of us. We use, of course, a common booklet we put out ourselves and a portable sound system tied into a cordless mike.

There is no reason why even an inner-city parish might not do this, erecting the crosses at places of drug dealing and killings.

In the evening we celebrate Tenebrae which is entirely conducted by the lay people, and well received. (We use the one-page foldover put out by Creative Communications for the Parish, 10300 Watson Rd., St. Louis, MO 63127).

5. Holy Saturday and Easter. The Easter Vigil is standard, except we have our "Now and Then" booklets handy for congregational dialogue and participation for the Easter Proclamation, the gospel (see below), and the reception of converts. An excerpt from that reception goes like this:

Celebrant: Then I ask you once again to renew the vows of your baptism, reject sin, and proclaim your faith in Jesus Christ, a faith held by the church into which you are being received.

Therefore, do you reject sin so that you might live in the freedom of the children of God?

Candidate: I do.

Celebrant: Do you wish to enter into the Roman Catholic tradition?

Candidate: I do.

Celebrant *(addressing the assembly)*: And do you, the People of God, so instrumental in bringing this man (woman) here, promise to continue to witness to God's presence and love?

All: We do.

Celebrant: Do you join in this happy moment, seeing in it an opportunity to recommit your own lives to Jesus Christ?

All: We do.

Celebrant: I ask you now, therefore, to bow your heads in prayer for _____ so that what he (she) is about to undertake in full view of this assembly may be assisted by that same assembly by faith and good works. *(pause)* I declare that you are now received into full membership of the Roman Catholic church. We, the members of both the local and universal church, receive you as a partner in our common journey and a friend in our common life.

All: You belong to us and we to you. May God be praised!

At the end we have the oldest member present lay hands on the candidate(s), and then lots of applause from the congregation.

On Easter Sunday we have the children bring flowers to church. Also, to simulate for everyone a kind of mini-celebration, we have all lights off in church (even though it may be sunny outside and hardly noticeable) and have the celebrant, dressed only in an alb, and ministers enter in silence. The readings are begun immediately and then the celebrant invites the congregation to join in the Easter Sequence (ancient poem, *Christians, to the Paschal Victim*), at the end of which he intones a threefold alleluia to which they respond. The lights are then put on, the organ peals, and the celebrant vests and leads the children around the church in procession. The children drop off their flowers into prepared vases. A hymn is sung. After the procession, the celebrant goes immediately into the dialogue gospel with the congregation. The congregational gospel goes like this:

Leader: The Lord be with you.

All: And also with you.

Leader: A reading of the gospel from the witness of John

All: Glory to you, O Lord.

Leader: Early in the morning, on the first day of the week, while it was still dark, Mary Magdalen came to the tomb. She looked and exclaimed:

All: The stone has been rolled away!

Leader: So quickly she ran off to Simon Peter and the other disciple and told them:

All: The Lord has been taken away from the tomb! I don't know where they have put him.

Leader: At that, Peter and the other disciple started on their way to the tomb. They exclaimed:

All: We must see if this is true.

Leader: The other disciple whom Jesus loved, being younger, outran Peter and reached the tomb first but he did not enter it. Instead he peered inside and said to the others:

All: I see the cloth wrappings on the ground.

Leader: Presently, Simon Peter came along behind him and he did enter the
            tomb. He too observed the wrappings on the ground and saw the
            cloth which had covered the head. It was not lying with the other
            wrappings but was rolled up in a place by itself. Then the other
            disciple who had arrived first went in and saw and exclaimed:

All: Truly I believe . . . We too believe!

Leader: This is the Easter proclamation of the Lord.

All: Thanks be to God.

            The homily and the rest of Mass proceed as normal. After each Mass
            we have an Easter egg hunt on the grounds.

6. *Pentecost.* This feast carries itself: the red vestments, the striking banner, the flowers and music. The only thing we add is to give out inflated red balloons as people leave Mass with a logo on them: St. Mary's Parish: The Spirit Blows Where It Will. Again, we have recruited people to inflate the balloons (by machine) and hand them out.

A Final Comment from Ebenezer Scrooge

From a pastor's point of view, the high holy days, in a sense, are the pits . . . or at least they cause tension. On the one hand, Christmas and especially Holy Week are such splendid and rich times. Holy Week, for example, has a nice rhythm of commemoration and celebration, even though it is quite backward. That is, the emphasis, inherited from medieval times, is all on the Passion. After all that drama concentrating on the suffering and death of Jesus, you hardly have any energy to shout "Alleluia!" on Easter Sunday. In addition, only

a comparatively few celebrate the Triduum—that's seen as an "extra"—so that the average churchgoer goes from Passion Sunday to Easter Sunday with no gradation. There's no slow-motion time to quietly enter into the mysteries.

On the other hand, it's the phone, the endless phone calls all day and all night. (Hell, for me, will be to be locked in a phone booth with a ringing phone.) It's the crowds. They make it so hard to do the Christmas or Easter liturgy well. The non-churchgoers have swelled the regular congregation. Once-a-year people are crowding the regulars to the fringes of the church or sometimes out the door and into the parish hall or gym. And they're there 45 minutes beforehand! They have various agendas. They are an unknown people with no common history, no parish family clues. And then, too, so much energy goes into logistics (parking lot, cutting off church crowding and sending people, grumbling, to the hall) that it's hard to relate to a gathering of strangers. You muster all your faith to give communion to those obviously unfamiliar with the procedure (Does the host go in the mouth, the hand, the nose, the eye?—you wonder if they're Catholic), or who take it so casually as they saunter back to the recesses of the crowd. Still, it's not for us to judge.

There is no room for sarcasm, no gain in substituting a Bob Newhart "See ya next year, fella!" for "Go, the Mass is ended," or making cracks about having poinsettias for Easter next year so they'll feel at home.

In one deep sense I enjoy these holy days with all their off-centeredness. My tactic is to show a good (tired) face, try to do things as nicely as I can, to preach as well as I can in the hope that the message might be, "See what you're missing all year round? Come back home."

Have a happy Easter.

Summary of Chapter 7

1. Advent includes a packet of home celebrations sent to all parishioners.

2. Have different neighborhoods decorate the church.

3. Consider a raffle whose prize is to decorate Father's tree. Proceeds go to the poor.

4. Have "kings" march in procession and be the offertory gift-bearers.

5. Try "Soup 'n Song" for lenten noon times for the workers.

6. Give the people more speaking parts in the Passion narrative.

7. The pastor might consider renewing his vows at the Holy Thursday liturgy.

8. Small loaves of bread might be given out at this liturgy.

9. Try an outdoor stations of the cross, no matter what your territory.

10. Try Tenebrae. People will grow to like it.

11. Consider a "mini" procession at each Easter Sunday Mass.

12. Pentecost is a feast of red: fire, Spirit, passion, balloons, etc.

13. It's Holy Week. Smile anyway.

I would like to buy three dollars worth of God, please.
I would like to buy just a little of the Lord.
Not enough to explode my soul or disturb my sleep,
Not enough to take control of my life; I'll keep
Just enough to equal a cup of warm milk,
Just enough to ease some of the pain from my guilt.

I would like to buy three dollars worth of God, please.
I would like to find a love that's pocket sized,
Not enough to make me love a black man.
Not enough to change my heart; I can only stand
Just enough to take to church when I have time,
Just enough to equal a snooze in the sunshine.

I want ecstasy, not transformation.
I want the warmth of the womb
But not a new birth.
I would like to purchase a pound of the eternal
In a paper sack guaranteed or money back.
You see, I would like to buy three dollars worth of God, please.

Chapter 8

Ordinary Time

Motto on board in front of church, "If you're done with sin, come on in." Written underneath in lipstick, "But if you're not quite through, call 272-0200."

Confession Time

You may have noticed that I take some liberties with the liturgy. I'm always nervous about that because I don't want to disobey the laws. Yet, I know from experience that often the prescribed texts and movements simply do not meet the occasion. The Eucharistic Prayers leave a great deal to be desired. They're stiff and unpoetic—and boring. The Opening Prayer, the Prayer over the Gifts, and the Prayer after Communion are archaic, remote, and frequently out of touch with present-day realities. Therefore, I admit to the following:

1. I always use the Prayer after Communion as a spontaneous time to summarize the spirit of the liturgy and the theme of the homily. I try to tie it all together at the end.

2. I will often interpolate the current Eucharistic Prayers with references made in the homily theme.

3. I will sometimes use unofficial Eucharistic Prayers that are moving and more to the point of the liturgy's spirit.

4. I will bow to practicalities. For example, we always have one (glass) chalice on the altar and another that is brought up with the preparation gifts. At communion, I pour from one cup to the other and leave both on the altar. Our experience has shown that having eucharistic ministers stand with the cup caused more traffic jams than we could manage. So we simply leave the two chalices on the altar and people can come up and drink as they wish. This procedure works very well.

5. I do not "do the dishes" at the altar any more than I do them in front of my guests when I have people over for dinner. The eucharistic ministers take the dishes back to the sacristy and clean them there.

6. I do not use the Sacramentary book. Rather, I photocopy the opening prayer, the gospel, and the canon and put them in a three-ring binder. Inserted after the gospel is my homily. I am one of those who never reads the homily and I do practice to be spontaneous, but nevertheless I feel more comfortable having the printed text handy, especially when I want to follow something closely or not miss a good punch line. In short, I have everything in one binder.

7. I also do this for weddings and funerals. I have separate three-ring binders for each. I find it very comfortable to have everything photocopied in one place, including the options I have chosen and the homily. I can therefore easily go from the first to the back page without mentally jumping

over all those rubrics and options.

8. We use real and recognizable bread. It is difficult to pretend that unleavened bread is real bread. We use red wine and a glass chalice so that the sign will be strong.

These are some of the "liberties" we take.

And just when I start to feel a bit guilty over all this, along comes a master liturgist and homilist, and a man of sense and experience, Father Joe Nolan. In a letter introducing his homily service (September 1993), he writes candidly:

> This is not about what some call "creative disobedience." Rather, it is about good liturgy and a sense of proportion. When people complain about the violation of rubrics (as they understand them), I would keep this in mind: don't take their complaints seriously as long as there is intelligent, good liturgy within the major guidelines—i.e., using bread and wine, the scriptures, an ordained priest, effective preaching and attention to the assembly as the body of Christ, exercising their share in the priesthood.
>
> . . . The blunt fact, attested by many liturgists, is that the four official prayers in general are deficient in content and style. . . .The point is that we have enough sensitive and informed liturgists to do better than this. . . .The first EP's [Eucharistic Prayers] in history were composed freely by the bishop from a model. . . .The freshness of language (from a priest who knows what he is doing) is often appreciated, not criticized, by most who are listening and praying.
>
> . . . Many of the same complaints could be made about the prayers offered by the priest alone. Despite the second edition of prayers by ICEL [International Committee on English in the Liturgy] they are often deficient in style, scriptural reference, and present awareness. Frequently they say next to nothing—"make us holy," "inspire us," "help us by your prayers." I would think any presider has an obligation to do better than this.

I leave the reader to ponder his words while we proceed to unfold Ordinary Time.

Ordinary Time

Ordinary Time is sprinkled with enough diversity and human-cycle realities to keep it fresh. Like most parishes, we have high involvement in the liturgy: ushers and greeters, lectors, acolytes, eucharistic ministers (and for those who bring communion to the sick we have a homemade booklet as a guide), bread bakers, cantors, cleaners, writers of the Prayers of the Faithful (one supervised person is in charge of each month's Prayers of the Faithful), flowers, organists, Moppet Choir, Traditional Choir, Contemporary Choir, and Ensemble Choir. All are volunteers and all take autonomous charge of their own area under the distant purview of the Liturgy Committee and the immediate supervision of their coordinators (who are members of the Liturgy Committee).

Likewise, as stressed before, both the expertise and the spirituality should be maintained. For example, we had an expert come in to evaluate and videotape our lectors (who are given the *Workbook for Lectors and Gospel Readers*, Liturgy Training Publications, 1800 North Hermitage Ave. Chicago, IL 60622).

One addition. In order to involve our youth, we ask them to give one month's service in any of three categories: eucharistic minister, usher, or lector. (The youth lector reads only the second reading while the usual lector does all the rest.) They meet with the coordinators who rehearse them beforehand. The names of our youth so involved are written each year in our annual Parish Booklet.

We mentioned bread bakers, both men and women. The recipe we use is a whole wheat altar bread from the Trappist Monastery in Gethsemani, Kentucky.

For five loaves:

5 1/3 cups unsifted whole wheat flour
3 tablespoons baking powder
1 1/2 teaspoons salt
1 3/4 cups warm water
3 tablespoons vegetable oil
2/3 cup honey (honey and vegetable oil already mixed)

1. Pour flour mixture into bowl
2. Add warm water
3. Add honey/oil mixture
4. Stir all ingredients for 2 to 3 minutes. Do not add any more flour.
5. Grease the outside bottom of a 9 inch cake pan (turn pan upside down).
6. Put dough in center of pan and pat out to edge of pan.
7. Score with a knife as per diagram.
8. Bake at 350 for ten minutes; brush lightly with vegetable oil and continue baking for another five minutes. Do not overbake.

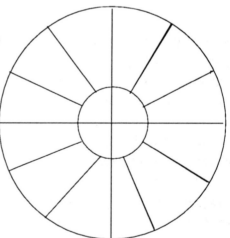

Outer circle = 2 lb. coffee can;
inner circle = 2 3/4" cookie cutter
Cut inner circle.
Score and cut to within 1/8" of cutting through.

Note: There is currently some serious discussion among the bishops that one day unleavened bread will not be required for the eucharist, but rather ordinary, everyday bread as we understand it. When that day comes it will be most suitable, I suggest, to take any bread left over from your soup kitchen or similar outreach situation and consciously use that bread at Mass. As the bishops write in their pastoral letter, *Communities of Salt and Light:*

> The most important setting for the church's social teaching is not in a food pantry or in a legislative committee room, but in prayer and worship, especially gathered around the altar for the eucharist....We support new efforts to integrate liturgy and justice, to make clear that we are one people united in faith, worship, and works of charity and justice.

Using the leftover bread from a food pantry would surely help in reminding us of that integration of liturgy and justice.

Some Ordinary Time areas worth commenting on:

1. Weekend Schedule. To help people avoid or attend certain styles of worship we have a fixed routine:

•The first Sunday of every month at either the 10:30 or 12:00 Mass, we have the Traditional Choir with the Family High Mass Servers.

•The first Saturday of each month is the Mass with Children.

•The second Sunday of each month we celebrate baptisms at the 12:00 Mass.

•The fourth Sunday of each month we have the Contemporary Choir at the 10:30 Mass.

•On the last Sunday of each month there is a food collection and Agape at all Masses. (No Agape at the Saturday vigil; people want to go home to eat.)

People can make whatever arrangement is suitable. It is just a courtesy to them to have a routine that can satisfy their needs and schedules. There is, of course, a cantor and organist at each Mass at which there is no choir.

2. Daily Mass Schedule. Because the same people tend to come every day to church, we have added variety to the schedule. Thus:

On *Mondays* we have four hymns, and at the Offertory we invite all members who so desire to join the giftbearers around the altar (90% of them come up). They return to the pews after receiving communion.

On *Tuesdays* we have a silent Mass with the Mass prayers spoken aloud.

On *Wednesdays* and *Fridays* we have the usual Mass with four hymns.

On *Thursdays* we do not have Mass but chant the Divine Office.

No Mass on *Saturday* mornings.

At all times, however, we have people who prepare the altar, bring up the gifts, cantor, and lector. There is a sign-up sheet at the back of the church and the daily attendees use it. (See Parish Papers, page 257.)

3. "State of the Parish" Address. On the third Sunday of every September, when everyone is back from vacation, I, as pastor, give a "State of the Parish" address with an overview of where we have been, our present challenges, and some visions for the future. Such visions are gleaned from people doing short- and long-range planning (see the chapter on planning). It's a good move, an important ingredient in the unity and cohesion of the parish.

4. Priests' Schedule. We have five Masses on the weekend, one on Saturday at 5:00 P.M. and the others on Sunday at 7:45, 9:00, 10:30, and 12:00. I have one priest helper come in for the weekends, so we rotate on a three-and-two basis. One month I have the 5:00, 7:45, and 9:00 (not to mention funerals and weddings) and he has the 10:30 and 12:00. The following month we switch. The benefit for the priests is that we always know what Masses we have, mathematically, to infinity. The benefit for the people is that they get variety (spiked, of course, with homilies given by our two deacons and lay people. See the end of this chapter). I mention these other preachers because I am not one that thinks the pastor should forever and always take "his" Mass. The people deserve better.

5. Prayers of the Faithful. These, as mentioned elsewhere, are written on a monthly basis by various parishioners. It gives an opportunity for people to speak aloud heartfelt needs or gratitude. I think of the wonderful essayist and novelist, Annie Dillard, who recently became a Catholic. She went for a year to a Catholic Mass before converting. It was not a good experience. The first Mass she walked into was a folk Mass. As she wrote, "It all seemed a pity at first, for I have overcome a fiercely anti-Catholic upbringing to attend Mass simply and solely to escape Protestant guitars . . .Who gave these nice Catholics guitars? . . .What is the pope thinking of?" Anyway, for all of the amateurishness of the liturgy, she was struck by the people, especially at the Prayers of the Faithful when a woman prayed out loud, "For my son, that he may forgive his father, let us pray to the Lord." She had discovered community.

The Prayers of the Faithful are different at the Sunday and weekday Masses. The latter have the same people who come day after day and have their own community and network. Often the Prayers of the Faithful are more like news bulletins or current domestic updates. For example:

"For the safe travel of my sister who is coming down from Buffalo, even though she's just getting over the flu and shouldn't travel, but her doctor said it was all right if she took it easy when she got here and will be arriving Tuesday, coming in on flight 202, let us pray to the Lord."

"That the Spirit may soften the hard heart of a certain husband who won't take a vacation with his grandchildren because they're too noisy, let us pray to the Lord."

"For proper respect for people's privacy and the Christian courtesy to acknowledge a personal sense of place and habits, let us pray to the Lord." (This one needs translation: "Move your butt out of my seat!" Some poor soul sat in Ellen's pew!)

I exaggerate, of course, but the close-knit daily group's petitions are definitely more personal and open than the larger, anonymous Sunday congregation. Anyway, here is an actual sample from graduation time in June:

1. For our church and its leaders that they might be filled with the gift of wisdom, we pray to the Lord . . .

2. That tolerance and acceptance of all people of our nation be fostered throughout our land, we pray to the Lord . . .

3. That those suffering the ravages of serious illness may feel the presence and love of family and the Lord in their lives, we pray to the Lord . . .

4. That the grade school, high school, and college graduates of St. Mary's continue to grow in wisdom, we pray to the Lord . . .

5. For all those baptized this weekend into our community, that they may be filled with the Holy Spirit, we pray to the Lord . . .

6. For Eileen Towne and Richard Besser and all engaged couples as they draw close to their wedding date, that they might find true love and lasting commitment, we pray to the Lord . . .

7. For (see below) and all who have asked for our prayers, we pray to the Lord . . .

Saturday, 5:00 P.M. Charles Bradley
Sunday, 7:45 A.M. Joseph Cawley
Sunday, 9:00 A.M. Frederick Wolf
Sunday, 10:30 A.M. Tom Haley
Sunday, 12:00 P.M. Rosemary Bordunovich

8. For all special intentions, burdens that weigh heavily or joys that cannot be shared, we pray to the Lord . . .

9. We invite you to speak out those intentions you wish to share with the community.

(To lector: Please conclude with your own petition.)

Observe Petition 5: It happened to be baptismal weekend so it is mentioned at all the Masses. Petition 6 is our way of announcing the Banns of Marriage. Petition 7 is our way of avoiding the announcement that this Mass is for so-and-so (the Mass Intention). The Mass belongs to all. This way we acknowledge the requested person and yet at the same time keep the Mass open as a sacrifice and celebration of all.

6. *The Offertory Collection*. It is worth observing that the first ones the ushers bring the basket to are the celebrant and other ministers in the sanctuary. As a member of the parish, I, too, am mailed envelopes. I use them and give as generously as I would want the people to give. When I have more than one Mass (always), I put in a blank envelope since I am convinced that the gesture is important.

As I wrote in *The Hands-On Parish*, we *never* have a second collection. We take any special needs out of the one general collection. We do, however, stress the need so that the people can remain sensitive to larger concerns. We do this in the interest of keeping the liturgy unencumbered by a constant basket passing, not to mention what an irritant this is.

When we have the annual missionary appeal, again there is no special collection. We simply give our entire weekend collection away to the missionary.

Likewise, we never permit the buying

and selling of tickets, even for the most noble cause, before or after Mass. People come to worship, not to be taken advantage of. Particularly, we would never allow a car, a raffle prize, to be displayed on the lawn. It is a competing icon and says in effect that whatever you heard inside, you can leave there: Materialism is the real world.

7. *Dialogue Sunday.* Once a month at rotating Masses, we have "Dialogue Sunday." This means that I stand in the pulpit and announce that I have a prepared homily, but if anyone wants to ask anything about the faith, about the church, about religion—about anything—now's the time. I await some profound theological conundrum, but someone raises his hand and wants to know how come Frank Sinatra was able to get married in the church! Oh well, we do pick up from there and really have an interesting question and answer period. These Dialogue Sundays are informative, at times entertaining, and always appreciated. When we first started them, I confess I had a shill or two in the congregation: people prompted to ask questions so we could kind of prime the conversational pump.

8. *Mass with Children.* Here, as in other parishes, the children have their own choir (the "Moppet" Choir), do the readings, usher, bring up the gifts, and read the Prayers of the Faithful. The homily is always a story told by the celebrant while sitting in front of the altar and inviting the kids to come up and sit around him. Refreshments follow. The adults rehearse with the children beforehand.

(The same dynamics work for Grandparents Day. They do everything, including the homily.)

With the cover on colored paper, an outline for the preparation of a Mass with children is put together by religious education coordinator, Marge Gilbert. (See the example of this on pages 244-248 in Parish Papers.) You may cut it out or reproduce it and fold it in half to make a small booklet. The names in it, of course, mean nothing to you, but they remain to show you how the plan develops.

9. *Liturgy of the Word for Children.* Under this section on children, we might mention the satisfying practice of our parish and many parishes: the Liturgy of the Word for children. The announcement is made by the cantor at the beginning of Mass that the children will file into the (attached) parish hall right before the Liturgy of the Word. The lector repeats this announcement right before he (she) reads, and the organist plays some background music while the children file into the hall. There they have their own Liturgy of the Word and follow up catechesis. When the celebrant begins the creed in church, word is sent back to the hall and the kids return. We have this at all Masses twice a month.

10. *Children's Bulletins.* At all Masses we have specially designed flyers for children, related to the Sunday theme, which the ushers give them as they come in. It contains something for the children to do, while at the same time providing a focus for them at this liturgy.

11. *Children's Christmas Liturgy.* In addition to the usual Moppet routine for Masses with children, we add two items: 1) We have some children dress up as Mary and Joseph, shepherds and angels. They lead the procession into the sanctuary where they form a tableau in front of the altar before Mass begins and then move to the first pew. They reappear beneath the lectern for the reading of the Christmas gospel. 2) At the Holy, Holy,

Holy Lord, five "angels" come into the sanctuary and do a wonderful and simple liturgical dance to this acclamation. The shepherds and angels are the offertory giftbearers and all recess out with the regular ministers at the end of Mass.

12. The last Sunday of each month is *Agape/Food Weekend.* After each Mass (except the Saturday Vigil: People are going home to eat) we have an Agape or mini-breakfast of coffee, juice, bagels, donuts, etc. It's a buffet affair with people mingling about. Hosting responsibilities for each Mass are parceled out among the parish organizations and parish families. "Hosting responsibilities" means to serve the coffee or juice and, for the last Mass, to clean up (as people for the first Mass prepared the tables and food). We send out letters (see page 305) and sign people up in the spring and so have all their names from September to the following August in our annual Parish Booklet, which is mailed to all by Labor Day. The parish pays for the food which is a standing order delivered by a local baker. Most people come back and it's a good parish mixer.

The food collection means that on the last Sunday of each month people bring bags of food or paper products and lay them in the sanctuary. At the end of Mass, just before the blessing, the celebrant calls up the food carriers to the sanctuary, who pick up the bags and stand there for the blessing and dismissal. It goes this way:

Celebrant: The community calls from its midst representatives to carry the donated food to the Sharing Shed.

(The carriers come forward, pick up a bag or box, and face the congregation.)

Celebrant: Let us pray. Almighty God, lover of the poor and friend of the outcast, bless those who gave this food from the goodness of their hearts. Bless too the hands that will distribute and the hands that will receive. And may all of us know that we have no right to pride, for, as disciples of the Lord and servants of one another, we are but doing our duty, beholden as we are to the gospel of Our Lord Jesus Christ. Amen.

(Here the celebrant sprinkles the carriers with holy water and then announces:)

This Mass is ended. Let us go to love and serve the Lord.

All: Thanks be to God.

(The carriers process out before the celebrant. They go directly out the front door and up to the Sharing Shed to deposit the goods on the shelves.)

Once more, these carriers—whole families, including the children—are signed up beforehand and have their names, dates, and times in the forthcoming Parish Booklet.

13. Ordinary Time is peppered with *various community celebrations*: the renewal of **marriage** vows on silver, or fortieth, or golden anniversaries (usually right after the homily), Mother's Day and Father's Day (we give out gifts), the betrothal ceremony, the Baccalaureate Mass, baptisms (second Sunday of every month at the noon Mass), Covenant signing for confirmation candidates when we celebrate that sacrament every other year, Mass of anointing, and the occasional departure ceremony for those leaving the parish:

Celebrant *(addressing the congregation after the homily, after having invited the family to the sanctuary to face the people):*

My dear friends, the _____ family is departing from our midst. We have known them and loved them. They have journeyed with us and now they move on. We shall miss them, but we also know that they shall carry the spirit of St. Mary's wherever they go.

Our prayers follow them, and so I ask you all to kneel for a moment for a brief litany to which you are to reply, "Lord, be with them."

Holy Father, give them vision and strength.
Glorious Son, show them the way.
Loving Spirit, surprise them with joy.
Holy Angels, surround them.
Saints of God, protect them.
Root them in your holy love.
Send them to plant the faith.
Make them witnesses of your truth.
Be their newness.
Be their adventure.
Be their laughter.
Be their memory.
Be their courage.

O God, you know that we shall miss the _____ family, but we

also know that you always send forth your people to new places, jobs, and tasks so that the gospel may be spread and your people may witness in all places to the wonders of your love. Comfort us with memories of them. Encourage them with memories of us. We ask this through Christ Our Lord. Amen.

The family is invited to say a few words and a parish gift is given them—and much applause. A touching moment.

14. Blessing of the Containers. Twice a year we ask people to take home aluminum or plastic containers, fill them with part of their dinner, mark directions on the container, and return them to the parish hall freezer during the week. The containers are in the hall, but some representative ones are on the altar as a visual reminder and these are publicly blessed just before the final dismissal in this way:

Loving Father, we ask your blessing on these food containers. Be gracious to those who prepare the food and those who eat it and are nourished. Let us be mindful of your constant care and mercy, and bring us all to your eternal banquet. Amen.

On page 280 of Parish Papers is an example of this notice.

15. Halloween. This seems to be a strange custom, and anyone walking in on us will call the Nut Squad forthwith. But all are invited to All Hallows Eve morning Mass dressed in costume. People do dress up and come and sit in different places to avoid identity. The church is filled with ghouls, witches, monsters, Darth Vaders, and Ronald McDonalds (remember, these are adults). Then, after Mass, as usual, we go to the hall for coffee and donuts. It really is fun, and it also provides a fruitful source of reflection on why we dress up, our connection with the Communion of Saints, and the masks we wear.

16. Lay Preaching. Although lay people do not normally preach, the New Testament seems to argue for it, even though, early on, preaching became linked with the office of bishop, priest, and deacon (although the record shows that some bishops called on laity to preach). Later, it became law that the laity were not to preach and the Council of Trent said it was anathema for anyone to say that all Christians had the power of the ministry of the Word. But times have changed, and such changes have led us to have lay persons preach once a month at rotating Masses (that is, not at all the Masses, but at a single Mass, a different one each month on a rotating basis).

The reasons for change are several. There is the theological emphasis given to experience, to the universal call to holiness, to how ordinary people discern the presence of God in their lives. This experience should be shared and encouraged. In 1988, the U.S. bishops issued *Guidelines for Lay Preaching*, which forbade the laity to give the homily but did allow them to preach at retreats, revivals, missions, spiritual exercises, and any large gathering of the faithful. Why? Precisely because the bishops readily recognized the gifts and experience of the people. And so by their very sensitivity to and acknowledgment of the work of the Spirit in the lives of the laity and their recognition that some laity indeed have the charism of preaching, the bishops have given a serious nod to a new reality. They have also admitted to "the deepened knowledge of scripture and theology which many lay persons possess" today.

Furthermore, Canon Law itself (canon 225) recognizes the obligation of the laity to spread the gospel, especially, as it says, "in those circumstances in which people can hear the gospel and know Christ only through lay persons."

Then, too, there are practical issues. More and more parishes are without full-time clergy. Some are pastored by religious men or women, or by lay men or women. Are such parishes to be without the preached word? Even where there is a parish priest, if he is there a long time (such as myself: twenty-two years alone in the same parish), the comment of Patricia Hughes Baumer, referring to her parish, is apt: "No matter how authentic, how could the spirituality of any one minister nourish and challenge this still growing community week after week?" (See her fine article, "Empowering a New Voice: The Potential for Lay Preaching," *The Catholic World*, March/April 1994.)

All of these factors—the validity of people's experience of God, their deepening scriptural and theological knowledge, their unique ability to evangelize—seem to me to argue, in these days of severe priest shortage and the growing demand for good homilies, that we might as well develop good lay homilists as opposed to no preachers at all or foreign preachers.

17. All Souls Day. On All Souls evening we have a lovely ceremony. Anyone who has lost someone to death in the past year is sent a special invitation to attend. The public is also invited by way of a bulletin announcement. Those who were personally invited are asked to print the name of the deceased on a card. All gather in a darkened church. There is an opening hymn, prayer, scripture reading, and homily. Then, one by one, the people approach the altar and hand their card to the server who in turn brings it to the cantor.

Do you recall the old Latin Litany of the Saints and how it was chanted?

> *Sancte Michael, ora pro nobis.*
> *Santa Lucia, ora pro nobis.*
> and so on.

In a similar way the cantor, in his deep baritone, sings out, for example: "Leonard DiMarcellis," and the congregation sings back in Latin, "*Ora pro eo.*" And so it goes, each name sung and responded to. As the cantor finishes with a name, a server takes the card and drops it in our fire bucket (someone made us a stainless steel container with a grilled cover and handles). Meanwhile, as each person hands the name card to the server, he (she) is handed back an unlighted candle which they light from a lone candlestand within the body of the church. The few lights that were on have been extinguished. At the end of our litany, the cards are set afire, and the people, holding their lighted candles, watch in silence (background music) while they burn. Then we close with the old reliable and moving *Dies Irae* as the ministers depart in silence. The high point is the public chanting of the names and the congregational response. Simple and very effective.

18. Music. Let us recall that we have several choirs. For most parishes I am in favor of having a full-time paid pastoral musician, in spite of the joke that dictators are easier to persuade than liturgists. Such a person, well paid and carefully understanding his (her) boundaries, can make a huge difference in the worship of the parish. It so happens, however, that all of our musicians and cantors and choirs are volunteers. I couldn't be happier because they do an excellent job and are full of spirit and expertise. They practice every week, seriously investigate new music, and attend workshops. It is consistently common for the congregation to applaud at the final song, not because they were satisfied with an entertainment, but because they were led so joyously in worship.

19. Family Mass Servers. On the first Sunday of the month when we have the High Mass at noon, we have a family serve as altar ministers or acolytes. This family may include a grandparent, parents, teens, and children. The Family Mass trainer meets with them beforehand and doles out the jobs.

Robed in white, the family servers process in with the celebrant. One, usually the father, carries the heavy processional cross and plants it in its holder in front of the altar. At the opening asperges, the water bearer (usually the mother carrying a clear bowl of water) accompanies the celebrant who sprinkles the people with a green branch. Then the family stays in the sanctuary and performs pretty much the tasks of the regular Mass servers. Two exceptions: Some of the family goes down and brings up the preparatory gifts, and others prepare the incense for the incensation of the altar and the congregation. They assist at Communion and

lead the celebrant back after Mass. This is, for a family, a one-time event and, nervous as they initially are, they seem to enjoy it very much and often ask for a repeat time.

Having Family Mass servers is a good witness for the people and a privileged and appreciated sharing for the family. (As always, "family" can be any arrangement.)

20. Morning Office. For many years we have had a group of men and women meet at 6:30 in the morning to chant morning prayer from the Divine Office. By mutual desire, the men meet on Wednesday mornings and the women on Friday mornings. This has proven to be a powerful and satisfying way to start the day. We meet in our spiritual center chapel with its large, open view of the rock garden and sky and, in the winter, sparkling stars. We get around 20 to 25 in attendance. The service lasts about a half hour with coffee and cake following for those who can stay and don't have to get on the road for work. We follow the outline in *The Catholic Liturgy Book* (Baltimore: Helicon, 1975. There are other fine books to use). Note that the leadership for this office is lay led and rotated. The procedure is as follows:

Opening hymn
Opening prayer
The psalm (now chanted by heart)
Prayer
Scripture reading
Homily, reflection
The Canticle of Zechariah (after which the leader incenses the participants and then the lit candlestand is placed in our midst as a sign of the Risen Christ)
Intercessions
The Lord's Prayer (chanted while holding hands)

Holy Communion
Prayers of the Faithful
Blessing and dismissal
Closing hymn

This follows standard procedure. The only break in the approved format is Holy Communion and this is given as a concession to the genuine piety of the people who want to start the day with Communion. Prayer, piety, and fellowship are wonderful fruits of this day's beginning.

I urge you to start this prayer routine, particularly among the men. They often have far fewer opportunities for shared prayer and, as a result, I have found them exceedingly open to and desirous of such a chance. The before-work time slot is most appealing to them. In fact, the men's morning office was in operation for many years before the women's. My point is that the men are much more susceptible to this kind of opportunity than you may think. Give it a try.

Cranky Thoughts

Let me close this chapter with some idiosyncratic musings. First of all, those Sunday readings. I realize that someone found a manuscript that indicated there were three readings in ancient times in some places and so thought it would be a good idea to restore them. Add to this the laudable desire to clean up the mishmash of saints and feasts and the desire to expose people to the entire Bible in the course of a three-year cycle. But the fact is that these three readings leave little impact on a people raised on sound bytes and one-note messages. As liturgist Father Joe Nolan says of the daily Mass lectionary, "It's time to say that people standing up to read dense passages from the book of Kings—or whatever—is simply a business of going through the motions" (*Good News* newsletter, April 1994). He's right. I bet nine out of ten parishioners can't remember what the first two readings were about on a given Sunday. (They'll remember the gospel. Do *you* remember last Sunday's first two readings?) Add to this, readings that only a Ph.D. in ancient Egyptology could connect together and gospels that contain multiple (and esoteric) themes and thoughts (St. John can drive you crazy), and you wonder how effective it all is.

And all those words! We have a first reading, a responsorial psalm, a second reading, a gospel reading, and a homily—all back to back. A visual, not audio, generation finds it hard to remember it all, even with pauses between them. The homilist, challenged to make connections among all three readings (sometimes he can, sometimes he can't), sticks with the well-known gospel. If he's smart, he'll cut it off after one solidly expressed thought or, at times, add the few verses unaccountably left out (for example, Luke 1:39–45, Year C, fourth Sunday of Advent, which omits the *Magnificat*).

Could we not reduce the three readings to the old two readings, bring in the pastors and the poets to choose them, and allow the Sunday gospel to be repeated on Monday so that the usual weekday crowd, who were all at Mass on Sunday, would have a chance to have the scripture theme unfolded even more? Could we not use for the first reading some of those magnificent lessons of the Divine Office from the Fathers of the Church and saints?

Second, there are those liturgists who find the notion of thematic Masses abhorrent, but I find them more in tune with where people are. By a theme I don't mean that it has to be explicitly announced before Mass, but I mean that the opening prayer could be adjusted to mention it, the homily expound it, the Prayers of the Faithful allude to it, and the closing prayer wrap it all up. Check the TV commercials. They repeat over and over again (to distraction) the single theme, brand, phone number, or motto till they feel they've made an impact on the audience. Well, that same audience is sitting in church conditioned to one message they can take home. A theme, I maintain, would help.

Third, as I have mentioned in the last chapter, on occasion we have dialogue readings; that is, congregational booklets that give people speaking roles in the gospel proclamation. It is very effective. I think that parishes or the commercial people should offer us cheap booklets for the major feasts of the year containing the people's participation in the some of the sequences and gospels. For example, Christmas, Passion Sunday (which the missalettes already do: I would add more

speaking parts for the congregation than presently), Pentecost, Thanksgiving, and maybe one or two more Sundays.

Finally, we should be ready to experiment, but with great respect for the rubrics. An example: Liturgist Gabe Huck offers this variation on the preparation of the gifts. After the Prayers of the Faithful, everyone is seated while two acolytes carry the empty chalice and the Sacramentary to the altar table and place them there. While they are doing that, two or three people from the congregation carry up the bread and wine and, along with them, the ushers with their baskets. The celebrant and acolytes go to meet the gift bearers and ushers and the celebrant says something like this: "Pray, brothers and sisters, that the money and other gifts we give today and throughout this week for the church and for the poor may, with these gifts of bread and wine, be acceptable to God." The congregation answers with the usual response.

Summary of Chapter 8

1. Take a second look at the Eucharistic Prayers and the priest's prayers and perhaps critique them with a small group or with your liturgy committee.

2. Consider, within firm guidelines, some variety, some more deeply human touches.

3. Have periodic evaluations of the liturgical ministers.

4. Discover how you can involve your youth in the weekend liturgies.

5. Look at the bread you use and evaluate its symbolism.

6. Weekend liturgies should have routine and expected variety.

7. Parishioner-written Prayers of the Faithful are better than the canned.

8. Use the Prayers of the Faithful to cover baptisms, marriages, and Mass intentions.

9. For the daily Mass attendees, have sufficient variety and engagement.

10. The *Lectionary for Masses with Children* has fine guidelines and Eucharistic Prayers. Use them.

11. Consider the Liturgy of the Word with children in another area.

12. Run off or purchase children's one-page bulletins.

13. A monthly food collection is a good project and a good symbol of the eucharist.

14. A monthly get together after Mass, if possible, over coffee and cider is always a good mixer.

15. Sprinkle the Ordinary Time with a variety of human passages and milestones.

16. Think about lay preachers, especially if there are too few current priest homilists.

17. Music: paid or volunteer? It's up to you.

18. Give a thought to the readings: How effective are they? What could be done better?

A young priest was dismayed to find a serious quarrel among members of his new congregation. During Sunday Mass half of the people stood up during the consecration while half remained kneeling. All decorum was lost as each side shouted at the other to conform.

Members of each group insisted that theirs was the correct tradition. Seeking guidance, the young priest took a representative from each side to visit the parish's founder, a 99-year-old monsignor living in a nursing home.

"Monsignor, isn't it true that the tradition was always for the people to stand at the consecration?" inquired the man from the standing-up side.

"No, that was not the tradition," the old man replied.

"Ah, then, it is the true tradition for people to stay kneeling?" asked the kneeling representative.

"No," said the old Monsignor, "that was not the tradition."

"But, Monsignor," cried the young priest, "what we have now is complete chaos. Half the people stand and shout while the others kneel and scream!"

"Ah," said the old man, "*that* was the tradition."

Want something to think about? Try Jim Bowman's thoughts in *Commonweal* (October 8, 1993):

A modest proposal, if you please, to return somehow, somewhat, to the old liturgy. I make it after worshiping five Sundays in a row at my neighborhood Tridentine-Latin Mass church. . . .I like their Mass. It has Latin and Gregorian music and incense and long periods when we pew-sitters have nothing to do but

let the music and the smell of incense and overall ambiance of set-piece
reverence wash over us. At the kiss of peace, we do not turn to shake hands with
our neighbors—the virtual highlight of the Masses I usually attend. Instead, we
concentrate on God above. . . .This Mass is in Latin, which is Greek to most of us,
I know. But that makes it a quintessential ritual language, special language for
church, language that says church is not an extension of the five-day week, but
something different, something out of the way. . . .I count myself a modern
churchgoer, but my baptism did not entirely take as a member of the new
church, it seems. For one thing, I relish the passivity of this worship experience.
No song leader is up there waving and weaving to get and help me be a good
Catholic by singing up a storm. No celebrant is looking me in the eye. . . .No
neighbor is looking for my hand at the Lord's Prayer. . . .I'm alone with God, and
I love it. . . .There you are, after running around all week, ready for something
different. It's natural. You love God, you might even like God. But God is
different from you and me. Extremely different. You would like to make contact.
You would like to walk away changed, if only a little. . . .Among the worshipers.
. . .are refugees from noise and frou-frou, balloons in the sanctuary, and all that.
They want something more reverential. For them, worship is no cabaret, no more
than life.

Planning

Chapter 9

Planning

> "Aren't you filled with the Holy Spirit?"
> " Of course I am. But I leak."

Let me start off by directing you to the pages of one of our annual Parish Booklets that we mail out to every family. (See Parish Papers, pages 249-252.) Look them over carefully. What was your impression? "My God, the place must be frantic!" or "Good grief, they've got something for everyone. Where do they get all these people?" Or your feeling might be one of frustration or disbelief. So some comments are in order and, in the process, hints on planning.

Getting Underwhelmed

To begin with, there *are* a great many items listed in these pages and there *is* a lot going on in the parish but, remember, no one does it all. It's like what C.S. Lewis wrote in *The Problem of Pain*, that there is a lot of pain in the dentist's office but no one is suffering it all. So, too, there's much going on, but no *one* is doing it all. So you have entries like the Heart Attack Support Group or the Craft Show or Lion of Judah Prayer Group or Pre-Cana Conferences or Stations of the Cross, but these cater to their own clientele—and in the process enrich the parish and the community. For example, two men who had experience with heart attacks asked me if they could start a support group for others who might need it. My invariable answer is, "Why not? Try it out. Talk to Joe." Joe is the coordinator of the Spiritual Center and he'll give them a classroom and time slot. Then they're on their own. They may have two or twenty-two attend. I have no notion, nor should I. They are responsible adults. The same with the Lion of Judah Prayer Group. They're a small group of charismatic people who get together in the Spiritual Center chapel every Friday night for prayer. They're on their own. And so it goes. These events and activities multiply and seem overwhelming when looked at all together, but they are separate items made to fit into an overall schedule and they provide wonderful opportunities for those who have particular needs.

There are, however, some controls. Five in fact:

First Control: The initiative of the people is a result of the *education* that I wrote about in the section "Getting to Know You." After years of self-understanding as a People of God, as co-laborers, people feel free to suggest, begin, and run events. It's their parish, their buildings, their property. I work with and for them and they pay my salary (not very much, I remind them). They, you recollect, are not "charged" for the sacraments, the use of the hall or materials.

They have the opportunity of the "no-strings" education and access to all buildings. This kind of climate fosters initiative and leadership, and that's why so many items in that index do not require my presence and why there is such a variety.

Second Control: The index is an expression of our *charism*. Every parish has its charism depending on its time and place and leadership. Virginia Finn mentions in *Pilgrims in This World* (Mahwah, N.J.: Paulist Press, 1990) that in Washington, D.C. there is a large inner-city parish with a quite diversified staff. They have adopted a sister parish and have a deep outreach to the inner city, an outreach firmly rooted in the scriptures and their scripture groups. Their charism is mission and scripture and everything in the parish in one way or another bends to that.

Another parish is in a business district. It has a mixed staff, full- and part-time. They have many discussion groups, seminars, lectures, workshops, the catechumenate, and so on. Because of their location and clientele, their charism is adult education and formation. Another suburban parish has full-time musicians and a music director. They do wonders with the liturgy, especially at the high seasons. There are several choirs. It's easy to see that their charism is liturgy. A city parish stresses spiritual formation. All parishioners make an overnight retreat and undertake intensive planning, guided by speakers and training sessions, evaluation, and so on. Their charism is spiritual formation.

Our charism is hospitality in the broadest sense. We're a semi-rural parish on 25 acres with a church and hall, a Spiritual Center, a meditation garden, a grotto, and a parish house with two apartments for guests. Because of the beauty of the place and its reputation as being innovative and sparked by shared and collaborative ministry, many people (and institutions such as schools) come here. They come to make retreats, to attend days or evenings of recollection, to hold seminars and, above all, to see how we do things and talk to the people to learn about the various ministries. We hold an annual fall Hands-On Workshop and open the apartments to anyone who wants to stay a while to observe. We send our Parish Booklet all over the world and respond to many letters. In short, we have a sense of mission not only to our own parishioners and the community, but to all. It is this charism, as we see it, that encourages us to learn, to do, to innovate, and to share.

Third Control: The initiative of the people comes from what we call *creating the threefold climate.*

a. The climate of freedom to 1) do, 2) experiment, 3) fail, and 4) know where things are. As I mentioned, people are encouraged to do things and to engage in ministry by having tools and services at their disposal. They are free to experiment and, if they fail, so what? We all know that experience. And, as to where things are, it is important that everyone know this. It is a form of control to have to run to the pastor to find out where the coffee or toilet paper is kept. Keys do give power but, like walking your dog, there are two ends to the leash and both are confining. Everyone has access to everything and every room has full instructions posted on the wall or door indicating how the heat, air conditioning, and lights work. Every (unlocked) cabinet has a list of the contents inside.

b. The climate of trust. People are free to run courses, to make decisions as to where our tithing money goes, to write our Prayers of the Faithful, lead morning prayer, borrow "their" tables and chairs, use the parish truck (keys always inside), and purchase whatever they need to do their job and turn the bill in to the office. I don't wish to imply that there is anarchy; people do touch base with the one in charge—but not me. Someone, for example, would ask the custodian if it's all right to use the truck or borrow chairs, and his permission is the final word. (Principle of subsidiarity!)

c. The climate of place, which I have already discussed. It's the openness of the buildings, the banner, the bulletin board, the photographs, the Guest Book, the fact that we can keep the buildings open 24 hours a day (a rarity, I admit, and I never, never advise this for other parishes). It's the sense of ownership that promotes initiative.

Fourth Control: The index of many activities and events are not entirely helter-skelter but are controlled by planning the *parish calendar* for the coming parish year, September to June. There are three steps to this:

a. Large white posters (22" x 28") are lined and marked for months, days, and dates for a ten-month calendar year (again, September to June). The standard civic and religious days are marked in: Labor Day, Thanksgiving, first Sunday of Advent, Christmas, Lent, Easter, holidays, etc. In June these ten posters are hung on the bulletin boards in the parish hall.

b. A notice is then sent to all the heads of the parish organizations, ministries, and outsiders who use the facilities, telling them that the calendar is up and they should mark

in their dates as soon as possible. June 20 is the final deadline. This forces them to do their planning and to get their preferred times on the calendar.

The calendar, therefore, has two positive aspects. It forces planning and resolves conflicts. For example, someone writing in a date for a dance might notice that another group is having one around the same time, and will make a change to avoid competition. Groups drawing on the same people will maneuver to spread the talent. In other words, the large calendar gives everyone an overview and they can act accordingly. Of course, where there are non-conflicting groups and many rooms are available you can have several things going on at one time—and this is obvious in the final edition of the calendar that eventually gets printed in the Parish Booklet. Page 253 of Parish Papers shows a sample of a typical month.

c. The final step is making dummy sheets of all the parish needs. For example, listing people to host the Agapes during the year or host the communal confessions or do the Stations of the Cross on a particular lenten Friday evening, etc. With these sheets, about a half dozen people connected with producing the Parish Booklet sit down and suggest names of potential volunteers, usually three, so that two can be alternates if the first choice refuses. Names are gleaned from personal knowledge, the Covenant signers who, you recall, listed a Christian service they would be interested in, and from a random gleaning of the parish census. ("Anybody know these people? Let's ask them and get them involved.")

The letters go out, appealing for help and underscoring the one-time commitment. The letters are very effective because 1) they are personally sent by the pastor, 2) they are asking for help, always a flattering and true resonance, 3) they usually ask for one thing and so are time efficient and appealing to harried people, and 4) they are sent early. (After all, anyone will say yes in May to decorating the church for Christmas. It's when December 15 comes that they panic. Then it's too late. Their names are inscribed in the booklet!) In the event of a refusal, another form letter goes out to the next on the list. The upshot is that we have 85% of our responses by mid-June. Where necessary, to round it out, we follow up with phone calls. Here are a few samples of the letters we mail out:

Dear Friends,

As you know, it has long been our parish custom to have an Agape or mini-breakfast on the last Sunday of the month after each Mass. Our organizations take care of the 7:45 and 9:00, but we need help for the 10:30 and noon Masses. And this is where, we hope, you come in.

Would you, along with other families we have listed, take care of the Mass whose date and time are written in below? What does "taking care of" mean?

Well, it *doesn't* mean 1) that you have to order the buns, coffee, or cider. We do that. 2) It doesn't mean you have to set up tables. We do that too.

What it *does* mean is that 1) you refill the coffee and milk pitchers and check the buns, 2) serve, so that when the people come into the parish hall after Mass the coffee and cider are already in pitchers ready to go. 3) Finally, you clean up so the next group can be served. It doesn't take long.

I realize that this time and date may not be convenient for you and your family, and I can understand if you are not available. You might wish to take another date. But if you could help, all of the parish community would be most grateful. Let us know by calling the parish office (780-2666) within the next ten days. Many, many thanks.

Sincerely yours,
Father Bausch

Date_____ Mass time_____
The families helping you _____ _____

Dear Friends,

As you know, on the last Sunday of each month we have a food collection for the needy. People bring up groceries and paper goods and place them in the sanctuary. At the end of Mass the food is carried up to the Sharing Shed and from there it is  distributed to many places such as Lunch Break or Mercy Center. This is a marvelous ministry and many people depend on St. Mary's for a steady food supply.

The way we get the food from the sanctuary to the Sharing Shed is to have individuals and families at the 10:30 Mass come up at the end of Mass, pick up the bags of groceries, face the people, and receive the final blessing. Then they march out with the celebrant down the center aisle and proceed non-stop up to the Sharing Shed to deposit the food there.

Would you and your family or friends do this task and commit yourselves on the date listed below?

I can appreciate it if you're unable to do this and understand if you are not available, but if you could either help out at this one instance or give us an alternate date, we would be most grateful.

Thank you for considering this.

Sincerely yours,
Father Bausch

On the bottom is a list of all the months and dates for the forthcoming parish year with a little check-off box. Notice that all the letters give a description, so there are no surprises, and there is a definite time limit and a way to say no. One final sample:

Dear Mary,

As you know, we are presently putting together our Parish Booklet for 1994-95. Our standard policy is to invite parishioners to take on the responsibility for coordinating an event or chairing a committee. Sensitive to busy schedules, we never ask anyone to make such a commitment forever but for a one-time event. And that person is always assured of the support and assistance of the staff and those who did the task before.

So, for the coming year we are asking you to coordinate the activity herewith described:

*Senior Citizens Day of Recollection: to organize and facilitate it for Sunday, October 24 at 2:00 P.M.

For replies and additional information, please call Sharon Sturchio, Program Coordinator, at the parish office, 780-2666.

Since our booklet goes to press at the end of June, we would appreciate hearing from you as soon as possible.

Thanks for considering this request. We are truly grateful for whatever participation you can give.

Sincerely yours,
Father Bausch

Two items to note: 1) This letter is a standard form and the asterisk could well read Father's Day gift, or the annual Christmas concert, or the Oliver celebration. 2) Sharon is, as noted, the Program Coordinator. This is an invaluable position. She keeps in touch, asks if there are any needs, explains the program or project if the people are still uncertain, hands over the log (we keep an ongoing log of each event so that the accumulated experience of others can help new volunteers), and in general acts as resource provider, encourager, and facilitator—but never does the work! She is there to get them to do it.

I readily admit that all this is hard work. But once the calendar is filled in, conflicts resolved, and people signed up, then we can relax and wait for the year to unfold, knowing that we will not have two groups meeting the same night, the same hour, in the same place, resulting in the ecclesiastical version of the Gunfight at the O.K. Corral. We are not so rigid that we don't know that the "best laid plans" go awry and so, once a month, we have a staff meeting to check corrections and adjustments.

Theme

Fifth and final controlling element in creating an index, producing a calendar that sorts it all out, and giving some unity is the year's *theme*. At different times we sit down with the staff, random groups, and the parish council and suggest a theme for the coming year. We go around with it until one is finally adopted and approved by the parish council.

For the parish year of 1993-1994, for example, our theme was "The Year of Evangelization," with its emphasis on appealing to inactive Catholics. It had several

components. One is that the previous year our theme centered around the formation of small groups, so we had in place many groups meeting to share scripture reading. They would be invaluable not only for prayer, but for being small enough to invite others to come to their group, people who might not at first come to church.

Next, we formed a committee who would work with the Paulist Evangelization program. We gathered names from the people at all the Masses (after much publicity) on "Invitation Sunday" and sent these names to the Paulist Center, which in turn will send five very attractive flyers to those people. Then we planned a parish mission with Paulist priest John Collins, who would center his talks on evangelization.

Finally, overall, we asked each parish organization to devote one of its meetings to the theme (speaker, video, etc.) and had the sick, the shut-ins, the prayer groups, and the children pray for the success of the program.

Thus, the annual parish theme (or "goal setting") is a cohesive force in giving all of us a common thread of consciousness while still allowing for the many diversified activities and parish projects. In other words, we have all kinds of people writing in on that calendar and appearing in that index, displaying all kinds of activities from a full religious education program with its first penances, communions, and Masses and parent meetings, to specialized gatherings such as the infant massage, Girl Scout leaders, drug rehabilitation, AA, Al-Anon, GA (Gamblers Anonymous), and bereavement groups. None detract from the theme and, in fact, all underscore it. The theme links the diversity to the unity of the parish.

Resource

For a sophisticated, computer-based analysis of your parish (breakdown tables, stats, sampling, survey, goal setting, etc.) check the program *Informed* by Tom Sweetser and Carol Holden. From PEP, 2200 E. Devon, #283, Des Plaines, IL 60018.

A practical postscript to planning. We have been speaking of the immediate planning for a parish year. We must also recommend the *long-range view*. That is, to get together with the parish council, staff, and other insightful parishioners and dream down the road. Where are we going? What are future goals? We do this in five-year stages. Following is a description of how it has worked out since I came in 1972. This is a synopsis from a report we sent to the people:

1972–1977: St. Mary's moves from mission status to an independent parish. The church was built in 1972 and in the next four years the grounds were expanded, sidewalks put in, playground equipment added, the parish house (rectory) built, and parish activities implemented.

1977–1982: Trees were planted to make a picnic grove, storage shed and the St. Francis meditation garden were built, and new ministries were added.

1982–1987: The Spiritual Center is completed and the Sharing Shed is built. Parish numbers grow from the original 150 families to 900.

1987–1992: The Grotto is built and extensive renovations to the church, parish hall, and grounds are completed.

1992–1997: The mortgage is paid off and the money given to charity. The catechumenate (RCIA) is in place, small faith communities (Koinonia), and the Bereavement Ministry have been introduced. Evangelization to be considered.

Prayerful dreaming, envisioning, wishful thinking, long-range planning—all these are much to be desired. They keep the parish alive and open to new possibilities.

A Challenge

In planning on the parish level the pastor or pastoral minister must have fortitude. Why fortitude? Not to deal with the home-front critics or naysayers, but to deal with the diocese—and that takes staying power and a good sense of self-identity and parish identity. You often get the feeling that the diocese does no or little planning or, to give it a charitable spin, it doesn't know how to stick to its priorities when it gets directives from Rome.

The problem is all those letters, all those programs sent to the pastor. Each one, let us say for the sake of argument, is noble, decent, worthwhile, redemptive. But, for cryin' out loud, how many in a given year can a parish do? Picture the mail coming to the pastor's desk requiring that: Each parish must implement an evangelization program, a social concerns program, introduce the new rite of penance or funerals, stewardship, the *Catechism of the Catholic Church,* instruct the people on the diocesan Synod and send delegates, march on the right to life, promote the missions, take part in the annual diocesan fund drive—and have people speak at all the weekend Masses promoting these to the people. The sad thing is that some parishes do all these things. The result is easy to surmise: fragmentation, lack of "wholeness" and vision, cohesion, and direction. The parish winds up doing many things poorly instead of one thing well. That's not planning. That's chaos.

You would think we would learn from the secular world that forms and shapes the minds of our people. Listen to the advertisements. They repeat over and over again one simple message, one phone number to call. It works. We can all identify Joe Camel, Roseanne, Calvin Klein, and Jessica Fletcher and the products they sell. Why can't we be as single-minded? I repeat: We can, but it takes fortitude. The fortitude comes in when the pastor or pastoral minister simply has to make a firm decision to put aside certain wonderful programs and projects and concentrate on just one for the year. Say, you choose the explanation and implementation of the new *Catechism of the Catholic Church*. Fine. You get the literature, the bulletin inserts, the homily outlines, the videos, audios, and the committee and make that the theme of the year as we explained above. Then you lead the people patiently and gently through the year (preferably, of course, the *following* year since it will take a year to study, pray, and work out a program that fits your parish) and *forget everything else.*

The diocese may put on pressure: Where are the names of delegates? Where is the report on this or that program that they sent?

With fortitude (again) you have to write to the people in the chancery and urge them to do some planning themselves, to have a greater sensitivity to the realities of the parish and people's lives and the limit in absorbing so many new ideas. It takes time for new thoughts and concepts to be absorbed and lived, and the distractions of 25 new programs or projects subvert that precious element. The diocese itself, of course, should resist the paper coming in from Rome and sit down and ask itself what it wants to accomplish in a given year. It would be wonderful beyond words if it offered us a five-year plan, and thus a sense of direction and vision, instead of the ever urgent latest program that must be done now.

Planning is a skill. It takes vision and effort—and fortitude.

Resource

See the fine article by Bishop Thomas Murphy on "Signs of Hope: Focal Points for Pastoral Planners" (*Origins*, March 19, 1992) and the work of Crozier Father John Sheets. See also *Whither the U.S. Church* by John A. Grindel, C.M. (Maryknoll, NY: Orbis Books, 1991). Get it for its overview and the challenging themes it offers for planning. But be warned: It's very heavy and demanding reading and short on parish appreciation.

Summary of Chapter 9

1. Multiple activities don't necessarily mean chaos.
    2. Some parish controls:
        a. the climate produced by education
        b. the overall charism of the parish
        c. the climate of freedom, trust, and place.
    3. Use a large planning calendar well before summer begins.

4. Notices should be sent to all interested parties to write on the calendar.

5. A committee might list all the jobs to be filled.

6. Send out letters of invitation.

7. Letters should always be specific as to task, help needed, and duration.

8. Provide a process for later adjustments and corrections.

9. Having an overall parish theme also helps keep order.

10. The theme is the result of brainstorming with various parishioners, the staff, and the parish council.

Once there was a rabbi who went on a journey with his servant named Jacob. Their cart was drawn by a very lively horse of whom the rabbi was very fond. Well, they came to this town and it was getting late. So the rabbi went into an inn and told Jacob to take care of the horse. While Jacob was doing that, a horse trader passed by, saw Jacob, saw the fine horse, and soon made friends with Jacob, and began to ply him with liquor. When Jacob was sufficiently intoxicated, he bought the horse from him for song.

Although Jacob was drunk, he was frightened by what he had done. What in the world would he say to the rabbi when he came back from the inn? Suddenly, an idea flashed in his mind. He placed himself between the empty shafts of the cart and began to chew the hay. When the rabbi came out to the courtyard and saw this, he was dumbfounded. When he finally recovered, he asked, "What is the meaning of this? Where is the horse?"

"The horse?" Jacob said. "The horse? That's me!" And he let out a loud whinny. The rabbi said, "Have you gone out of your mind?" He said, "Please, Rabbi, don't get angry with me. You see, years ago a great misfortune happened to me. When I was a silly and foolish young man, I was tempted and I sinned with a woman. And so, to punish me, God turned me into a horse, *your* horse, and for these 20 years, actually, I have been that horse. Now it seems that the punishment is over and today I am once again a man."

The rabbi didn't know what to make of this. He was still awestruck, but even while he was pondering this, he nevertheless needed a horse to continue his journey. So he went into town an lo and behold, saw his horse there at the horse trader's barn. He was amazed. But there it was, munching away at the hay. Going up to it in alarm, the rabbi whispered into its ear, "For goodness sake, Jacob, so soon again?"

Chapter 10

The Parish Booklet

In religion class the teacher asked a little girl why she thought the priest in the Good Samaritan story passed by on the other side. "Because," she said, "the man lying by the roadside had already been robbed."

Why the Booklet?

Thanks to a couple of brilliant women who are computer whizzes, we have the production of our annual Parish Booklet down to a science. Which is not to say, as we mentioned in the last chapter, that there is not a lot of hard, tedious work: putting up the calendar, recruiting volunteers via letters, pulling a theme together, and tapping all this information into the computer. We've been producing this booklet for over twenty years and a reasonable question is why? Is it necessary? No. Is it helpful? Yes. There are a half dozen reasons why:

1. The production of the Parish Booklet with its need to be in the people's hands by Labor Day forces *us* to act, to plan, to recruit volunteers before the summer arrives.

2. The Parish Booklet contains all our policies, spelled out carefully and fully, so you don't have to fight each and every separate battle. The guidelines for baptisms, marriages, funerals, and so on, are all there in everyone's hands. No one can plead ignorance. Moreover, since the Parish Booklet is sent to every home, there is no excuse not to know the parish activities and dates for important events.

3. The Parish Booklet helps those who want to plan their year and attend certain activities or lectures or spiritual exercises.

4. The Parish Booklet is a way to let everyone know the theme, even those who don't go to church and otherwise wouldn't know what's going on.

5. The Parish Booklet contains not only the theme, but each year it is dedicated to a certain person or group, thus offering the opportunity for public acknowledgment and praise.

6. The Parish Booklet is good public relations both for the parishioners (remember, a good many of their names are there as volunteers) and for the many who write from all over for a copy.

There *is* an expense to the booklet, of course, but it is compensated somewhat by the fact that we now do most of the layout and give a completed copy to the printer, so it's cheaper. Also, we do not have to mail out many notices during the year since everything is already contained in it. In any case, in relationship to other activities, this is a chosen expense that we feel has a good return.

However, the Parish Booklet is but one way. Many parishes prefer to print up a monthly calendar sheet and put it in the bulletin or mail it out.

Some Themes and Dedications

It might be interesting to see a few of the themes and dedications over the years. The first year, for obvious reasons, was called "The Year of Community," and the dedication was to the founding pastor who had died an untimely death at 48. It sounded the note, the thrust that we are a People of God, responsible to and for one another. We're not a club, we're a community. The second year was "The Year of Faith," dedicated to the priests who had served the parish over the years when it was a mission. The note sounded here was that of education, an explanation of Vatican II.

Other themes were:

• "The Year of the Spirit" for the first time we had confirmation

• "The Year of Signs" when we spent the year explaining the sacraments

• "The Year of Renewal" focused on spiritual development and direction

• "The Year of Vision" brought us to a consideration of where we were headed and the need to expand and build our spiritual center

• "The Year of the Family" underscored the programs for helping families

• "The Year of Time Remembered" reviewed for newcomers who we were and the theology of collaboration

• "The Year of Preparing the Way of the Lord" was the year we introduced *Renew*

• "The Year of Marketplace Spirituality" speaks for itself

• "The Year of Koinonia" is the year we began the formation of small faith sharing groups, called Koinonia.

Some of the dedications were to the former pastors, the staff, the volunteers, our senior parishioners, deceased members, our retiring bishop, the sisters who have helped out, the secretary, the sexton, the deacons, our oldest parishioner, and so on.

The Tradition of Seven

The Parish Booklet is divided into seven sections:

Section I is "Education" and lists the courses, lectures, and workshops for adults as well as the schedule and program for the children's religious education.

Section II is "Worshiping," which contains not only our Mass and service schedules but also those of our neighboring parishes. It also includes the year's offerings in spirituality, for example: spiritual direction, retreats, scripture sharing, spiritual reading, morning office, and senior citizen, staff and ministries days of recollection. This section also gives a short directory of houses of prayer and retreat and, finally, a summary of our sacramental policies and practices.

Section III is "Helping," and lists all the help that the parish offers, from AIDS counseling to social concerns, and all that the community offers, from marriage encounters to assistance to Alzheimer families.

Section IV is "Playing," and lists all of our year's social activities from plays, dances, trips, and attic sales to concerts, bowling, bread baking, and quilting classes.

Section V is "Organizing," and lists all of the parish organizations, volunteers and their phone numbers, and members.

Section VI is "Exploring," and lists all of the new things we hope to try out. Many of the things that work become mainstream for next year.

Section VII, finally, is "The Calendar" itself, and lists all events from September to June.

Feel free to send for a copy: St. Mary's Church, P.O. Box H, Colts Neck, N.J. 07722.

The Helping Hand

I want to return to Section III, "Helping," for a moment. In that section of our booklet we have a whole list of resources which either we ourselves offer or the diocesan Catholic Charities or other civic organizations or even nearby parishes offer. Even if you do not produce a booklet, it might be well, now and then, to insert a flyer, or print in your Sunday bulletin, a list of such resources. People are hurting and often they do not know where to turn. Resources recommended by the parish would be helpful. Such areas might be:

- AIDS hotline (many dioceses have this)
- AA and Al-Anon and Alcoholism
- Aging
- Counseling
- Marriage Encounter
- Charismatic prayer groups and Cursillo
- Birthright
- Exceptional children
- Divorced and separated Catholics
- Compassionate Friends (parents who have lost children)
- Adoptive parents
- Crisis pregnancy counseling
- Alzheimer help (Indiana University Medical Center helps hunt for genes that may cause this disease: 800-526-2839)
- Gay and Lesbian Catholics (Catholic hotline: 609-228-7438)
- Bereavement
- Advocate for the handicapped
- Rainbows (children suffering loss through divorce, death)
- Drug hotlines

Again, it should be easy to compile a list of reputable resources. Start with Catholic Charities or your diocesan directory. (See more listings in Parish Papers, page 254.)

A Parish Newsletter

If the parish can support it with both money and personnel, a parish newsletter, to supplement the Parish Booklet, is always welcome. It can range anywhere from a full blown newspaper to a two-page magazine. The emphasis of any such newsletter should not be on heavy theology or parish announcements for the year, but on human interest. People, places, events, fun things, "St. Mary's salutes…[mostly the behind-the-scenes people], photos, etc. make it appealing and read. Our four-page production, put out two or three times a year, is called *The Mustard Seed*, not terribly original, but catchy. If you decide to inaugurate a newsletter, your parish might have a contest for its title and logo.

The parish newsletter may be a simple mimeographed affair, but with so many parishes and individuals having computers, a nicely computerized print is better. Also, there are always some people who can do desktop layouts and printing. A few dedicated (and clever) volunteers with a sense of humor can do wonders. Technology has made printing affordable, so you can send a prepared newsletter with photographs and clip art to the local printer. Copies could be inserted into the Sunday bulletin.

Start small. There are many resources, usually from homily service companies, which give good advice as to layout and ideas. (For example, *Bright Ideas,* from Liturgical Publications, Inc., P.O. Box 432, Milwaukee, WI 53201). A parish newsletter adds considerably to parish spirit. Photographs of new parishioners, events, parties, and the like are indeed worth a thousand words.

Computers

Because they are so ubiquitous, I must close this chapter by saying a word about computers. I do so with a certain sheepishness because, as a parish, we still don't have a computer system—but are in the process of getting one. We have only a thousand families with no school and a small staff. We own an old and venerable Addressograph, which the Smithsonian has its eye on, which pounds out plates. We have a manual census with cards in catalogs and scored cards on which we write the weekly contributions. That has done us well all these years. I do have a personal computer which, like many people my generation, I have not mastered. I use it as a glorified typewriter. On it I am writing this manuscript and on it I create flyers and letters. One woman who is a computer whiz puts out the Mustard Seed referred to above. So we are content to be computerless.

But not really. With so many dioceses now demanding standardized financial reports from the parishes, with so many of the younger generation raised on computers, with more and more networking systems, it's time to move into the twenty-first century. In pursuing options, I can make these recommendations. Primary is this one: The average parish will want a flexible but simple system with software support and personnel support, a system that trains the users and backs them up. Then it will want capacities for census, ledgers, inactive Catholics, reports, schedules, family identification numbers, records (parish, school, CCD) and contributions, mailing labels, personalized communications (not only having people's names on the letter instead of "Dear Parishioner," but also the capacity to send out birthday and anniversary greetings), payroll, and other postings that fit its situation. Any system should also have the capacity to take transfers from other programs and to have secure passwords. There are many programs for parishes available and you'll see them advertised in religious magazines. Whoever supplies your envelopes, for example, likely has a program. The Parish Data System, Inc. is in use in over 6500 parishes (14425 N. 19th Avenue, Phoenix, AZ 85023). Or, if you have a computer expert in the parish he (she) can recommend the proper hardware and software and set up a system for you at half the price. Your best bet is to find out what your neighboring parishes are using and go with someone who can speak computer language, check out what they have and do with computers, and listen for the pros and cons.

A Note on Staff

As for the staff itself, I have my own philosophy and practice. The staff understands its role strictly as *servant* to the community. This may sound banal, but it's really important. What it means is that our staff does not make policies and does not plan and does not decide on programs. Members of the staff, of course, like any other parishioners, may have input on all policies, plans, and programs, but they are not the final word or the direct initiators. If they have a great idea, they too must pass it through the regular process. In our parish that process is this: Planning and programs (done after Easter for the coming parish year) are done by an independent ad hoc committee and passed through the parish council. The significance of this is that people do not have to "walk around" the staff, get the staff's permission, or feel that they have to answer to the staff as they would if the staff were the chief architects of everything. The staff is there for *their* needs, not the other way around. The staff should not be the collective old stereotyped housekeeper that simultaneously runs the parish and protects the pastor. The staff facilitates the parish's needs, and serves those needs. It does not make the needs for people to serve. That attitude and policy, I think, are critical for parish health and freedom.

I might add that if at all possible, I would never let the staff have its offices in the rectory. The priest's (or pastor's, lay, religious, or cleric) private life and work should be just that, private, and people should not be subject to the gauntlet of peering eyes and knowing nods when they come to visit the priest either socially or professionally.

Summary of Chapter 10

1. A parish booklet is optional, but there should be some means of announcing all policies and events.

2. At least there ought to be a notice in the bulletin regarding where people might go for help.

3. A parish newsletter adds interest and bonding to the parish.

4. If not now, later: Go computer.

One night a woman dreamed that she walked into a brand new shop. Much to her surprise, she found God working behind the counter. She asked God, "What do you sell here?"

"Everything your heart desires," God replied.

It was incredible. She was talking face to face with God. God had just told her she could have anything she desired.

"I want peace of mind and love and happiness and wisdom and freedom from fear," she told God. Then almost as an afterthought she added, "Not just for me, but for everyone on Earth."

God smiled. "I think you've got me wrong, my dear. We don't sell fruits here. Only seeds."

Sowing Seeds

Chapter 11

Small Faith Communities

> "Dear God, please help me to be the person my dog thinks I am."

The Spiritual Landscape

Since starting in Africa and South America, the small group phenomenon has come to the United States in full force. Whether these groups are called Small Base Communities or Basic Christian Communities or by another name, the first emphasis is on the "small." We can see this almost as a reaction to the large churches and denominations, both Catholic and Protestant. An article in *Newsweek* (August 9, 1993) entitled "Dead End for the Mainline" examines the precipitous decline in "money, members and meaning" of seven mainline Protestant denominations. The gainers? The small, personal, direct evangelical churches—a new one opens almost every day. Some of the losses stem from the large corporate headquarters these Protestant denominations have that often send down highly liberal agendas, out of touch with the ordinary people.

Catholics have fared no better. Evangelicals are winning over traditional Catholic Latin America. They claim some 50 million members, all former Catholics. One Baptist preacher comments: "I believe a lot of people feel let down and are looking for something else. People don't want impositions from above. They're looking for a chance to participate, and if there is something that

characterizes evangelical churches, it's participation." A Catholic liberation theologian comments: "These people have a far better chance of being esteemed and recognized as individuals in the evangelical churches than they do in the Catholic church which is highly centralized." Or, to use the words of Father Art Baranowski, a strong advocate of small parish groups: "You can't bring one person into a parish of 1000 people and expect community to develop automatically. People need to see each other believing and making connections between their faith and their lives."

Restructuring the Church

These quotes exemplify the kind of atmosphere that encourages small gatherings of people, who pore over scripture, build personal community, and are inspired to carry their faith into the world. We can add other reasons for the growth of small faith communities.

1. People do have a need for community, especially in these alienated and alienating times of broken families and fractured neighborhoods. There is an obvious sociological reason for the proliferation of youth gangs. The quest for belonging is one reason why more than 15 million Americans

127

are in some kind of small group from AA to GA (Gamblers Anonymous).

2. The success of such evangelical groups as we mentioned above. Even the Vatican report on cults faulted large, impersonal parishes. Novelist Madeleine L'Engle writes:

> I have a friend who became an alcoholic as a teenager. She then spent ten years as a young adult participating in Alcoholics Anonymous. She was thirty years old and planned to drive from New York to California alone. I felt greatly concerned about her doing this. It was an awfully long trip to take alone. But she said, "Don't worry. If I'm lonely, I'll just call AA." I thought, "If I'm driving across the country and I call the local church saying, I'm lonely, how would they respond? It's likely that I'm not going to get as much compassion as if I had called AA—which is a terrible indictment of the church. . . .we are not fulfilling our obligation to be communities within communities within communities."

(My guess is that if she called the local church, she'd get the answering machine.)

Msgr. Tom Kleissler, the founder of *Renew*, tells the story of the time he was flying home from Australia and discovered that his seatmate was a fallen-away Catholic, as were his brothers and sisters. When he asked Tom what he was doing in Australia, Tom told him he was establishing *Renew* there. Pressed as to what *Renew* was, and having little time left before landing, Tom simply said *Renew* was a small-group process that involved five things: 1) People got to know Jesus personally, 2) they reflected upon scripture and came to a deeper appreciation of the word of God, 3) they found it easier to pray and to share prayer with others, 4) they felt a sense of belonging and mutual support, and 5) they connected their faith to their daily lives. His flying companion just muttered, "It's too bad we didn't have that a long time ago. I'd still be a Roman Catholic today."

3. Youth have much more affection for small, active groups than the large "corporation" church.

4. There is a real need for a forum for listening. In a fast-paced society, who really listens to us? To our children? There's a need to "process" faith and scripture and life. For some, Sunday Mass is simply not enough.

5. There is a need to connect faith and the world, and that need is more easily fulfilled in a small, supportive group than in a large assembly.

6. Small groups, as we shall see in the next chapter, are natural allies to evangelization.

Besides these reasons favoring small groups, there are also negative criticisms of even good and active parishes. Some criticisms are:

1. Even in the active parishes, people get quite used to the service mentality and may tend to look at the parish as one more consumerism group. They're always coming back from vacation bringing a new idea from another parish. The prayer life tends to get superficial and personal formation suffers.

2. The busy, active, popular parish tends to wear people out, especially the volunteers.

3. The staff comes in as professionals and they take over. People follow their programs and are passive before their demands. Thus the people lose their initiative.

4. The active parish seems to present its new parishioners with such an array of activities that it subtly suggests, "You will belong if you do something."

5. Finally, the large parish, by its very size and organization, subverts the leadership and charisms of the laity, at least in the interesting sense as Tad Guzie proposes it. The church, he says, started out as household churches characterized by: 1) fellowship, 2) familiarity, and 3) smallness (what he calls the micro-church). Later the households grouped into larger and larger assemblies of households and you had: 1) organization, 2) anonymous members, and 3) largeness (what he calls the macro-church).

In such a macro-church the focus is rightly on the large assembly and worship, and therefore we have devised official books such as sacramentaries, lectionaries, and rituals. In this church we have, as we should, large-minded liturgies and a hierarchy that helps us to remember that we do indeed belong to a past and a future and that our stories belong to the larger universal story of salvation. For this large assembly, the priest is indeed the proper celebrant.

The trouble comes when the priest is co-opted into the micro-church, that is, when he replaces the natural, small group "households" and their leaders. You see this when a priest celebrates a home Mass. What does he bring? All the official books written for the large assemblies! You see this when he is required to be present at the parish council, the Rosary-Altar Society, wake services, prayer services, and Masses in the locker room every time the parish team wins.

But these are the territories of the micro-church, the place for natural leaders, and by inadvertently replacing them the priest of the large church has undermined the development of the lay leaders of the small church (and, of course, this has gone on so long that the lay leaders *want* the priest. Otherwise, somehow, it's not "official.")

Ordination is a function of the macro-church, to keep the small micro-churches from becoming too inward and to connect them to something larger, more universal. Baptism is a function of the micro-church to keep the macro-church from becoming too outward, too impersonal, and losing connection with the gospel as it is lived in everyday life. In a word, we have here a paradigm and a justification for small faith communities within the larger *ecclesia*.

Small Groups

Authors Bernard Lee and Michael Cowan remind us in their book *Dangerous Memories* that there are four core experiences of what the church is all about. They apply the Greek words found in scripture to these experiences (a translation and explanation of the Greek follow).

Kerygma, or Word: scripture, preaching, evangelizing
Leitourgia, or Worship: prayer and worship
Diakonia, or Welfare: service and ministry
Koinonia, or Witness: shared fellowship, community

The parish is a place for this, but a parish must have an eye to creating small communities that often can fulfill these descriptions more effectively. Not that everyone has to be part of a small group. In fact, my opinion is that small faith communities are essential and helpful, but are not necessarily required of all, although perhaps of most. Perhaps the reason for this is that Americans are notoriously individualistic and notoriously private. Realistically, most of the parish will not be a part of a small group. And that's all right. But such groups should exist, be encouraged, and have strong mechanisms to tie them into the larger parish.

There is no need, when you think of it, to look very far for groups, since all parishes already have natural webs and weavings of relationships, already existing ministries and gatherings. It only remains to invite them to add some shared scripture and reflection time to their meetings, with some guidance and help, of course.

Getting Started

1. As in any project or new idea, gathering the leadership and resources is the first act. You want converts to the notion. I called a random group of parishioners—some 50 people (35 came)—and tossed the idea out to them using the basic information above.

2. After presenting the notion of small groups, some history, and the experience of others, you seek two things: 1) a temporary small core committee that will really catch fire, go through the process of study, understanding, and experience, and eventually own and oversee the development of small faith-sharing groups, and 2) potential group leaders or facilitators willing to be trained. This should take about a year.

3. The initial ad hoc core group not only studied many sources, but also went through the actual experience of faith sharing.

4. Then they invited other select people to go through a pilot program for Lent. This was followed by an evaluation.

5. From all of this—the temporary core group and the pilot lenten group—a final core group emerged.

6. This core group began surveying what actual faith-sharing groups there already were and then turned their attention to facilitators.

7. Promotion was done by a member of the core group speaking to each parish organization and ministry (including the staff). A member also spoke briefly at all the weekend Masses. For the children there was a poster contest on the theme of small groups. Finally, invitations seeking facilitators were mailed.

Facilitators

1. Facilitators were gathered (see #3 below) and taught what to avoid and what to embrace. For example:

Avoid:

- bringing your personal "bad mood" to the group to be aired
- being controlling, critical, judgmental
- putting people on the spot
- allowing others or self to dominate or take too much time
- garlic breath!
- acting disinterested

- canceling meetings
- being negative or inflexible, or too formal
- not listening.

Embrace:
- a clear meeting focus
- being a good listener
- keeping the sharing moving
- clarifying the expectations
- being tactful with dominant members and non-participating members
- asking clarifying questions
- providing a relaxed and comfortable atmosphere
- being an enabler.

2. Sessions for the facilitators should be repeated twice, so all can make them. Training and input would cover:

- scriptural and historical background
- contemporary realities
- a better understanding of a faith-sharing approach to scripture
- developing personal reflection skills
- group dynamics
- dos and don'ts for facilitators
- practice sessions
- evaluations and feedback.

3. Our initial bulletin flyer went like this:

We need your help. . . .
The Koinonia core group is looking for individuals and couples with
- a capacity to learn
- a practical prayer life
- a desire to experience and help build faith-sharing (Koinonia) in the parish
- time and interest to be trained as facilitators.

A training program will be given to prepare facilitators in personal and skill development in the fall and early winter, approximately three 2-hour sessions in the fall and three 2-hour sessions in the winter. Groups will be formed to meet during Lent.

If you know folks in the parish with the above qualifications, please give us their names, addresses, and phone numbers. We will send them an invitation to our facilitator training program.

(place here for names, addresses, and phone numbers)

4. The name Koinonia was arrived at after much discussion and has become a parish by-word. To get the name into the public consciousness, this blurb appeared in the parish bulletin:

Koinonia
A Greek Word for Fellowship, Communion

The word *koinonia* occurs frequently in the New Testament to express a central feature of the early Christian community: fellowship, sharing, and participation. Then, as now, a truly Christian community must be seen in contrast to an individualistic, self-absorbed society. Koinonia describes the sense of community that unites because of a common participation in the same spirit or life.

When did the early Christians experience koinonia? Whenever they gathered to break bread, to share the Word of God, and to live the gospel in service of others (Acts 2:42–47). Today, we followers of Jesus desire the same experience of Koinonia in our local faith communities. We see a renewed sense of reaching out toward koinonia when the global community—united through the transforming power of the Spirit and the love of Christ—is drawn into union with God and one another.

This year, St. Mary's community of faith continues to foster the development of a spirit of koinonia. We will continue to call forth one another's gifts—personal and material—to serve the needs of others, locally and beyond. We will continue to seek a greater integration of gospel values in everyday life by encouraging and forming small faith-sharing groups. These groups will gather to reflect on the Word of God alive and active in our hearts, homes, neighborhoods, workplaces, and world.

As a people chosen to proclaim and build up the reign of God, let us join in koinonia for all peoples, places, and times.

5. The core group met frequently, voicing their hopes (ownership, trained facilitators, parishioner enthusiasm, galvanizing the community) and their fears (not enough facilitators, people who fall through the cracks, expecting too much, quitting too soon).

6. It was decided to take advantage of

the natural parish groups (Martha/Mary, Lazarus, staff, etc.) to promote faith sharing among them.

Getting Ready

1. Announce in the bulletin that you are taking a year of preparation. Let the people know something is happening and in fact start some educative material in the Sunday bulletin.

   2. Be aware of the many excellent resources available, in written, audio, and video formats.

   3. After the year's training (and always, ongoing meetings and formation both of the core and leaders groups), have the core group speak at all the Masses to introduce the concept of small groups.

   4. On a given weekend, have a sign-up Sunday. Here's a sample of the card handed out to our people at Mass:

St. Mary's Koinonia Faith-Sharing Groups
Sign-Up Card—Lent 1994

Name(s) _____

Address_____

Phone _____ Bus. # _____

Indicate all acceptable time preferences.

	Mon.	Tues.	Wed.	Thurs.	Fri.	Sat.	Sun.
Morning							
Afternoon							
Evening							

My group preference is:

Young Adults _____ Singles _____ Couples_____ Mixed_____

Note: When a conflict arises between time and other preferences, placement will be made according to time.

---

5. Have limits. Start with exact times. For example, we began our Koinonia small groups for Lent and confined them to those six weeks. We wanted to give people a definite time to experiment and a time to legitimize their leaving if they did not want to continue after Lent.

   6. At the end of the six weeks we had a convocation. After Easter, there was a large gathering of all the groups and their leaders and the core group. We wound up with 28 groups of six to twelve people each.

   7. Afterwards, for the core group, there was a thank you dinner that included making plans for the coming year.

8. Have evaluations so that inept group leaders can be released and the unforeseen  difficulties that arise can be dealt with.

9. All new participants now receive orientation.

10. A reminder: The new year's Parish Booklet was entitled "The Year of Koinonia."

Conclusion

There are an estimated 15,000 small Christian communities in the United States, mostly peopled by those seeking a "roundtable" church where power, authority, and leadership are shared and a more personal, "hands-on" Christianity is sought. The movement is growing as evidenced by the 400 delegates who met in Minnesota in August 1993, whose mood was not to diminish participation in the larger parish, but to find a more authentic Christianity, to have a more personal forum in which to tell their stories, which mega-parishes (especially in these days of clergy shortage and merging parishes) do not foster.

In fact, some delegates, with more of a bent toward social justice, look with suspicion on such large parishes precisely because they so easily lose contact with the poor and the marginal: the homeless, the deprived, the ex-convicts, the chronically unemployed. As a result, these pleasant and privileged parishes become in effect isolated and isolating gatherings for people who wish to come, remain anonymous, and return home after worship. That kind of distance is hard to achieve, they maintain, in small communities.

Also, the parish is usually middle class and well off, cocooned from the less fortunate. In a word, the argument goes, the average parish cannot be easily identified as the church of the poor—the very ones Jesus came for. To that extent it betrays the gospel.

Those who defend the large parish readily admit and bemoan the fact that for some Catholics the anonymity and homogeneity of the parish are attractive. Catholics like the physical and emotional distance of the large parish. And they admit that smaller communities would put pressure on people to get to know each other and eventually be concerned and build real community. (Members of small communities also put pressure on the homilist to go deeper, since they have already plumbed the scriptures during the week.)

But those who argue for the parish (myself among them) tend to be realistic. We are not going to change that much in our church. Besides, there is something to be said for the large parish. For one thing, for privatized and individualized Americans, the parish church may be their only contact and their only feel of community. For another, our large parishes more authentically reflect the biblical notions of inclusiveness; they are like the great dragnet that pulls in all kinds, the good and the bad, or like the king who sends out to the highways and byways to bring everyone into his banquet hall. The New Testament impulse seems to be large-minded and broad, and perhaps the parish reflects this. Besides, many an anonymous church-going Catholic winds up doing some pretty specific ministries. Small groups, after all, can become inbred and exclusive. Finally, parishes offer helpful activities that are often beyond the abilities of small groups.

I return to my own opinion stated above: Most Americans will not gravitate toward small communities. Nevertheless, it is my conviction that a healthy parish offers both and encourages the latter: the larger parish and the smaller faith communities with strong connections between the two. But, having said this, I also insist that independent grassroot communities, not connected with or initiated by the parish, have a place. Such free-floating communities are often ecumenical and somewhat outside the mainsteam, but the parish should in no way try to absorb them, but rather give them encouragement and acknowledgment. Challenges and changes in structure will come from them.

Resources

Check the series by Father Art Baranowski, *Called to Be Church* (Cincinnati: St. Anthony Messenger Press), and any books by Father Pat Brennan and articles in the trade magazines. There's also the Serendipity Small Group Resources (P.O. Box 1012, Littleton, CO 80160) and the (Protestant) Small Group National Conferences, P.O. Box 861480, Plano, TX 75086.

Look into *Community of Faith: Crafting Christian Communities Today* by Evelyn and James Whitehead (1992), *Forming a Small Christian Community: A Personal Journey* by Richard Currier and Frances Gram (1991), *Good Things Happen: Experiencing Community in Small Groups* by Dick Westley (1992)—all by Twenty-Third Publications, Mystic, CT 06355. You might also contact: Communitas, P.O. Box 4546, Washington, D.C. 20017, the National Alliance for Parishes Restructuring into Communities, P.O. Box 1152, Troy, MI 48099, and the North American Forum for Small Christian Communities, 430 No. Center St., Joliet, IL 60435.

Summary of Chapter 11

1. Get the literature regarding small faith-sharing communities.

2. Call in and form a core group who will take a year to study and assimilate the material.

3. Start a pilot program, perhaps during Lent.

4. Promote, through the bulletin, explanations to the various parish organizations and ministries, etc.

"The denominational families with which most of us have had a love-hate relationship for years may have already become antiquarian relics. God may have a more challenging future in store for us, calling us out of these structures altogether." —Loren Mead, founder and president of the Alban Institute in *The Once and Future Church: Reinventing the Congregation for a New Mission Frontier* (Washington, D.C.: Alban Institute Publishing, 1991).

Chapter 12

Evangelization

> The woman was late. She tiptoed into the large auditorium where the speaker was holding forth to a gathering of Evangelical Pentecostals. She spotted an empty chair near the back. She went over and whispered to the man next to it, "Is this chair saved?" "No," he answered, "but we're praying for it."

Catholics would never respond as the man in this story. Unlike our evangelical brethren, we don't ask our plumber if he is saved. We're too polite for that. Religion, we have been led to believe, is a private affair, like your love life, and you keep it to yourself. This, of course, is the opposite of evangelization: sharing one's faith and reaching out religiously to others. But, truth to tell, sharing the faith has not been a strong characteristic of American Catholics from our first entrance into this land until the present time. There are potent reasons for this lack of vigor and it might be worth our while to explore them.

Timid Beginnings

It is hard for us now to imagine how very small were the numbers of Catholics in America when it was founded—less than one percent of the population. Or maybe this will grab you: The diocese of John Carroll, the first American bishop, was the entire country! Moreover, the few Catholics who were here were prohibited from worshiping publicly. No Catholic parishes were allowed to be formed, so people met in homes. Convents were burned. Priests were tarred and feathered. It is quite understandable,

therefore, that Catholics did not, could not, witness to or evangelize the hostile Protestant majority. The best they could do was to defend the faith from the constant slurs and attacks.

The vast mid-nineteenth century immigrations alarmed the Protestants, for suddenly Catholics became the largest single denomination in the United States. Therefore, all the energy of the church went into preserving the faith of these immigrants from the pervasive anti-Catholicism of the time and into building a unity from the incredible diversity of Catholic peoples: Poles, Irish, Germans, Italians—you name it. Tremendous and heroic amounts of money, time, and effort went into erecting churches, schools, and social organizations for these "foreigners" who were not welcomed and even ostracized from the mainstream. All this effort was fortified by a strong allegiance to authority and the bonding and renewing role of the popular parish mission. The point of this is to note that, being so busy trying to respond to both immigration needs and Protestant hostility, the American church never got into the posture of evangelizing American society. It was too busy trying to survive.

There were a few exceptions to the lack of large evangelizing efforts. John Slattery, leader of the Josephites in the late 1800s, pioneered the evangelization of African-Americans, but racism and lack of support in the church itself soured him and he left the church. (The Josephites have continued evangelization work to this day.) Katherine Drexel reached out to the American Indians. Perhaps the most influential evangelizer was Isaac Hecker, founder of the Paulists. In the 1850s he proposed to evangelize the whole American culture. In 1908 Frances Kelley founded the Catholic Church Extension Society and *Extension* magazine and the railroad "chapel cars." In 1911 James Walsh and Thomas Price founded Maryknoll for overseas evangelization and Father Judge founded one of the first lay apostolate organizations, from which emerged the Trinitarians.

These beginnings were small, but they were being made, and there was some hope of effectively reaching out to others. But even these meager hopes were dashed by the defeat of Alfred Smith in the presidential campaign

of 1928. This defeat revealed how deep and strong anti-Catholicism still was. To meet this challenge, some new forms of evangelization gradually emerged: 1) The Catholic Evidence Guild, 2) The Catholic Lay Apostle Guild, 3) The Catholic Information Society, 4) Street Preachers, 5) The Catholic Truth Guild, and 6) in 1939, The Home Missioners of America, or Glenmary. But the fact remains that early American Catholic experience demanded survival tactics and no strong and pervasive evangelization thrust was forged.

Modern Times

That was then, and modern times have not seen much of an improvement. We have our own set of problems. Catholics, for example, have gone mainstream and, while anti-Catholicism is still very strong and prevalent, it is no longer overt. Catholics, in fact, have adopted the culture. Their attitudes and church-going rates are indistinguishable from the rest of the population, and their embrace of diversity and multiculturalism has led to indifferentism and relativism. As William Portier expresses it:

> The greatest obstacle to Catholics becoming more evangelical is their general acceptance of American religious pluralism as a kind of ideal natural state in which people are best left alone with their own beliefs. This secular-pluralist approach to church-state separation dates to the beginning of our century and ignores the need for public discussion about the deepest shared basis for this culture. In such a view, imagining effective ways to share faith with inactive Catholics or the

unchurched appears as somehow in poor taste, an impolite invasion of privacy or even un-American. Catholics who are really serious about evangelization as transformation of culture from within must learn to behave more as fired-up evangelicals than as civil republicans or pugnacious immigrants. (*The Catholic World*, July/August 1992, p. 155. I am indebted to his whole article for this survey.)

There are other inhibitions. For one thing, most parishes are just too large to evangelize effectively. People get lost in the numbers. We are reluctant to redress this and make parishes smaller because we do not have enough priests to go around. We don't have the money and the will isn't there. We, too, are caught by "Bigger is better." For another, traditionally the clergy were the ones "to seek out the lost sheep." But clergy numbers are down and no one else has been trained for the task.

Another reason is that often the parish is already under stress, due to lack of finances or personnel, and it has all it can do to maintain the status quo. Who wants to go looking for more work? All pastors publicly lament those tremendous hoards who crowd our churches at Christmas and Easter, but secretly we say to ourselves, "My God! What would I do with all these people if they all came every Sunday? How would I handle them?" Another problem is simply Catholics themselves. Pressured, as we recall, by a long-term inferiority status in "Protestant America," excluded until comparatively recently from the mainstream and now immersed in it, they are reluctant to share the faith.

Nor, to be honest, can we neglect to mention that our evangelizing indifference has been brought on by the fact that we too have bought into the "American consumerist dream" that both erodes and teases our spiritual foundation. As Pope John Paul II wrote in *Redemptoris Missio*:

Our times are both momentous and fascinating. While on the one hand, people seem to be pursuing material prosperity and to be sinking ever deeper and deeper into consumerism and materialism, on the other hand, we are witnessing a desperate search for meaning. . . . Not only in cultures with strong religious elements, but also in secularized societies, the spiritual dimension of life is being sought after as an antidote to dehumanization.

In addition, American culture itself makes evangelization difficult with its built-in prejudices and resistance to religion. Modern times have relegated religion to what David Tracy calls a "sacred reservation," and the need to reduce everything to computer language leaves no room for religion, which deals with mystery and thus defies the computer. Moreover, our culture often enshrines elements that are simply opposed to the life of faith: polygamy, ritual murder, sexual promiscuity, abortion, violence, salvation-products.

In his well received book, *The Culture of Disbelief* (New York: Basic Books, 1993), Yale Law School professor Stephen L. Carter laments the culture's ingrained tendency to trivialize religion, which insists that people with religious beliefs and language can only get a hearing if they convert those beliefs and language into secular terms. A recent study (1993) by the Freedom Forum First Amendment Center at Vanderbilt University has concluded that a "chasm of misunderstanding" exists between news organizations and religious leaders in this country, resulting in coverage that is often inadequate. This study found that the news media simply refuse to take religion as a matter deserving of serious coverage and that there is basically "a lack of well-informed reporters and an intellectual laziness about getting the facts straight." For instance: When Billy Graham returned to the U.S. after preaching in Eastern Europe, a reporter asked him why he had gone. "To preach the gospel," Graham replied. After a pause, the reporter said, "Right, but why did you *really* go to the Soviet Union?" A faith motivation was simply beyond his ability to grasp.

Television, the Freedom Forum study concludes, fares no better. It covered religion only when the stories involved pageantry or scandal. Other researchers have found that television virtually blanks out religious realities on prime-time programs. After examining 100 fictional programs on ABC, CBS, NBC, and Fox TV networks, a team of scholars in communications from three universities concluded, "Overall, the message being presented about religion by network television is that it is not very important, because it is rarely a factor in the lives of the characters presented on TV or in the society in which they are portrayed." This is in contrast to the findings that 94% of Americans believe in God and 75% pray daily and consider religion very important in their lives. "Religion," it concluded, "is a rather invisible

institution on fictional network television." Even that fine journalist Bill Moyers, on his acclaimed series *Healing and the Mind,* never talked to anyone engaged in Christian healing. Buddha was mentioned and ancient Chinese medical practices but no single chaplain, minister, priest, or rabbi was interviewed in the series. Jesus was not mentioned once.

Hollywood does no better. In the *New Republic* (April 20, 1992) Morton Kondrake criticizes the movie *Grand Canyon* and its director for making a movie on faith and then merely "tiptoeing up to the subject." He wrote:

> [Religion] oughtn't be that difficult for [the director] or for others in Hollywood to portray. People in the audiences believe. Polls consistently show that between 70 percent and 90 percent of all Americans consider themselves religious. No other topic, no matter how personal, embarrassing, or perverse (witness *Silence of the Lambs),* is out of bounds for Hollywood, but religious faith somehow is taboo.

Well, the obvious point of all this is that the culture itself makes evangelization difficult, or at least suspect.

The Wound of the Inactive

So that's where we have been and are. These are the problems and the inertias. But we must move on. The country is in need of recapturing its soul, and our fellow Catholics who have left us or simply drifted away must be touched by our concern and invitation to come back home. Their absence wounds us.

Why should we be worried about their

absence? Because we're losing numbers? Because the collection is down? Because it makes our parish look bad? No, we worry because large numbers of inactive Catholics strike at the foundation of the church itself. Remember, we have an incarnational church, a Communion of Saints. We in the Mystical Body have always believed that Christianity is communal. The solitary Christian worshiping at the seashore (or at the golf links) is a contradiction. Revelation takes place in community. The Risen One is where two or three are gathered in his name. From the Trinity on, community is the essence of God's definition and outreach. God gathers a people to himself. Abraham and Moses were but prophets; Israel was God's goal. Jesus selected apostles and disciples to multiply themselves throughout the world. He broke bread in company. The gathering, the base community, the domestic church—all are phrases that bespeak what church is all about. In a word, large numbers of separated, inactive "communal" Catholics betray what it means to be an assembly, a church. These "believers without belonging" (to use George Gallup's phrase) undermine community and betray the meaning of church.

Who Are the Inactive?

As we all know—and some of us know from experiences in our own family—Catholics, like mainline Protestants, have dropped out. They form the biggest sub-population in every parish. They resurrect, perhaps, at baptism time or religious education time, only to disappear once more. Who are these inactive Catholics? They are people who fall into three categories: 1) the alienated, 2) immigrants, and 3) youth.

We won't deal with the last two categories. Suffice it to say that by the year 2050, the Census Bureau estimates, non-Hispanic whites, now 75% of the population, will be 53% and the Hispanics will increase from their current 9% to 21% of the U.S. population. Unless we reach out to them, they will be increasingly inactive and increasingly the target of Protestant evangelists. It is alarming to note, for example, that while Hispanic youth are thought to be predominantly Catholic, proselytizing efforts by Protestants have had an effect. According to Gallup, only 53% of teenagers of Hispanic origin now say they are Catholics by preference.

Catholic teenagers of all origins, according to sociologist Patrick McNamara, distrust authority and trust their own consciences to the extent that only 11% felt bound to form their consciences solely according to church teaching. Nearly 80% were of the opinion that they should listen to what the church has to say and then make their own decisions. Sexuality in the teen world is "strictly personal" and not even within the range of church authority. But, as I said, let us look to what we commonly consider the alienated or inactive Catholic. A fun list of the inactive, of those who don't go to church, includes those with these excuses (from the *Southern Nebraska Register*, March 8, 1992):

1. I stay away from church because it rains. *You go to work in the rain.*
2. I stay away from church because it is hot. *So is the golf course.*
3. I stay away from church because it is cold. *It's warm and friendly inside.*
4. I stay away from church because I am poor. *There is no admission charge.*

5. I stay away from church because I am rich. *We'll take care of that.*

6. I stay away from church because no one invited me. *People go to the movies without being asked.*

7. I stay away from church because I have children. *God loves them.*

8. I stay away from church because there are hypocrites. *You associate with them daily.*

9. I stay away from church because my clothes are not expensive. *It's not a fashion show.*

10. I stay away from church because the church always wants money. *So does your grocer.*

11. I stay away from church because I have company. *They will admire your loyalty, whether you bring them along or ask them to wait until you get back.*

12. I stay away from church because I have plenty of time to go later. *Are you sure?*

For a more serious list of the inactive, let's build on and expand the categories given by Father Pat Brennan from Chicago. (Read his book, *The Evangelizing Parish*, Tabor Publishing):

•*The Anti-Institutionalists:* those who don't like institutions: the military, corporations, government. This includes the church with its "self-serving and self-maintaining hierarchy."

•*The Locked Out:* the gays, the divorced, the marginal, the handicapped, the singles. They believe that the church doesn't want them and has made that known explicitly or implicitly by its pronouncements, policies (dances are $10 per couple, not $5 per person), and omissions. For instance, a gay man, Andrew Sullivan, writing in *America* says:

Natural law! Here is something [homosexuality] that seems to occur spontaneously in nature, in all societies and civilizations. Why not a teaching about the nature of homosexuality and what its good is. How can we be good?

Teach us. How does one inform the moral lives of homosexuals? The church has an obligation to *all* its faithful to teach us how to live and how to be good—which is not merely a dismissal, silence, embarrassment of a "unique" doctrine on one's inherent disorder. Explain it. How does God make this? Why does it occur? What should we do? How can the doctrine of Christian love be applied to homosexual people as well?

•*The Nomads:* the always moving, the "always changing addresses" group. There's no time to form community. They're like the gospel parable seed that fell on rocky ground: no roots.

•*The Lifestyler:* Their lifestyles are simply incompatible with Catholic or Christian living: murderers, drug dealers, chronic abusers, child pornographers, etc.

•*The Incredulous:* can't accept the authority of the church or its teaching, for example, on sexuality. The encyclical *Humane*

Vitae was a final straw for many.

• *The Angry:* These include some women, some ethnic groups who feel unwelcome. One woman in the church, a professor of pastoral theology (Rosemary Chinnici, *The Catholic World,* Nov./Dec. 1991), writes:

> During moments of reflection it is not uncommon for women to come to the realization that the church is not a place of liberation but rather a place of oppression. Examples of this abound. A woman works on a parish team, is a member of the local parish council, or is a eucharistic minister, and almost overnight she discovers that she is no longer allowed to participate in these activities because the priest who supported her has been moved to a different assignment and the new pastor does not believe in collaborative ministry. . . . Women choose different methods for dealing with these experiences. Some leave the church, others continue to participate; some speak out against the injustice they see and are labeled "angry feminists"; some live with the tension by attending church liturgies and women's liturgies; some attempt to be content with the slow progress that they see; some throw themselves into church activities and try to ignore their feelings.

• *The Drop-Outs:* The lifestyles of these people are far from the church's teaching; or these are simply the burned-out crowd, or those who feel they are not being spiritually nourished.

• *The Scandalized:* Instances of priest pedophilia, for instance, have made many feel betrayed; or the exposure of the sexual exploits of Bishop Casey of Ireland or Archbishop Sanchez of Santa Fe has rocked their faith and confidence. Here's a church whose leaders preach one thing and do another.

• *The Wounded:* those hurt by some church person or event, real or perceived. Not all Catholics, contrary to media noise, grew up hating the church. Many have fond memories. The popularity of books like *Growing Up Catholic* and the long-running play *Nunsense* testifies to the good-humored appreciation of what was gained. Still, there are the horror stories. One man, now returned to church, remembers that he dropped out at 17 because at 15 a priest preached distressfully against altar boys and refused to give them (himself among them) communion. At 16, he recalls, a priest punished some schoolboy infringement by requiring some boys (again, himself included) to lie spread-eagle in the school entrance hall where he then walked across their fingers! (Paul Vallely, *The Tablet,* March 13, 1993).

• *The Simply Unawakened and Drifters.* These people never had any kind of feeling or conversion experience. They're ethnic or cultural Catholics. They are lazy, not only physically, but intellectually. They don't challenge God's existence or enter into any open or searching dialogue with the church.

• *The Cyclers:* These are the anticipated, sociological 18-23 routine drop-outs. This group tends to drop out, disengage at this stage of their lives, but often returns later.

• *The Populist Ecumenists:* They can easily change religions because of a new neighborhood, a new spouse, etc. It's all one big happy family and they understand ecumenism to mean "It doesn't matter what you believe as long as you're sincere."

• *The Nuptially Swayed*: those influenced by spouse. There is a strong correlation between one's spouse and the influence that a spouse has on religious practices and church loyalty.

• *The Prophetically Alienated*: those who left to take a stand against what they perceive is a church policy not in keeping with the gospel. Often they are right and the church is wrong. This is a church that pays less than just wages to its employees or is racist or sexist. These people will not be back until the church lives its own gospel.

• *The Disbelievers*. In a highly secularized world with its very deep sense of historical consciousness or relativism, some people simply do not believe. The young are leaving the church, disappointed in seeing so little palpable evidence of holiness. The sins they know about. Where is the measurable holiness in the church? Some simply don't believe the church is authentic or true.

• *The Spiritually Starved*. These are the people who find no spiritual nourishment in Catholicism, at least as they find it at the parish level. They are looking for a deeper union with God, with answers or at least directions for their lives and struggles, and they come up empty. So they search elsewhere.

Responses

In spite of all this, evangelization is once more in the news. It is a newly focused priority, and rightly so. Significant numbers do in fact return to the church; others would if asked. Pope Paul VI, in 1968, provided the first

official impetus to this asking in his masterful encyclical *Evangelii Nuntiandi,* laying out the principle of evangelization. Our own National Council of Catholic Bishops has issued another fine, practical document, *Go and Make Disciples: Shaping a Catholic Evangelizing People* (U.S.C.C.) with its three goals:

1. To bring about in all Catholics such an enthusiasm for their faith that in living their faith in Jesus, they freely share it with others.

2. To invite all people in the United States, whatever their social or cultural background, to hear the message of salvation in Jesus Christ so they may come to join us in the fullness of the Catholic faith.

3. To foster gospel values in American culture, promoting the dignity of the human person and the common good of our society, so that our nation may continue to be transformed by the saving power of Jesus Christ.

Most notably the Paulist National Catholic Evangelization Association (hereafter referred to by its initials of PNCEA) has devised resources for evangelization. There are now many processes for evangelization such as *Landings,* developed by Paulist Jack Campbell, *Re-Membering Church* from the North American Forum on the Catechumenate, the Stephen Ministries, etc.

Our Plan

As a parish launching into formal evangelization, we have made both a remote and proximate preparation.

I. Remote Preparation

1. The remote preparation for evangelization is captured in the whole point of this manual: We want people to "come back home," but

home should be worth coming back to. It's as simple as that, and no process or program will be worth its salt if there is no good news awaiting. This manual has tried to offer suggestions for making the parish alive, and for moving from maintenance to mission.

2. We have put into place Greeters, male and female, who not only act as ushers, but who are trained to be genuinely warm welcomers to the people who come to worship.

3. We have already started our small Christian base communities, called Koinonia groups (see the previous chapter). These groups are invaluable because a) they provide a forum for people to be formed in the Word of God and to be filled with a desire to share that word with others. In short, evangelizers are born here. b) Such groups are often more attractive to returnees and sometimes provide a bridge to the larger community.

4. We have Bible study and prayer groups that provide a place to unfold scripture and offer that necessary prayer without which evangelization is fruitless.

5. The catechumenate (RCIA) is in place already, offering its public steps and meaningful liturgies.

II. The Proximate Preparation

1. Our first step was the formation of a core group to meet, study the documents (Pope Paul VI's *Evangelii Nuntiandi*, Pope John Paul II's *Redemptoris Missio*, and the bishops' pastoral, *Go Make Disciples*) and other resources, and attend diocesan meetings to tie in with the diocesan office.

2. Meanwhile, each parish organization and ministry, the staff, and the parish council were "indoctrinated" by teaching (such as in

this chapter), using the ten-minute Paulist video "Go, Make Disciples" and literature (mostly from PNCEA).

3. We also purchased a series of five videos on the theme of evangelization from the charismatic meetings in Steubenville, Ohio, and have offered them to the parish at large, especially for those more attuned to this style of evangelization and spirituality.

4. We have, as indicated elsewhere, introduced a series of lay homilists to help forge the connection with "ordinary" life and the life of faith.

5. We preached on the theme of evangelization and included its intentions in our Prayers of the Faithful.

6. There is a superb manual called *The Catholic Way of Life*, written by David Byers, Neil Parent, and B. Allison Smith and put out by the PNCEA. It is a fine, relatively brief work of 100 pages. It can be used as a resource or a study book for possible returnees. But it has additional use. What the PNCEA has done is to break down its 22 chapters into two-page flyers (four sides) so they can be given out individually. That was an option. But we asked, why have them available only for possible candidates who want to return? Why not use them to *educate everyone*, bring everyone up to date, so to speak? Make evangelization an opportunity to educate the whole parish?

We pondered how to do this. We finally decided not to put them in the Sunday bulletin as an insert since, we reasoned, only those who came to church would get them. We decided, rather, to mail them, twice a month, to each one of our thousand families: the good, the bad, the indifferent. That, of course, would be a large task and it would be costly, some $6000. So we made this a project of our two major parish organizations and they agreed to underwrite more than half of the cost. It was a matter of priority and we felt that the cost and effort were worth the investment. Again, if nothing else, the whole parish had a chance at some good adult education.

7. We provided a Parish Mission given by Paulist John Collins the week before "Invitation Sunday." The mission included a Book Fair.

8. Invitation Sunday is a process whereby we garner names and addresses of people who are inactive Catholics by leaving envelopes and papers in the pews and asking the congregation to write up to six names of inactive people anywhere in the world that they know. They are asked also to give some donation toward mailing expenses. We then collect the envelopes with their contents of names and hand them over to the Paulist Center (whose plan this is), which in turn sends five very well written, attractive flyers to these people, basically saying, "Come home again." The congregation, of course, had been well prepared for this day.

9. In addition to all this, we invited people to return to church via newspaper notices, posters, and local radio ads.

10. We also put up a highway sign advertising our parish mission and urging: "Come Home Again."

11. We offered a special "Listening Session" for anyone who wanted to come and air his (her) views, disagreements, or hurts. It was billed as a time of listening and healing.

12. Since the parish has a certain discretion of choosing the yearly calendar (usually underwritten by the local funeral director) which we distribute to the people (see Chapter 13), we chose the one whose theme was evangelization.

13. Thanks to the formative experiences of the small faith-sharing groups (Koinonia), people were also willing to visit homes and invite people to church.

14. We thought about how people could return to church if they wanted to. Do they just slip back and come to church, lost in the crowd? Do they have the option of some public ritual of return? Do they have to see the priest or deacon? Our answer was yes to all these questions. We let it be known that people had options. They could just go to confession somewhere and return quietly. They could engage in some public ritual. They could talk with the priest or deacon, or they could talk to people whose names and phone numbers we had made public. Finally, they could call a "hotline." We offered them the equivalent of an 800 number: a number to call and talk to a trained person who would offer advice and resources.

15. At Christmas and Easter, we left little printed invitations in the pews at all the Masses inviting people to come back again to church.

16. Since it is a sad fact that a good many parents send their children to religion class but do not regularly attend church, we mailed each family a letter: short, sensitive, and inviting. Here is a copy:

Dear Parent,

As a member of St. Mary's, you and your family are important to this community. When you became members of this parish family and signed the Parish Covenant, you indicated that you agreed with this realization and that you would actually be part of this community by worshiping with us. Since then you may have made worship part of your family life. Perhaps you had to prioritize your activities or rethink your views on or reasons for worshiping with a church community. Although this may have been difficult at times, you have shown your children that God and a community of believers are important and are a value for your life.

If you have not made church worship part of your family life, we urge you to "come back." Your reasons for not worshiping with your family may be one of many: your own experience as a child, a past negative encounter with church people, an overburdened schedule, even laziness or plain habit. Yet we think that your child is so important to you that you realize, today more than ever, the need for values in your child's life. With all of society's influences touching and affecting your child's mind, we urge you to *give God an equal chance* by making worship in church a regular part of your family life.

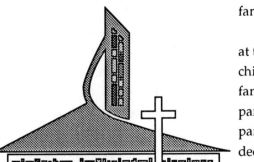

Is church-going difficult or boring at times? Of course it is! Will your children always like it? Of course not! But families that have made weekly worship part of their lives have said that once a parent (or preferably both parents) decided that weekly worship would be part of their family life, children accepted it. "I know you may not always like it, but this is what we are doing because we think it is important" is a direct and simple response that has worked for parents. You may even try negotiating: "When would you prefer going to church: on Saturday evenings at 5 or on Sunday morning?" As with many things in life, once parents decide that something will be part of their family life because they see it as a value, children will accept it.

Church is a place to hear other values, see other people, be part of a larger reality. It is a place to encounter people in need of God's mercy trying to make God part of their lives. Here, in common worship, people are renewed. Here we remember that God, who gives each of us life, loves us and strengthens us in our life journey.

If you have made St. Mary's your parish family and have gathered here to worship with your own family, you are giving your child an advantage that can have long-term effects. If you have not worshiped with your family on a regular basis, please give your children this advantage.

Sincerely yours in the Lord,

17. Finally, we felt it was essential to give regular progress reports to the parish via the Sunday bulletin and occasional mailings.

Summary of Chapter 12

1. We noted the cultural climate of disbelief and the alienation of many, including our youth.

2. We responded by forming a core committee to study the documents.

3. We presented the notion of evangelization to the people through the annual State of the Parish Address, making it our Parish Booklet theme for the year, giving presentations to all organizations and ministries, and enlisting the prayers and actions of the already formed small faith communities.

4. We offered evangelization videos, the witnessing of lay homilists, and a Parish Mission on the theme, plus the usual radio, newspaper, and poster spots.

5. We worked with the Paulist Evangelization project in having an Invitation Sunday that gathered the names of inactive Catholics.

6. We also got our organizations to underwrite the cost of sending the 22 chapters of the *Catholic Way of Life* manual to all of our parishioners.

Resources

The best and most sophisticated resource is the Paulist National Catholic Evangelization Association, 3031 Fourth Street, N.E., Washington, D.C. 20017. Other resources can be gleaned from the religious press flyers, but I would mention two worthwhile books, *Welcoming the Stranger: A Public Theology of Worship and Evangelization* by Patrick R. Keifert (Fortress Press) and the outreach program *We Miss You* (Sheed & Ward).

See also my recent *While You Were Gone: A Handbook for Returning Catholics—and those thinking about it* (Mystic, Conn.: Twenty-Third Publications, 1994).

If we do not evangelize, we offer the world by default to those who paganize.

If we do not evangelize, we offer the world by default to those who advertise.

If we do not evangelize, we offer the world by default to those who dehumanize.

If we do not evangelize, we offer the world by default to those who idolize.

If we do not evangelize, we offer the world by default to those who militarize.

If we do not evangelize, we offer the world by default to those who terrorize.

Rhythms
&
Reflections

Chapter 13

Parish Potpourri

> There I was, sitting at a table for two in an elegant restaurant. I looked across the table and I suddenly realized that I was having lunch with God. Fantastic! Then God sneezed—and I didn't know what to say.
>
> —Comedian Allen Rossi

Here are some ideas for miscellaneous programs and some thoughts on how to accomplish them. We've done them all. Some continue to flourish; others did flourish and, after a time, dwindled. In that case, we discontinued them, perhaps to be resurrected at another time. We have no trouble with this. Often parishes keep projects and organizations on the books long after they have died. Parishes are littered with dead organizational or three-member, chronically-ill ministries because "That's the way it's always been," or "The founding pastor started it in 1912 and it was a huge success for a long time." Now it's a huge corpse and everyone's afraid to bury it. That's why parishes need evaluations. In any case, here are some programs and their descriptions.

1. A.M. Table Talk. We started out with both an evening and morning Table Talk, but the evening session did not go over well, so we discontinued it and kept the morning. This was very popular for several years and then, for some reason, declined. We have discontinued it but likely will restore it in the future.

The A.M. Table Talks are simply a continental breakfast served in the parish hall at 10:00 A.M. with a speaker present. Since you're getting mostly women and retirees, the topics are heavily focused on family life, raising children, family spirituality, current topics, Catholic teaching, etc. Local community colleges, parishes, or other institutions are a good supply for speakers. Volunteers arrange for the speakers, host the breakfast, and clean up. They were well received and well attended, and they are simple to do and arrange. We charged $3.

2. Cassette Tape Ministry. If you have speakers in to give courses or lectures, have them taped, with their permission. In our parish we also tape all homilies: Sunday, funeral, and wedding. The latter two are given to the interested parties, the former is brought to shut-ins. All taped talks and lectures are available for study groups, nursing homes, and just friends or interested people. Every parish has a taping buff. The parish supplies the tapes and it would help to invest in a tape-copying machine. An appreciated ministry.

3. Cracker Barrel. This is a kind of "town hall" meeting with the pastor. It's informal. We have peanuts (you *must* throw the shells on the floor) and other snacks and drinks. It's a chance for the public to ask about policy— parish, church—or whatever is on their mind. An ecclesiastical talk show without the phones.

4. *Telecare.* Telecare is a group of trained parishioners who contact each family by phone once during the year (although not every year). Their main concerns are: a) to offer a hello, a greeting, an encouragement to a fellow parishioner on behalf of the parish, and b) to see if the parish is meeting their needs and ask their opinions.

Personal problems and strong anxieties are off limits and such people are referred to a compatible resource or ministry. It's not a gripe session, just a hospitality call for people who might fall through the cracks.

We had a three-night training program that included listening skills, referrals, and role-playing. These were given by some contact people, a professional calling group, or anyone who is certified to do so. Calls were made mostly from the homes, although they could be made from the parish office. Callers give a commitment to do this just one time. The parish census is broken down so each caller has about 20 people to call. This is a great ministry for the sick and shut-ins. And it was well received by the people. Obviously this is not something you want to do each year.

5. *Home and Hearth Week.* This is in response to people's busy lives—and the parish's. We have one week where we have no organized activities. We urge people to stay home and offer a delightful array of home activities that they might enjoy. It's an attempt to legitimize a sabbath time by having the whole parish slow down. (See the invitation on page 264 of Parish Papers.)

6. *Monthly Birthdays.* On the third Tuesday of each month, at and after the regular 9:00 A.M. Mass, we celebrate the birthdays that fall in that month. A volunteer cuts out different stencils with the birthday names on them and pastes them to the wall behind the altar. We give each birthday attendee a corsage and at the end of Mass sing "Happy Birthday." Then we go into the parish hall for the birthday cake and coffee. Obviously, only those free in the morning can come, but that's a pretty good number and it adds to the parish spirit.

7. *One-on-One.* This began accidentally when I consoled a woman who was about to undergo a mastectomy. After it was over and she was back on her feet, she told me one day that if any other woman was to have the same experience, she would be happy to talk with her. It hit me that this would be true of many life experiences. So I talked to people and asked if they would be available to share their experiences and encourage others, if needed and called upon. The result is the one-on-one ministry. A reprint from our annual Parish Booklet explains it all:

"Bear one another's burdens," St. Paul has written. And there is no one who can bear another's burdens as well as someone who has been there himself or herself. The people whose names are listed here are "wounded healers," ready to listen and help. All have personal experiences in the categories mentioned.

Adoption	Steve and Elaine Carroll	946-0419
Adoption International	Joanna and Peter Tonacci	946-7146
Adult returning to school	Ginny Phelan	946-9420
Alcoholism	Marge Cron	741-0431
	Joan Henderson	431-2784
Alcoholism, young adults	Paul Hartman	938-2006
Abortion, post		229-0403
Amputee	Marilyn Montski	842-7987
Aging parents	Alta Barnett	946-4276
Anxiety, obsessive-compulsive	Cecelia Eldred	431-9278
Arthritis	Joan Weaver	566-3175
Cardiac visitation	Bill Bender	741 5837
Chronic illness	Irene Nichols	431-0686
Children on drugs	Mary Ellen & Jim FitzGerald	577-1986
Corneal transplant	Mary Beth Koch	747-9562
Crisis pregnancy	Cal & Irene Weller	842-8628
Diabetes	Betty Guenther	431-5059
Divorced and remarried	Roger & Barbara Kane	462-9391
Family of cancer patient	Marilyn Romano	741-8896
Gamblers Anonymous	Terry Zehl	577-9732
Handicapped	Anne Henderson	431-2784
Heart attack	Hallie Gardner	946-9517
Hypoglycemia	Gloria Ziemienski	462-9396
Loss of job	Ed Toutounchi	946-3187
Loss of a loved one	Tish Boro	671-5287
	Pat Whelan	758-9074
	Eileen Connair	741-6433
Lyme Disease	Gloria & Al Stravelli	780-7867
Mastectomy	Eileen Flint	462-3830
Teaching, helping handicapped	Barbara Drober	842-3751
Terminal illness	Barbara Luchinger	741-7837
Widowhood	Rosemary McCann	747-5240

8. Nullities. Every parish has its quota of failed marriages and sometimes those in need of annulment. For over fifteen years we have had a couple who, in gratitude for their own nullities, have undertaken as their ministry helping others in this. If a call comes in inquiring about a nullity, we simply refer it to this couple. They do everything. They explain the process, assist with the questionnaires, type them out, gather the necessary papers and certificates, and send the final product into the chancery. Of course, having been through it themselves, they have instant rapport with the one seeking the annulment, and, after all these years, considerable knowledge and savvy. My suggestion is to send several couples for training. Most chanceries, in deference to the priest shortage, now will conduct sessions for such people. Contact the chancery.

9. The Blessing of the Calendars. Every parish gets, courtesy of the local funeral director or other business, New Year's calendars. Rather than just have the ushers hand them out, how about a little ritual? The calendars are placed before the altar and after, or in connection with, the homily are blessed with this lovely prayer:

> Lord, you who live outside of time
> and reside in the imperishable moment,
> we ask your blessing
> upon your gift of time to us.
> Bless our calendars,
> these ordered lists of days, weeks, and
> months,
> of holidays, holy days, fasts, and feasts.
>
> May they remind us of birthdays and
> other gift-days,
> as they teach us the secret that all life
> is meant for celebration and
> contemplation.
>
> Bless, Lord, this new year, each of its 365
> days and nights.
> Bless us with happy seasons and a long
> life.
> Grant to us, Lord, the New Year's gift of
> a year of love. Amen.

At the end of Mass the calendars are carried by the ushers to the back and given out at the doors.

10. The Tree of Love. The flyer says it all. (See an example of it on page 259 of Parish Papers.)

11. Thanksgiving. A very simple suggestion. On Thanksgiving Day the morning Mass is wonderously crowded with parishioners who are not under legal obligation to be there, but want to be. Part of the homily consists of my sharing what I am thankful for. Then I ask the people to call out what they are thankful for. One of the joys of being in a place so long is that you know all (or most of) their names, and so it is sheer spiritual delight to be able to call someone by name who has raised his or her hand to tell what they are thankful for. The statements are invariably touching, deep, and meaningful.

12. Hunger Sensitivity. An activity for adults or a youth group or religion classes designed by Oxfam, the food relief agency (Oxfam-American, 15 Broadway, Boston, MA 02116, phone: 617–482–1211). A luncheon is prepared for those attending, who are divided into three groups, representing first, second, and third world countries. Of this group 60% are served one cup of plain rice with water; 25% are fed a simple meal of rice, beans, and water; the remaining 15% are fed with a full course meal—*and* they eat it in the same room as the others, and at decorated tables. The first two groups eat on the floor. That's one way to remind us all that each day 60,000 people die of hunger, 40,000 of whom are children under 5.

13. The Elderly. We should become conscious that the elderly are the largest group in America. We should also be conscious that suicide among white males over 65 is four times the national average. The root cause is that such people feel they have no reason to live. Our elderly must be made welcome in the parish and absolutely must be visited and sent cards when in the hospital. There are a million tasks they can do around the parish and all ministries must be open to them. Courses, days of recollection, and planned organizations are needed. Involve them. We call our senior group the "Holy Spirits" as a nod to their age and accumulated wisdom. They brown-bag it once a month at the parish for a combination of spiritual and social events. Resource: a fine six-session small-group discussion process with older adults called *A Time for . . .* by Daniel Mulhall and Karen Rowe (Los Angeles: Franciscan Communications).

14. *The Unemployed.* Like many other places, our area and our parish has been hit by unemployment. This is a most difficult time, especially for men who have so much identity invested in their jobs. All these people need a combination of spiritual and practical help. We have a professional person and dedicated parishioner who volunteers her time in holding seminars and support groups for the unemployed. If you have no such professional person, you might want to cooperate with other parishes either in tapping the resources of each parish or perhaps hiring someone collectively from a local college or business.

15. *Keep in Touch.* When the kids go to college, put a notice in the bulletin asking their parents for their complete college addresses. Then when you have them all, have some volunteers put the information on a label and send them communications two or three times a year. Use a large brown envelope. What goes in it? The Sunday bulletins (they know a lot of people), some reprints or flyers, such as a meaningful "Updates," clippings from the local paper, a personal note from the pastor, whatever. The point is contact, that they are known and remembered. Even if they toss it, it still speaks of the home faith community. The freshmen, of course, are very happy to get these things. Maybe the Rosary-Altar Society could fund the postage.

16. *Care Cards at the Door.* Tucked in your book rack you might have "care cards." Thus:

St. Mary's Parish Care Card
Colts Neck, N.J.

If you know a parishioner who is ill or a shut-in or who needs some help, please fill out this card and drop it into the mail slot [we have a mail slot in our sacristy door facing the vestibule for book-rack money] or mail it in.

Request for _____
(Name and Address)

Phone _____

[ ] sick [ ] elderly [ ] at home [ ] in the hospital (which one?)

[ ] would like communion [ ] needs sacrament of the sick

[ ] needs assistance in getting to church [ ] would like visit from a priest

[ ] include in the Prayers of the Faithful [ ] other (use reverse side)

17. *New Drivers Blessing.* On occasion put a notice in the bulletin that all new drivers (mostly the kids) and their parents are invited to a Mass to receive a blessing. At an appropriate time, parents (who have the car keys) stand on one of the sanctuary and the youth on the other.

Celebrant:

My dear friends, today we are blessing new drivers and so we pray: "Almighty God, giver of all good gifts, look upon the joy and expectation of the new drivers gathered here today. Give them sharpness of eye, keenness of hearing, and alertness of mind. Above all, give them sense and sensitivity, for in a new way precious human life is being entrusted to their care and responsibility. In their work and play may their driving be both a source of joy and service to us all. May they continually earn the trust of their parents and this community. We ask this through Christ our Lord. Amen."

Turning to the new drivers, the celebrant asks them to repeat after him:

Before my parents and my faith community/I pledge: Never to drink and drive/never to let anyone who is drinking drive my car./I pledge I will drive safely/for I know that driving is both a privilege and a responsibility. /I intend to remember the first and honor the second/for all life is precious. /God keep me and my friends safe. Amen.

Now the parents come over from their side of the sanctuary and hand over the car keys to their offspring (with a hug!). The celebrant sprinkles them all and they return to the pews.

18. *Parish Logo and Motto.* A little contest here. Ask parishioners to come up with a logo and motto that best describes the hopes and mission of the parish. The logo can be one made up or chosen from clip art or other sources. The logo and motto then go on all official stationery and notices. To this extent they become a small token of parish identity and cohesion. We have a dove for our logo and our motto is: A Christian Community in the Roman Catholic Tradition. "Christian" identifies us as those who are disciples of Jesus Christ. "Community" unites us with all humankind. "Roman Catholic Tradition" says that within that Christian identity we walk, celebrate, and live in a particular way.

19. *Fall Name Tags.* We do this every four or five years. It works very well. The challenge is that we go to church often, see people Sunday after Sunday, but never know their names, never put names and faces together. So we send out a parish mailing stating that for the month of September (coming home again), we ask everyone to wear a name tag, several of which we have included in the mailing. We encourage them to write their names large and, when they come to church, to look directly at each other's tags. No sideways glances or casual peeking. A direct, frontal look. And furthermore, at the beginning of Mass we ask people to turn to one another and introduce themselves and then give the Sign of Peace (which we omit at the usual place). For those who forgot to bring their tags, the ushers have a supply. We always have fun with this and it is always appreciated.

20. *The Affirmation Affair.* Here we ask

our children in our religion classes to write letters to a particular group in the community showing them appreciation and gratitude for their calling and vocation: for example, teachers, fire  fighters, the police, first aid people, store merchants, doctors, nurses, sanitation workers, etc. We're trying not only to say thanks but to give the lesson of "marketplace spirituality" to our children.

21. *Vacation Map.* This requires a large map of the world to be hung on your bulletin board or church wall. Ask people who are going on vacation to send a postcard to the parish. Take the cards and tack them all around the outer border of the map along with a colored thread or yarn connected to where they have been. The people love to come back to discover where everyone was and that some were at the same place and didn't even know it.

22. *Garden for the Poor.* Somewhere on the parish grounds there must be room for a small vegetable garden—or perhaps people would like to donate some space in their own gardens. In any case, have volunteers prepare the ground and plant the seeds or plants: onion, tomato, pepper, celery, squash, zucchini, etc. Then you need volunteers who will keep it weeded. Near mid-summer the vegetables should be ripening and, when ready, given to the poor or some organization that feeds the needy. The janitor or the pastor (often the same person) can water early in the morning or early evening. We've had this for years and get terrific yield, all of which goes to the local "Lunch Break" that feeds the hungry daily.

23. *Freezer Meals.* For this you need plastic or aluminum containers and lids where they can easily be picked up. Then you announce in the bulletin that these containers will be available after each Mass next Sunday. Some are placed on the altar as a reminder. Before the dismissal, the celebrant blesses these containers and then asks the people to go to the hall (or wherever) to pick them up. There are directions there saying that when they cook a meal during the week, they should make some extra, put it in the container(s), write the directions on the lid (bake at 350 for an hour, etc.), and return during the week to the freezer in our Spiritual Center. We do this twice a year; it helps mightily to feed the shut-ins and elderly and those in sudden need. The people are very responsive and generous. An easy but critical outreach.

24. *Staff Mystery Ride.* A minor suggestion, but each year two of the staff collaborate on a day away. The destination is unknown to the rest of us. The two receive sealed envelopes in the parking lot stating the first destination, where they may have lunch. Then they get another sealed envelope directing them to their final destination: some point of interest or fun. Then they have dinner together (tab on the parish). A community builder.

25. *The Parish Council.* It may seem strange to insert a major parish organization here under a catch-all chapter, but I didn't want to get into its details since there are many fine books (Rademacher's *The New Practical Guide for Parish Councils,* Mystic, Conn.: Twenty-Third Publications, 1990) and articles on parish councils and most dioceses have guidelines. I just wanted to share what we have found to be most workable. We have

a design that has two parts, like two concentric circles. The first circle is the Parish Council proper. It is small, with only nine members, since the bigger the council, the more ineffective. Four members are ex officio, there by diocesan law. The other five are nominated by the parish at large. From the list of nominees, the current council votes in new members. Members serve on a rotating basis so that all council members don't end their terms all at once. Two members retire every two to three years. The president is voted in by the members.

Ours is what we call a "discernment model" council, which means that the first, most serious task of the council is to ask of any important matter, "Is this of the gospel? Does it advance the spirit of Jesus?" There must be much prayer and reflection. Only this council votes. It meets every other month.

The second circle is called the Parish Assembly and it too meets every other month. Its members are the heads of every parish organization and ministry (one of the members is, of course, the Parish Council president, who gives a report of what went on at the Parish Council). The members have two tasks: 1) Each ministry gives a report so all can catch the overall view of what is happening. This is quite impressive when you put it all together and get a sense of what is going on in the parish. 2) Members may lobby for any ideas or needs they think important. No voting is done at this time.

There is a third element. Since we have so many critical people at the assembly, some timely topic of church or society is tossed out for discussion. As I mentioned, they meet every other month, and alternate between an evening time and on Sundays after Mass, so

the public, which is always invited, can attend. Minutes of both the council and the assembly meetings appear in the Sunday bulletin.

Note: The finance committee representative is also present at the meeting to give a report, but he (she) is merely one of the non-voting assembly members and does only that: report. He (she) may not forbid or allow expenditures. It prevents this person from wielding undue influence and determining how the parish should go.

26. Family High Mass Servers. We have a modified High Mass on the first Sunday of each month. Music is provided by the Traditional Choir and we alternate between a full-blown sung Mass in all its parts and just the usual four hymns and responses. We begin with a procession, using the asperges and incense. The Mass is served by families. This includes the parents, teens, children, any elderly folk living at home (and any singles). They are trained by the High Mass trainer, dress in robes, and share the jobs such as carrying the processional cross, the water bowl, and the incense. It's really simple. The family does it only once. They seem to enjoy it, even the teens. As usual, we recruit them in the summer and their names are in the Parish Booklet.

27. Parish Library. We have a parish library in our Spiritual Center, but any room or even a few standing shelves will do. Good Catholic reading is hard to come by. People will be glad to donate books. Publishers sell remainders cheaply. A few wise purchases will get you started. It's a good ministry and library use will surprise you.

28. Environmental Quilt. With environmental sensitivity running high, ask people, under the guidance of someone in the parish who knows quilting, each to make a patch for the quilt. This can be an on-going project. Teens and children contribute. You might hang it in the sanctuary or somewhere in the church or hall if you celebrate Environmental Sunday or Earth Day. (See the sample invitation for another quilting occasion on page 278 of Parish Papers.)

29. Talent Auction. At some fun time, say, your parish picnic, raffle off talent and time from both the people and the staff. Offer babysitting, cooking a meal, weeding a garden, teaching a skill such as skiing or painting, or whatever talents people have. It's a fun thing, a community builder. I once raffled myself off to babysit. I wound up with two energetic boys, and I got to sleep the next day!

30. Grandmothers This Side and That. The basic concept here is based on the recognition that, due to so much mobility and family breakup, the very young and the very old are bereft of each other's company. Many kids, especially those with unwed mothers, don't have grandparents, and they are already deprived of half their heritage and relationships—on their father's side. Then there's that army of latchkey kids. So gather some grandparents and local teachers and let them find a forum to make connections—something they can easily do. Then arrange for a Seniors luncheon and have a drawing for "adopt a grandparent." The bargain can be as simple as a latchkey kid having someone to call (or vice versa) when he (she) gets home, or a real exchange of birthday gifts, cards, and all the things that grandparents do. "This side and that" reminds us that we can do the same for overseas

children. We have a connection with an Irish woman who cares for orphans. She tells us that there is nothing in the world that the orphans want more than a grandmother, and they want her picture to hang over their beds. Your local Catholic Charities will give you foreign contacts.

31. Grandparenting. Theresa Cotter (*Church*, Fall, 1993) reminds us of the old African saying that it takes an entire village to raise a child. Thus grandparenting by Seniors is to be encouraged on every level by the parish. She cites these gifts of grandparents: affirmation, storytelling, example, homemade gifts, listening, prayer. It behooves a parish to recognize grandparenting, provide space for storytelling, offer Grandparents' days, and include Seniors in all parish liturgical and social events. You should also be aware of grandparenting resources. Here are some of them:

•The American Self-Help Clearinghouse is a nationwide database that offers tips on how to start a grandparent self-help group and a listing of such groups in your area. Write: Self-Help Clearinghouse, St. Clare-Riverside Medical Center, Denville, NJ 07834, phone: 201–625–7101.

•A free copy of the newsletter *Vital Connections* can be obtained from the Foundation for Grandparenting, P.O. Box 31, Lake Placid, NY 12946.

•GAP, or Grandparents as Parents, is an organization to network grandparents in an area. Write: Psychiatric Clinic for Youth, 2801 Atlantic Ave., Long Beach, CA 90801.

•There is a support/advocacy group called Second Time Around Parents from Family and Community Services of Delaware County, 100 W. Front St., Media, PA 19063.

For our Grandparents Day, see the notice on page 285 of Parish Papers.

32. Midweek Revival Lunch. If you're in the city or suburbs, why not have a good old noontime revival of prayer, song, and preaching (or video), after which you give out a bag lunch of sandwiches (or sell them reasonably). It's lunch hour break time. Several teams of men and women can prepare the sandwiches. Hold this once a week or once a month. The emphasis here is on revival. It's not quiet time. It's energizing time, singing time, open prayer time, inspiration time.

33. Walk Time. This is common. Some kind of walk-a-thon for a cause. Join the national Crop Walk Sunday, or make up your own agenda. This does draw people, especially the young.

34. Wilt Thou? We hesitate to let people know that it is fitting and proper to leave estate gifts to the parish. As a result, when a parishioner dies he (she) leaves a will that just about names every charity in town—except the parish. Many people would leave something to the parish. Why don't they? Most common reason given: They weren't asked. Now and then a gentle reminder is in order that a lifetime gift can reduce estate taxes as well as help the parish. Don't be pushy. But occasionally a word in the bulletin will help. People could bequeath just a percentage if they want. Even a modest 1% can bring a few thousand dollars to the parish.

35. Spaghetti Video. Sounds like watching a Spaghetti Western starring Clint Eastwood. Actually it's quite an effective and simple idea. Hold a spaghetti dinner for the family. That's always an attraction. But after the dinner, show a family movie either in the same room with a large TV set or move to another room. Charge, say, $5 per adult and $2 for kids. Pre-sell tickets so you can control the numbers, since you're likely to have only one sitting. (See the notice in Parish Papers, page 268.)

36. Historical Wall. No matter how young the parish is, there are beginnings, roots, pioneers. These things, these people, should not be forgotten. If yours is an old parish, then all the more reason that memories should be preserved. Find a wall somewhere: the hall, parish center, wherever. Have some handy person put up a wallboard (either paste it on or put up studs first and nail it on). Paint it and you have a surface ready to go. Then go ferret out the photographs: the dedication of the church, school, hall, etc. Talk to the oldtimers and get photographs and memories from them. Check old newspapers (parishioners may have them; certainly, the newspaper itself has archives) and clip out notices, marriages, parish events. Ask the people for dedication booklets. You'll be surprised at what some people have saved.

Then write up some blurbs, say, a listing of the pastors from the beginning till now, along with their pictures. Or a newspaper clipping showing the dedication of the church or other newsworthy items. Show the church now and then. Then ask someone with a good eye to arrange and fix them on the wallboard. Put up a colorful title of large letters and finally cover it with glass or plexiglas. The historical wall will stand as a memento, a shrine, for the people and a point of interest for the visitor.

37. The Peace Tree. In times of crisis, say, the Persian Gulf War, or just as a reminder any time, erect a "peace tree" in church. It could be a small live tree like a dogwood or a similar tree. Then in the bulletin explain the various colored hearts hanging on the tree. Let's use the Gulf War as an example. The *Yellow Hearts* represent those in the war for whom we are praying. People can write names on these hearts and fix them to the tree. (The hearts are kept in a little container with pins, etc., beside the tree.) The single *White Heart* represents all those who work for peace. The single *Lemon Heart* is for all people on both sides who die and grieve like everyone else. The single *Green Heart* is for the environment, which war always ravishes. Finally, the single *Red Heart* is for the enemy (here in our example, Saddam Hussein).

This red heart is hard for some to tolerate and you may get some resistance and some anger. But the simple fact is, not to pray for him is to truncate the gospel. "Love your enemies. Pray for those who persecute you," taught Jesus. "Father, forgive them, they know not what they do." For those who angrily ask "How can we pray for Saddam Hussein?" the proper Christian response is "How can we not?"

38. Teddy Bears. This is a project to help AIDS patients (mostly children) or any children with chronic illness. People purchase a teddy bear (or any toy, for that matter), write a note to be pinned on it, and bring it to the parish for distribution.

39. Sharing the Bounty. I pass this one on from Judith Dunlap. Two weeks before Trick or Treat, parishioners receive a flyer in the mail asking the parents and adults to donate some of the goodies they will receive to be sent to those away in the service and at college. The source of these names comes from parents who are asked to write their away-from-home children's names and

addresses on the outside of an envelope with a few dollars inside to help cover postage. Then, after Halloween, in the parish hall, volunteers (parents and kids) write notes, separate the goodies, and wrap packages. End the evening with a prayer service.

40. Ministries Fair. A good time for a Ministries Fair is in the fall. After each Mass on a September or October weekend, set up well-marked tables or booths in the parish hall or, if you have room, around the church. Have people stationed there with flyers about their ministry, one-page explanations and other material, and ready to answer questions. Tying this in with some kind of Commissioning Sunday would be helpful.

41. Adopt a Family. This impulse at Christmas or Thanksgiving time is appealing to neighborhoods, organizations, and staffs. Such groups adopt a single family (or several families) whose name is suggested by the Social Concerns committee or any in-touch agency. The names and ages of family members are known and each member of the organization or neighborhood buys something for a particular individual. Then they meet at someone's home to wrap and label the gifts, which they deliver in person to the recipient family's house or apartment. (Page 267 of Parish Papers has a sample notice.)

42. Returnees. It is estimated that some 320,000 former Catholics return to the church each year. They come back for a variety of reasons: They feel a spiritual void; they feel guilty over being away, especially from the sacraments; they're facing a mid-life crisis; or, most strongly, they want something to pass on to their children, or simply they want to commit themselves to something. In any case, there is, surprisingly, no ritual for them, or at least no known process for them to return. Think about it. Those who want to return really don't know how to go about it. All they know is that they're embarrassed. I guess most just slip back to Mass, but they're still uneasy, knowing something more should be done. I suggest three things (besides the official Re-Membering Program from the Midwest).

First, (if you'll pardon me) give them my small book, *While You Were Gone: A Handbook for Returning Catholics—and those thinking about it* (Twenty-Third Publications, 1994). It will help them regain their Catholic bearings, especially if they've been away a long time.

Second, often all that is needed is a talk with the priest and the rite of reconciliation, but people have to know that. So advertise in the bulletin now and then. Something like this: "If anyone wishes to return to the Catholic church, or if you know of anyone wishing to do so, please call for an appointment to see the priest. You will be met cordially and joyously, and you will receive information and help with your return or the return of someone you are concerned about." Or a variation is to say to the would-be returnees or their friends who wish to get information for them: "Come to a meeting on Wednesday evening in the parish hall at 8:00 to find out what can be done."

Third, there are, in my experience, always a few who are quite open to a public ritual at Mass. For such people, we have them come up after the homily, share something of their journey with the congregation, and then I offer a simple prayer, such as :

O God, Gentle Father of the Prodigal, Shepherd of Lost Sheep, and Seeker of those you love, receive into your community once more your son (daughter) whom you have always claimed. Embrace him (her) as your own once more, for you desire that all be one as you and the Father and the Holy Spirit, one God, forever and ever. Amen.

43. Used Books. Many of us have books in perfectly good order that just sit on our shelves. We have put such books we no longer need on a public book rack in our parish hall foyer with the directions that they are a gift and people can feel free to take them, keep them, pass them on to others. This continues to work very well. The books do move.

The saint loves people and uses things. The sinner loves things and uses people.

—Sidney Harris

I said to the almond tree: "Speak to me of God." And the almond tree blossomed.

—Nikos Kazantzakis

A vision without a task is but a dream. A task without a vision is drudgery. A vision and a task is the hope of the world.

—Church sign, Sussex, England. 1730

Jan Green tells of putting her young son to bed for the umpteenth time. Her patience was worn thin. When she heard him cry "Mamma" again, she yelled at him, "If you call 'Mamma' one more time, I'll spank you!" After that, there was quiet. Then just as she sat down, she heard a wee whisper, "Mrs. Green, may I have a drink?"

Chapter 14

The Parish Attic

Bulletin Announcement: This being Easter Sunday, we will ask Mrs. Brown to come forward and lay an egg on the altar.

The title of this chapter suggests that, like items in an attic, we have some odds and ends, so let's list them and make some suggestions.

Leadership

A persistent question whenever I gave workshops on the parish had to do with the Reverend Bottleneck. That's the pastor who is regressive and won't let anything happen, certainly very little of what's listed in this manual. Depending on my mood and the mood of the audience, I would initially suggest assassination but, noting that the law (not to mention God) takes a dim view of that, I suggest that we come up with other creative ways to deal with the Reverend. Here are six:

1. Start small. You tell the pastor that old Mrs. Smith is ailing and homebound. Is it all right if you visit her? "Of course. Why not? By all means." As time goes by, you mention to Father that Mrs. Smith is such a religious woman, she would like you to pray with her. Can he recommend any pamphlets or booklets or prayers? Yes, he thinks he can do that. "Be happy to recommend some prayers." As time goes by, you mention that Mrs. Smith would like to receive communion and you know how terribly busy Father is. Could you bring her communion if he shows you how to do it?

Even if he says no at this time, what is happening is that you are establishing credibility for another day, the credibility of a concerned parishioner about another, and the frequent contacts with the pastor give him a chance not to be threatened by you. It's a start.

2. Invite the pastor to your meeting, prayer group, home. Let him see that you're regular, good people. Get him off his turf so he can relax. Then you might suggest a moderate way that you and others could assist at the parish or help with a ministry.

3. Confront with moderate people. Don't bring the crazies or the confrontational people. Bring sensible, respected people to talk over ministry and possible activities.

4. Start a prayer chain for his conversion, removal, or reward, whichever is likely to happen first.

5. Send a respectful letter to the bishop and—this is important—a copy to the diocesan personnel director. *Be specific* and note that, as a result of the pastor's position, the following is happening: a) There is a loss of participation in the parish; b) there are transfers out of the parish, and c) money has declined. Ask to meet with the bishop.

6. Consider the pastor's fears. For example, his fear of losing identity if others take over what he thinks is his job. Perhaps personal problems: alcoholism, loneliness. Today, with all the publicity about pedophile priests, his image is not that great and he's not feeling good about himself. We know such poor imagery has gone mainstream when the *New Yorker* magazine starts printing cartoons about it and the subject is a regular staple on the six o'clock news. In a word, the pastor is the way he is for a reason. Try to understand him, even if you're frustrated. If indeed there are problems, they should be presented to the bishop when you meet with him.

But, you know, there's another side to this story. Anyone in leadership labors under certain handicaps, perhaps a pastor more than most because he projects a father figure, and that aura entices dependency and a kind of parent-child expectation. Or, to put it bluntly, people tend to keep Father isolated and immature, or they take the attitude and position of children rather than co-workers and collaborators, thus forcing him into an authoritarian position.

The fact is we project too much on our leaders, demanding that they be all-providing, accessible at all times, and always ready to care for our needs. We insist they be perfect, hold them to high standards, and make them superior in every way. The upshot of all this is to justify our own irresponsibility. As long as Father is superior, we don't have to be responsible. We can count on him to make things better. In a word, we unconsciously foster co-dependency. So take a look, courtesy of Father Joe Giallanza ("The Myth of Authority," *Human Development*, Fall 1991), at seven unreal expectations that drive the leader bonkers:

1. The Pick-Up Expectations. The pastor really is in charge of all unclaimed jobs. He does what others simply don't want to do.

Somehow he is more responsible than others. He is expected to pick up after everybody, to turn out the lights, lock the doors, and fill the empty Coke machine. Father Giallanza mentions an incident where at a meeting of about 50 people in the parish hall, the phone was ringing and ringing and ringing until someone said in exasperation, "Why doesn't Father Shea answer it?"

2. The Transmitter Expectation. Father is expected to relay all information to others whether he shares in the agenda or not. For instance, "When is Father going to tell her to stop bothering me?"

3. The Encyclopedia Expectation. Father, of course, should know, process, update, and distribute all information. "How could the pastor not come and visit my mother in the hospital!" That he had no idea she was there is not considered. Of course, he knows all things.

4. The Maintenance Expectation. Whatever is broken he will fix. Whatever is empty, he will fill. Whatever is left on, he will turn off. His adult "children" would never think of taking responsibility.

5. The Dart Board Expectation. The leader is presumed to be a natural target for ventilating all anger and frustration.

6. The Low Affirmation Expectation. A regular diet for most leaders. Father is seldom fed affirmation. Honestly now, when was the last time you complimented him? See, you never even think of it. Sooner or later this poor diet shows.

7. Self-Destruction Expectation. Patterns of overeating, undersleeping, and never playing are bad news for any priest and this should be reported forthwith to the bishop and personnel director. Why not? Isn't the pastor part of your parish family?

I guess I'm saying that while there are indeed Reverend Bottlenecks around who stifle creativity and co-ministry, we should also look to ourselves as being partly responsible for making them what they are.

Conflicts

Writing in the Alban Institute publication, Roy W. Pneuman (its senior consultant) often works with troubled Protestant churches. As a result of his experience, he has found common trouble spots, nine of them in fact. They're worth sharing with, and adapting to, Catholics. (By the way, the Alban Institute is an excellent resource for all parish and ministry matters. Send for its journal, *Congregations,* at 4125 Nebraska Ave. N.W., Washington, D.C. 20016.)

1. People disagree about parish goals or objectives; what they are; what the parish is all about. In other words, parishes that don't have a clear mission statement flounder. Form one or get outside help to do so.

2. The parish structure is unclear. Who is responsible for what? What's the role of the pastor, the staff, the parish council, the volunteers? And, as parishes grow or decline, how are these roles realigned? Clarification is needed here.

It should be evident that this source of conflict is becoming more serious for the Catholic church. The simple reason is fewer priests and more laity on staff. Priest pastors always had the automatic aura of ordination, authority, and education about them. They were the bishop's men on the scene. The parish reflected the priest's style and priorities. He was undisputed master and leader. He was in charge. But no longer. More educated and degree-holding lay staff calls for more shared leadership. With this comes problems, problems that arise simply from not having the opportunity or necessity to confront them in the past. What problems? Those such as: unclear expectations, lack of work appraisals, lines of accountability and communication, explicit job descriptions, and simple justice in pay and work hours. All of us may need help here from the diocese or from professional leadership seminars. (Good source for help: National Association of Church Personnel Administrators. See page 310 for the address of this and other useful resources.

One serious issue should be mentioned here in connection with parish structure. The issue is justice. The shameful fact is that often the church (which intoned in its 1971 World Synodal Document *Justice in the World:* "While the church is bound to give witness to justice, it recognizes that anyone who ventures to speak to people about justice must first be just in their eyes") often treats its own employees unjustly. Unilateral and secret firings, sudden and unexplained dismissals, penalities for unionizing, denial of benefits, and the like are rampant. Women especially, who make up almost 80% of those who work in church ministry, are victims of unjust treatment. This new relationship between clergy and laity, this new partnership and collaboration, this search for clarifying parish structure must be supported and sustained by honest justice with all the due processes of fairness, open hearings, and redress. Otherwise, all our summonses to justice in the persecuted parts of the world and in our own nation lose credibility. (Read the revealing five-page lead article, "Injustice in the Church Workplace" in the *National Catholic Reporter,* January 21, 1994, by Tim McCarthy.)

3. The pastor's role is unclear. This is an outgrowth of the above. We Catholics think we know what the priest's job is, but do we? (Does he?) What are our expectations of him? What time off is his, *should* be his? Must he attend every one of our meetings? Maybe we ought to sit down and write a job description. I know that is foreign to Catholics, but misunderstood expectations cause too much hurt.

4. The parish no longer fits the people. Maybe numbers have shrunk or expanded. Maybe several ethnic groups have become predominant. Maybe the staff is too large now. Maybe the parish has grown so large that it's unrealistic to expect that same old family feeling as when it was smaller. Maybe we need to form small groups.

5. The pastor and the parish leadership styles don't match. A quiet, bookish man may replace Father Charismatic. An authoritarian pastor may replace a consultative one. A new pastor is at odds with the way things "have always been done." This tension becomes especially acute after the long reign of a former pastor. And, speaking of a long-term pastor, usually no adequate grieving time is allowed or provided for when he leaves. Someone should be conscious of this and of the process necessary to make a transition, and ritualize the bereavement. When there are changes, the diocesan personnel board should come to the parish and talk with the people.

6. A new pastor rushes in changes. There is a conflict when too many changes are made too quickly without due regard for the heritage and feelings of the people. New pastors ought to be given Father Phil Murnion's pamphlet, "Seven Rules for New Pastors" (National Pastoral Life Center, 299 Elizabeth St., New York, NY 10012).

7. Blocked communication lines. Poor communication is always a source of conflict. There must be mechanisms for dialogue: regular staff and parish council meetings, the printing and distribution of minutes, adequate bulletin notices. Sometimes an outside consultant is called for. Communication between pastor, staff, and heads of ministries and volunteers needs attention here.

8. Poor conflict management. Conflict is inevitable and can be creative, so it's no shame to have it. In fact, it's probably necessary for growth. One caution: We have to be careful of "triangling," that is, complaining to a third party about a second party.

Under this heading I want to include a sensitive issue beyond the in-house staff conflicts: parishes with open tragedies or scandals. I mean such things as a school bus accident, a charge of sex abuse by a teacher or coach, a priest accused of pedophilia, a secretary confronted with embezzlement, etc., in a word, something significant that will bring the media running to the parish doorsteps. A conflict situation is here, especially in relation to the media: How much should you tell the press? How do you deal with reporters? Wanda Vassallo, writing in *Celebration* (May 1994) gives some sage advice. First, she says, you *must* deal with reporters. Putting them off only sows the seeds of rumor and less reliable information. Hassling, denying, minimizing only sow the seeds of the suspicion of a coverup. She advises giving the facts as you know them and that, as things become clearer, to hold a news conference at a certain time that day. At such a conference, give what details you know, show caution as to what you don't ("As far as we have been able to ascertain so far...") and give plans the parish or church intends to take to rectify the situation and keep the public appraised of the problem.

She quotes Donald Blohowiak's book, *No Comment! An Executive's Essential Guide to the News Media* (Westport, Conn.: Greenwood Press, 1987). "Reveal bad news in total. The slow drip, drip, drip of damaging facts piques public interest and surrounds the story with an air of a drama unfolding....Revealing all there is to tell right off the bat allows the media to tell everything in one shot." She also advises not waiting for a crisis to happen but to have a well thought out and rehearsed crisis communications plan in writing beforehand, such as a ready spokesperson, an on-site "newsroom," a note taker, and so on. In-house or public conflicts will occur. It's best to be prepared. Get hold of Vassallo's article or Blohowiak's book.

9. Not listening to all segments. We all tend to stack our staff with people who agree with us. But other segments of the parish need to be heard. Suggestion box, open meetings, town meetings (our Cracker Barrel), printed names, addresses, and phone numbers of the parish council members who thus may be contacted—all are ways of being available to everyone's agenda.

So, these are possible conflicts a parish may encounter. Is there help? Yes. Believe it or not, there's a leadership hotline called Convergence, Inc. It assists people in leadership positions to focus on the issues, develop the skills, and initiate the action plans that will help their parishes. Call Sister Elizabeth Vermaelen, S.C., or anyone at Convergence, Inc., phone: 312-743-5461.

Social Concerns

I have left out social concerns in this work. Not in the sense that this manual is not filled with many helpful suggestions, but in the sense that we have not discussed the deeper issue, not of charity, but of justice. This is a tough one. Most people don't like the church to be directly involved here, although that is certainly our mission and mandate. They don't like the church engaging in "politics," and this has been a large factor in the downfall of the mainline Protestant churches and the failure of liberation theology in Latin America. The huge success of the evangelical churches is due to an intense focus on the gospel, the "personal Savior," and community, and they let any social justice flow indirectly from that. Something for us to think about. (Read the challenging *Fullness of Faith: The Public Significance of Theology* by Michael and Kenneth Himes, Mahwah, N.J.: Paulist Press.)

Nevertheless, as we shall indicate in the next chapter, never have parishes been so involved in social activities and concerns as in the present time. The United States bishops have noted this. In their pastoral, *Communities of Salt and Light,* their introductory remarks state:

> In the past decade, we have written major pastoral letters on peace and economic justice and issued pastoral statements on a number of important issues touching human life and human dignity. But until now, we have not specifically addressed the crucial role of parishes in the church's social ministry. We offer these words of support, encouragement, and challenge at this time because we are convinced that the

local parish is the most important ecclesial setting for sharing and acting on our catholic social heritage.

We agree, and all over the country parishes are doing heroic grassroots work in meeting local needs. Without getting overtly into the "politics" that have divided many a parish, we still must be involved, not only in the everyday social needs of the community and beyond, but also in the restructuring of the very fabric of society. For some parishes, direct and radical action is the way to go; for others, indirect support of lobbying groups such as Common Cause or Bread for the World is the way to go.

Family concerns are high as the family continues to disintegrate. One response is not to despair, but to realize that families can make themselves heard at the highest government levels. Therefore I strongly recommend, along with Dolores Curran, that families join Parent Action. It focuses on 1) public awareness, 2) family-friendly legislation, 3) networking among parents, and 4) corporate partnerships that help employers implement policies that do not force parents to choose between family and job. Join! Fee is a suggested $25. Parent Action, B&O Building, 2 North Charles St., Baltimore, MD 21202, phone: 410- 752-1790.

Lay volunteers can be so helpful to the world, and an incentive to the parish community, when they are aware of global needs. We've had young people give up a year of college to help others through accredited organizations. You should be aware of some of them. A good resource is: *The Response: Lay Volunteer Mission Opportunities Directory*, put out by the International Liaison of Lay Volunteers, 4121 Harewood Rd., N.E. Washington, D.C. 20017, phone: 800-543-5046.

"For What We Have Done, For What We Have Failed to Do"

These words from our common Confiteor at Mass, "for what we have done," mean that what has been shared here is not the last word, but an interim one. We have done all these things, have found them helpful and community building, but they don't and won't work everywhere. You have to pick and choose, use or discard. Some resources are limited. Still, there are enough good ideas here to be helpful to most parishes to some degree.

"What we have failed to do": We have not mentioned spirituality, a subject about which we are very serious, for we do not want to fall into activism: movement without spirit. So we offer many opportunities for prayer with and without the clergy. We chant the morning office twice a week at 6:30 A.M., one day for the men and the other for the women (they want it that way). It's a powerful day's start, and I would recommend this heartily. Each ministry is required in its bylaws to have at least one day or evening of recollection a year. We have many prayer groups and scripture study groups as well as a variety of offerings, from healing Masses to charismatic prayer groups to parish missions and spiritual direction (we have a full-time spiritual director).

We have also, in one of our more creative moves, built a Spiritual Center, so that people would not have to always "go to the mountains" (they should at times), but realize that right at the local level there is provision for their spiritual needs. It contains a large meeting hall, a chapel, reconciliation rooms, a library devoted to scripture and spiritual reading, counseling rooms, spiritual direction rooms, a theater, and rooms for scripture study, prayer group meetings, and whatever else will help nourish the spirit.

We have built a grotto on our spacious 25 acres, and it continues to draw great numbers of people. Most remarkably, it draws by far not the older people I expected, but young men: men in their late teens, mid-twenties, and thirties. I'm not sure what is operating here. Perhaps Bishop Kenneth Untener of Saginaw, Michigan, is right when he says that Mary will be the new focal point of a renewed spirituality in the future. Anyway, each parish has its charism here.

I asked you in the introduction to read this manual as if you had limitless money and personnel. The fact is that most parishes have neither. But I remind you that the majority of items in this manual are easy and free, or minimally costly. Most are more concerned with "approaches" and style, the way we might do things. The biggest factor is volunteered time and talent. Most people are indeed pressed for time, but they will give some time and effort if they are asked.

And there is help out there. Tim Unsworth publishes a monthly four-page newsletter called *U.S. Parish,* which contains "parishable ideas" (put out by the Claretians, 205 W. Monroe St., Chicago, IL 60606). Twenty-Third Publications (P.O. Box 180, Mystic, CT 06355) publishes a magazine, *Today's Parish.* There are centers, such as the Center for Parish Development, 5407 South University Ave., Chicago, IL 60615, (phone: 312-752-5093) that offer seminars. We offer a two-day workshop about the parish each fall. These are only a few of the aids a parish might be aware of and tap in to.

"Come to the Feast"

This directive is, of course, from the gospel parable where the king throws a banquet for his son and sends out his pressing invitations to attend. The same kind of urgency is present from the pastor or the DRE when they send home letters saying that it is parish policy that people must attend certain meetings in order for them or their children to receive the sacraments or in order to get married. And there's the rub—or the tension. On one side are the people. They are already overhassled, overextended, and overprogrammed. On the other side is the pastor or deacon or DRE saying, "Come, or else!" More rules, it seems; more hoops to jump through. And the people thought the church had changed.

It's a dilemma. As one book's title put it, how do we "challenge people without crushing" them? After all, people *do* have responsibilities. The parish exists to supplement them, not substitute for them. People should not just "use" the parish for ceremonial occasions any more than the parish should show interest in them only at money-raising time. That's hurtful and demeaning—and, from the people's side, it sends a definite message to children: Church is there for holiday time; it's not a way of life.

And, besides, so much has changed. Do we both understand what we're talking about? Some parents' idea of baptism (bleaching out original sin so their child has a shot at heaven) and the church's idea (initiation rite into a faith community) might be worlds apart. Their idea of extreme unction (greasing dying grandma into bliss) and the church's idea of the sacrament of the sick (anointing the unwell living) might be worlds apart. And so it goes. The two sides simply have to get together to see if they're talking the same language, sharing the same theology. Hence the sensible demands: Come to the meetings.

But how rigid should these reasonable demands be? After all, people have a journey and they have a story. They should be heard. Perhaps we need better mechanisms to help us to listen to and be gentle with the recalcitrants and the reluctant. We need to learn how to challenge them without turning them away, to invite without rejection. It's an art. Perhaps every parish or region needs a grievance board made up of clergy and laity who will review conflicts in the area of parish policy and rules. There is something to be said on both sides and a gentle confrontation might be the sincerest form of evangelization. People skilled in management conflict could do a lot here in finding middle ground between reasonable rules and personal stories. Rules always need to be flexible in honoring people's circumstances and special needs. Still, people should be aware of how necessary it is to be more than skin-deep Catholics in these urgent times. To sum it up: As far as the rules go, leniency should be the norm, fidelity the challenge, dialogue the procedure.

The Future Is Now

The parish, as we have stated in the first chapter, is here to stay. Whether it's large, such as the very vibrant, much sought after 17,000-member parish like St. Michael's in the Archdiocese of Chicago or the small two-dozen member alternate community in the Tucson Mountains in Arizona, the desire of people to gather around word and bread is strong. But large or small, the parish of the future—and many right now—will be challenged by the 50-60 new immigrant groups flooding the country all the time.

Hispanics, for example, 90% of whom are Catholic at least in name, are the largest non-English-speaking group coming to the United States. By the turn of the century they will be the predominant ethnic group in some large dioceses. A very large number of immigrants are Asians, the largest group of these being (the mostly non-Catholic) Chinese. Vietnamese and Filipinos often bring their own priests, but most groups do not. In any case, there is a great challenge for the parish to absorb and welcome them.

Why? Because, unlike former times, you can't build churches all over the place just for them. There's not enough money or clergy. This means that existing parishes must be open to the immigrant, Catholic and non-Catholic alike. Into this polyglot we must forge new centers of unity and new people of unity. Some suggestions: 1) It might be well to prepare or obtain some flyers or bulletin inserts giving a background on the new immigrants (especially those who might be impacting your parish) and what the church is doing for them. Start sensitizing the people. It's a matter of building bridges, expanding minds and hearts and preventing undue, un-Christian prejudice. 2) Prepare some parish leaders and volunteers now to study about and meet ethnic people, so that they may be parish representatives or liaisons who are attuned to the culture and ways of the immigrant. 3) Support and finance (at least partially) teaching the immigrant language; say, a Spanish course at a nearby community college or high school.

Tap into your diocese or the United States Catholic Conference, 3211 Fourth St., N.E., Washington, D.C. 20005 or The National Center for Urban Ethnic Affairs, P.O. Box 33279, Washington, D.C. 20033 for all kinds of help and resources.

Like Pentecost of the past, the Pentecost of the present and future is diverse, challenging, and enriching, demanding from us all an openness of heart.

Some News Items

One out of four Americans has switched faiths or denominations at least once from the religion in which they were born. Of those who switch, 81% end up in the Protestant denominations and 9% in the Roman Catholic church. Most often cited reason for the switch: marriage to a person of another faith; next, a positive feeling toward the new faith, and, finally, convenience, as in a move to a new neighborhood.

Think of it: The Catholic parish has taken over the work of religious orders. They used to do all those charitable, educative, social things. Now they're all part of average ministries in most parishes.

Ruth Wallace, in a lecture published in *Review of Religious Research* (June 1991), tells what's happening in some of the 300 Catholic parishes in America that are led not by priest pastors but by religious or lay women. While clear about the tensions and problems, Wallace summarizes her learning: "What my data indicates is that these women . . . are not simply reproducing the structure, they are transforming it."

Reflections

A friend, Dr. Rich Glenn, devised a nice series of reflections when he gave us a workshop. They are rich and evocative, and I share them with you.

I. The People of God. (Read Exodus 19:1–6; Jeremiah 31:31–34; Romans 9:25–26; 1 Peter 2:9–10.)
Questions to Ponder
    1. Do church members today feel that the church is called into being by God

or established by human beings? Is it biblical to speak of the church possessively as "my church?" Is it not God's church, of which Christ is Lord?

2. Do you feel that St. Mary's manifests itself as God's "pilgrim people" in movement toward the Kingdom? How about the larger Catholic community? If so, how? If not, why?

3. Does a continual harkening of the past prevent us as church from following God's call into a new future?

4. Can you identify your own covenant with God? Can you explain it?

II. The Body of Christ. (Read Romans 12; Ephesians 4:4–16.)
Questions to Ponder

1. If the church is the Body of Christ, why is there so much divisiveness in the church today? Why do we not have more unity?

2. Does today's church hold koinonia (fellowship) and living for the sake of others (mission) together in creative balance? Do we spend more money and attention on ourselves than on reaching out in Christian love to others?

3. Is St. Mary's living a sacrificial life, thereby endeavoring to carry out the ministry of Jesus Christ?

4. Do you see yourself as one called to "ministry"?

III. The Community of the Spirit. (Read Acts 2; 1 Corinthians 12–14.)
Questions to Ponder

1. Do you see evidence of the sustaining and reforming power of the Holy Spirit here at St. Mary's? In the larger Catholic community?

2. How can there be a diversity of gifts and also unity in the church? Does St. Mary's possess both diversity and unity?

3. What are some of the ways in which you see the Holy Spirit equipping us for the purpose of Christian witness?

4. In what ways do you see yourself as God's servant in the world?

IV. The Church at Worship and Study. (Read Acts 2:41–47; 1 Corinthians 11:20–26.)
Questions to Ponder:

1. Do the members of St. Mary's place high value on the liturgy? If not, where does the problem lie?

2. Does St. Mary's place a high priority on the teaching and learning ministry from small children through adulthood?

3. What do you think it means to be a people holy to the Lord God?

V. The Purpose of the Church. (Read Matthew 10; Luke 4:18; 10:1–29.)

Questions to Ponder

1. Does St. Mary's understanding of mission separate the great commandment from the great commission? Is this theologically defendable for the church when both are grounded in our Lord's own ministry?

2. A good indication of the church's understanding of its nature and mission is the church budget. Study St. Mary's budget. What does it say about your church's understanding of its nature and purpose?

> Among the rich nations, we are number one in the percentage of children living below the poverty line (20%), number one in teenage pregnancies (one million a year and the latest census shows a marked increase), and number one in murders of males between 15 and 24 years old. In 1989, at least 900,000 children were physically or sexually abused. The number of children in foster care is now 340,000 and the number of homeless children is estimated to be 200,000. Twelve million children are uninsured and have little or no access to health care.

Chapter 15

Parochia Semper Reformanda

Cartoon of church sign: THE LITE CHURCH: 24 percent fewer commitments, home of the 7.5 percent tithe, 15 minute sermons, 45 minute worship services. We have only 8 Commandments—your choice. We use just 3 spiritual laws and have an 800 year millennium. Everything you've always wanted in a church—and less!

Deconstructing the Parish

The title of this chapter is, of course, a play on the ancient adage, *Ecclesia semper reformanda*: "The church is always in need of reformation." By changing the first word to "parish," I mean to call attention to the obvious fact that the parish continually needs to undergo change and renewal. Many parishes today are a far cry from the parishes of fifty years ago. As we pointed out in the first chapter, there have been large paradigm changes in ministry (clerical-lay collaboration), focus (not always Mass at the parish church, but prayer groups in homes), place (marketplace holiness), authority (more diffused and collegial), and dialogue (more voices being heard).

Changes and challenges continue. For example, I know several parishes that have boldly canceled the first three years of religious instruction for children and instead teach the parents. I know of a parish in Harlem, New York City, that has 200 baptisms a year and four marriages, so the parish concentrates on the meaning of baptism and helping single parents. It embraces the need for community and structure, and designates each Sunday as "Sunday Alive!" which means that religious and social activities go on all day long. So it goes: Many parishes are putting their emphasis on openness, healing, reconciliation, and justice issues. Virtually every parish I know of is involved in some ministry to the poor through twinning, soup kitchens, food banks, food and clothing collections, shelters, community outreach, and the like. People are involved as never before. Truly, the parish is alive. The parish has changed.

But, for some, not enough, particularly for those who see the parish being used as a consumerist enterprise. That is, they claim, people go there anonymously, put in their hour at Mass, take what they need (such as the sacraments for their children), and remain fundamentally unconverted. These critics call for the deconstruction of such parishes, by which they mean their metamorphosis, or reconfiguration, into intentional small Christian communities. For some, the whole issue has become a question of the parish versus such communities.

Balancing the Act

It's hard to argue with the critics and the arguments I cited in Chapter 11. The "parish of programs" is not adequate any more. Many parishes are large and anonymous and often out of touch with the needs of the people. Such parishes are hardly evangelizing, hardly compelling. Many still are in the mode of providing services, rather than building community where people gather to help one another and discern the meaning of their lives in the light of the gospel. Even the parish liturgy, as liturgist Father John Baldovin, S.J., has commented, has turned into entertainment rather than a deeply experienced communal event of worship and prayer.

Add to this the fierce economic and social pressures on the parish. The inner-city and the rural parishes are dying. The suburban parish is growing but sometimes growing into megachurches. And all parishes are facing the crisis of clergy shortage. An instance: In 1977, 44 parishes in Brooklyn, New York, were served by a total of 128 priests. These same parishes are today served by one priest each. As Father Richard McBrien remarks: "Either local communities will simply have to get along without the eucharist, or lay members themselves will assume eucharistic leadership and Catholicism in the United States will gradually be replaced by a new form of American high-church congregationalism." (See "The Shape of Things to Come" by Tim Unsworth in *The Critic*, Fall 1993.) These facts argue for the demise of the parish and new forms of Catholic life, such as small faith communities.

There is no question that small faith communities or intentional communities are an asset and, as I argued in Chapter 11, should be in every way encouraged and recognized. They are a potent factor in formation and

evangelization and I count them among the great developments of our time. Still, such small communities are not without danger. They can become ingrown, self-selective, exclusive, and particular (cut off from the universal church) and, to this extent, can accidentally betray the Catholic, universalist spirit. After all, the local parish, like Robert Frost's home, is a place that has to take everyone in—the good, bad, and indifferent.

Furthermore, the parish need not be only consumerist, although I feel we have to tolerate the consumers as much as we dislike their attitude. We have to reach out to them and challenge them because they're not the type of people to join small faith-sharing groups, and how else can we reach them, connect with them? How else, except on the occasion of a baptism, First Communion, or marriage, can we dialogue with them, challenge but not crush them?

In addition, there is something to be said for the mechanisms of the parish that can coordinate not only parish picnics, dances, trips, and rummage sales, but also clothing drives, food pantries, twinning, tithing, counseling, and large charitable enterprises. There's something to be said for a parish that can bring together diverse people for a common project. There is something to be said for a large meeting and worshiping place that gathers many from far and wide. There's something to be said for a parish that can be "home" to many singles, alienated, and dispossessed. There's something to be said for larger financial and social combined resources that help the community and go beyond the local community.

I would like to see the parish reconfigure into many small faith-sharing communities, and there is no reason why the polarizations cannot be handled. Small faith communities can keep firm the mechanisms that tie them to the parish church and the church universal. The parish can transcend its "programs only" and consumerist image by challenging the activists to consider why they're doing what they're doing, by providing a spiritual component to every project, by demanding that every ministry be itself a small faith-sharing reality.

I think the creative friction between the parish and the small group will be with us a while. I see the groups growing, but I also see a firm and lasting place for the parish. True, not the same old parish of 50 years ago, not even the same new parish of 25 years ago, but one that, while "always in need of reformation," will form a valuable and needed role in the life of the church.

Planning

As part of its ongoing reformation, a parish must constantly look to the wider view. The guiding emphasis of this view is one we don't examine too often—we just take it for granted: What are we all about? What are we, as a parish, here for? These questions seem obvious, but I am as convinced that we take them for granted as I am convinced that they should be asked at every parish council meeting. As an example of "getting back to basics," let me cite a survey that asked parishioners what were the two most important items they wanted to see in a parish. The first item, by a whopping 86%, said good Sunday liturgies. The second, by the same impressive percentage, said the spiritual formation of parishioners. When asked how effective their parishes were in

responding to these goals, 85% said that their parishes met the first goal but only 28% said their parishes met the second goal. What are we here for?

The wider view of a parish means basically having access to wide information. Every parish is a "plant" in that it must consider the very realistic operational costs of staff salaries, building costs (new or maintenance), and programs. Urban parishes, plagued by white flight and shifting demographics, reduced by falling baptisms and rising funerals, find that contributions do not match needs. To meet expenses, programs are cut (musicians, staff, teachers) and maintenance preventions are dropped. At some point, the parish needs to reflect on all that energy going into raising money and so little energy going into the mission of Jesus. At some point, that parish needs to see where it is situated in the larger community demographics and development. It needs information. It needs skills to discern what's going on with its neighboring parishes and neighborhoods. It needs experts to check out the larger community context. Above all, the parish needs clergy and staff who must *think* differently and be ready for radical changes. Else they'll continue to try to support buildings that are a burden to all and sell off the gospel in the interests of survival. Worse, they'll try to continue seeing the parish as it was in its heyday when power, prestige, and privilege ruled instead of loss, disdain, and drugs.

Again, the question has to be asked: What are we here for? Maybe the urban parish as it exists in some places has to die. Maybe a whole new approach has to be tried. Maybe the store-front church may be the place to begin. Maybe the small base communities that meet in homes have to return. What did the first Christians do before they had churches?

The suburban churches fare better in contributions, but often they are not enough to cover the interest debt. People in the suburbs tend not to register (until the kids need to register for religious instuction), so the clergy and staff need to be aware of the building that's going on and go knock on doors. These suburbanites are better educated and affluent, so they look for a good parish style and expect good homilies and liturgies. They do vote with their pocketbooks and their Mass attendance runs around 37%. But their needs expand and parishes do not see them or meet them or have enough information about them. Often the suburban parish has a school and finds 60-70% of its income going toward its support. Then the money raising starts. I know of one parish that has five bingos a week! I cringe at that when I realize that that means that the parish hall cannot be used for something more substantial those nights. I cringe that no one is noticing that the tail is wagging the dog, that the parish is now basically in the business of raising money. As one who believes totally in Catholic education, I simply say that such a picture has to be looked at, that perhaps that school and all parochial schools ought to be turned over to the laity and let the parish get on with its other work and mission.

The bottom line is to come back to our questions: What are we about? What's a parish for? The crying need is for leaders to be trained in those skills needed to meet the challenges. It is interesting to observe how exceedingly many theological and spiritual growth opportunities there are for church leaders and how many take advantage of them. It is equally interesting to observe how very few, if any, opportunities are offered to increase the skills needed for today's church and how few dioceses make use of planning and information services to help them gain the wider, broader view.

We desperately need leaders with creative skills and visions who are willing to change or renew the old structures. The old-time pastor will not do in today's church. The clerical caste system is an obstacle as its privilege is obsolete. The isolated rectory and convent are social and religious anachronisms.

I Was the Way

St. Luke tells us that Christianity, before it became Christianity, was called The Way. That means discipleship was a way of life requiring some dramatic changes. You might recall that the catechumens had to have an apprenticeship of many years before they could be received into the church. The least of that apprenticeship was instruction. The time, rather, was spent on scrutiny: Can the candidate hack it as a Christian? Witnesses were brought in to testify to his or her prayer life and charity. Certain occupations, such as serving in the military, were considered incompatible with being a follower of Christ. Public penitents in the early centuries often gave up their jobs to spend time repenting and were supported by the community. Disciples, in a word, were expected to be converted in the fullest sense of the word. They were expected to be different and often were persecuted for being so.

Well, we've come a long way. The old poster slogan comes to mind: If you were hauled into court for being a Christian, would you be released for lack of evidence?

What happened? What happened was that Christianity also grew up in a gnostic atmosphere where knowledge was considered crucial. Knowing the secret truth would set you free. So the emphasis on head knowledge began. Also, the Greeks were at it with their philosophical questions that had to be answered. The early church Fathers responded with reasoned replies and apologetics and unwittingly started a habit. The habit was to cast Christianity into intellectual terms only. An academic tradition grew up and great systems of thought. These were started by the early Fathers and picked up by the medieval schoolmen and found their way into our catechisms. Knowing the questions and answers were important; you were even graded on "religion." Of course, the tradition that one had to *act* as a disciple continued, and heroes and heroines were held up for emulation. But action got sidetracked, especially as Christianity went mainstream and became the dominant culture which people were simply born into, not converted into. This has led into a split between belief and action, between assent to truth and living out that truth radically.

Perhaps the great modern depiction is that famous scene from *The Godfather* where the camera cross-cuts between the simultaneous scenes of Michael's baby's baptism and the horrific, bloody slaughter of Michael's opponents. Michael and the Godfather certainly believed in and got a church baptism and a church funeral, but that they were acting as Christians becomes absurd in the very asking. The result, as youth are quick to remind us, is a church that is hardly credible. By virtue of the Phil Donahue Show and Oprah and the rest, youth are well acquainted with fraud, dishonesty, and sexual misconduct. They do not know of love, service, and heroism (although these certainly exist). They see a gap between the gospel preached and the gospel lived in their parishes. The average parish is not always a credible sign. Yet, they and we are drawn to what? To Weston Priory, Mother Teresa, the L'Arche community, and Taizé, the interdenominational monastery in France. Youth by the literal thousands traverse the land to make the Taizé pilgrimage where they find the word preached and lived.

An article dated October 10, 1993, from the *New York Times* front page, "Pilgrims Crowding Europe's Catholic Shrines," points out that so-called secularized Europe, whose churches indeed lay empty and where religious vocations have dwindled, is on a spiritual journey. Pilgrimages are growing, to the old venerable shrines of Lourdes, Santiago de Compostela in Spain, the basilicas of the Sacred Heart at Paray-le-Monial and St. Anne at Auray in France, as well as sites in the Netherlands, Portugal, and elsewhere. Is it a Catholic revival? Are the astonishing numbers of pilgrims a sign of disillusionment with all of the broken promises of politics and materialism? Is this a flocking to "warm" places where something more intense, more emotional occurs, a reaction to a cerebral liturgy our university liturgists have devised? Are the symbols—the Virgin, the Gregorian chant, the processions, the habits of the ecumenical monks at Taizé or the Benedictines at Weston Priory—more resonant of the transcendent than the more horizontal liturgy the average parish offers? What needs do Taizé and Lourdes meet? How does the parish measure up against this backdrop? Our survey at the beginning of this chapter tells us that, while most like their parish liturgies, few (28%) said they were spiritually formed there. Is our preoccupation with programs, money, building, and personnel diverting too much energy away from simple witnessing?

It was understandable that we were initially preoccupied with the focus on the revised Mass and participation and the presence of Christ in the congregation. Without meaning to, we often dropped the devotions and rituals and with them an outlet for feelings and expression. Sometimes we even disdained them. Yet, in my experience, people who will not worship at Mass, will come out in droves for a good mission or a procession. I have already cited the number of people who come to our grotto, to healing Masses, and attend the outdoor Stations of the Cross.

Mitch Finley, in *Living Prayer* (March/April 1993), remarks on how his children perceive Mass: "We don't call for a return to the old Latin Mass, but our kids' hankering for ringing bells tells us that the post-Vatican II liturgy is long on verbalizing, short on signs, symbols, and symbolic actions." Citing a study of fifteen liturgically reform-minded parishes by Lawrence Madden, S.J., from the Georgetown Center for Liturgy, he noted that scholars commented on the impact of scripture on people's lives and an increased sense of being gathered as the Body of Christ. That was the positive news. The negative news was that "the study revealed that there doesn't seem to be much depth to most people's participation in the Mass. . . . The scholars who examined the data the Center collected noted 'what may be a certain shallowness and a loss of the sense of

the transcendence of God' in the Mass."

That's why I've often thought that at one place at least, at the beginning of the Our Father, the celebrant should also turn and face front, in the same direction the people are, in an expression that the *whole* congregation is in a united gesture not facing one another, but all facing toward the Other.

Again, I ask if the lack of a sense of spiritual formation and transcendence is behind our failure to move religion from a belief to a practice? Liberation theology, for all of its limitations and failures, has taught us once again that being a disciple demands a change of life and heart, that to witness requires tangible signs. Pope Paul VI in his encyclical on Evangelization (*Evangelii Nuntiandi*, no. 76) asks:

> Either tacitly or aloud—but always forcefully—we are being asked: Do you really believe what you are proclaiming? Do you love what you believe? Do you really preach what you live? The witness of life has become more than ever an essential condition for real effectiveness in preaching.

Because we have so concentrated on knowledge alone (catechism instructions, oaths against modernism, professions of faith, etc.), we have a serious problem now with Catholic identity. Church leaders are far more preoccupied with and troubled with what they consider unorthodox beliefs than by unorthodox conduct. The chancery will come down heavily on any priest who publicly denies the Trinity, but not at all if he is uncharitable or self-serving or even merely inadequate as a pastor. Senator Edward

Kennedy and Madonna are both Catholics. So are the people in the pew who are not challenged as to whether being a disciple of Jesus has any bearing at all on the size of the house they live in, the hours they watch television, the ingrained consumerism they indulge in, the number of children they have, or the decisions they make at work. Indeed, to raise these questions is to evoke protests to keep "politics" out of religion. This leaves us with no distinctions—not even the old meat-on-Friday abstinence or Mass attendance. There is, truth to be told, only one criterion for being Catholic and that is to be baptized into the same church as the pope. Period.

But, as Michael Warren says, "The fact remains that religions are not simply ways of thinking; they are also ways of living. . . .To believe is to practice. . . . We become Christians by acting as Christians." He also gives us a good practical guide for an examination of conscience. One's life structure and one's life values are readily found in:

•one's checkbook

•in a list of the things one has read over the past week or month

•in what one watches on television, or how one watches it, or whether one watches

•in the tickets one buys and for what

•in one's phone bill

•in the kinds of liquids one consumes and under what circumstances

•in one's credit card statement

•in one's ways of spending leisure time

•in the patterns of eating

•in the mileage of one's commute to work or school

•in one's pattern of religious practice or lack of it.

The point of all this is that it is a rare parish or parish council that asks itself whether it is prophetic or not. It is a rare preacher who not only challenges his flock but offers them concrete ways of being a disciple. It is a rare parish that makes any demands of conduct for fear of being regarded as rigid, dictatorial, or old church—and indeed abuses never lurk far behind any challenge. But as we have striven in this manual to offer suggestions that might make a parish more hospitable, appealing, active, and collaborative, we have to ask ourselves, "Why?" We are always tempted to make any enterprise a "success." We like to "run a tight ship" and have a good reputation and brag about our parish. But the overall judgment of Matthew 25 hangs over each parish and each parishioner, and any success must be measured against that. A parish is a collective Christian that must do Christian things. We have to ask ourselves whether we spend as much time teaching people how to live the faith as we do in how to understand the faith.

In her book *On Pilgrimage* Dorothy Day looks back on her life and writes:

Children look at things very directly and simply. I did not see anyone taking off his coat and giving it to the poor. I didn't see anyone having a banquet and calling in the lame, the halt and the blind. And those who were doing it, like the Salvation Army, did not appeal to me. I wanted, though I did not know it then, a synthesis. I wanted a life and I wanted abundant life. I wanted it for others too. I did not want just the few, the missionary-minded people like the Salvation Army, to be kind to the poor, as the poor. I wanted every home to be opened to the lame, the halt and the blind, the way it had been open after the San Francisco earthquake. Only then did people really live, really love their brothers. In such love was the abundant life and I did not have the slightest idea how to find it.

We have to challenge our ministers to find conversion in their ministries. We have to redesign our rectories and perhaps even jettison them in favor of real neighborhood living. We surely have to redesign our clergy and our pastoral leaders so they think and see in a new way. We have, most of all, to redesign our bishops, allowing no one to rule over us who has not tasted the streets and tested the community (and been tested *by* the community!). We have to be open to those people who know how community works, who offer the charts and graphs and projections in the service of the gospel.

Look, for example, at these sobering 1993 statistics from the *Official Catholic Directory* for the United States. Then compare them to ten and 25 years ago.

	1993	1983	1968
Catholic population:	59, 220,723	52,088,744	47,468,333
Hierarchy:	402	370	267
Priests:	51,052	57,870	59,803
Women religious	94,022	109, 699	176,340
Seminarians	5, 891	12, 054	39,838
Teaching priests, sisters, scholastics, and brothers:	20,528	41,074	116,893

You have to really pause over these figures and see the severe crisis that confronts the church. We have not even noted, for example, the mean age of the priests, which is around 63. This aging is true for the religious as well. Think of the drastic downsizing of any comparable group in the United States—say, teachers, doctors, nurses, or engineers—and you get a sense the absolute panic the country would be in. The last two categories in the chart are astounding; there is no one behind the current clergy to replace them. Who will lead us to new forms of ministry and ordination? We need such bald and searing statistics to force us into reflection and action. Perhaps we even need to consider that our present crisis is a cleansing action prompting us to take a look at the overgrowths of the centuries that have choked off the gospel and are forcing us to go back to the roots of our faith: the Christ who had no place to lay his head, but who was the freest of all to announce the Good News.

Yes, our durable parish will endure. How it will endure will be up to us. What kind of a parish we can pass on to our youth who are leaving it in droves is up to people of vision.

Connections

A final aspect of the ongoing reformation of the parish is, first, to hold fast to a sense of connectedness. Once more, we must see the parish not as a totally independent unit, but as part of the overall expression of the church. If indeed the parish has its own validity and is not a mere subdivision of General Headquarters, as I argued in the first chapter, it is, nevertheless, connected. That is why, even in earliest times, when the people put forth their own candidates for bishop, that candidate was consecrated by three other bishops to demonstrate the solidarity of the whole church.

Parenthetically, don't fail to note the admirable idea of the community choosing its own leaders. Some quotes worth remembering: "Let him be ordained as bishop who has been chosen by all the people...by the consent of all, let the bishops lay their hands upon him" says the 3rd century *Apostolic Tradition* of Hippolytus. Pope St. Celestine in the 5th century wrote, "Let a bishop not be imposed on the people whom they do not want"; and his successor, Pope St. Leo, wrote, "He who has to preside over all must be elected by all. . . . Let a person not be ordained against the wish of the Christians and whom they have not explicitly asked for." (We should also pause and reflect on the complete, very recent, novelty of the pope alone appointing all bishops.)

All this meant that the community could propose its leaders, but not be the ultimate source of its ministers. Thus Schillebeeckx:

"There is an ancient awareness that no Christian community can call itself autonomously the ultimate source of its own ministers"(*Ministry*, 1981); Kenan Osborne: "Any suggestion that originally there was a completely democratic or congregational Christian community cannot be authenticated" (*Priesthood*, 1988, p. 146); and, finally, Bernard Cooke:

Is it humanly possible to have a unified grouping of humans, no matter how idealistically Christian they might be, without some organization? Is it possible to avoid chaos and consequent effectiveness in ministerial activity unless there is some authoritative direction? The response to both questions is an obvious "no." Among the charisms given to individuals by Christ's Spirit for the sake of the community's life and mission is the charism of governance, a clear recognition that able administration of the structured elements of the church's life is a gift to be cherished. This means that those who are in directive positions must possess the power and authority needed to guide and unify the community, and to some extent at least this involves something like jurisdiction (*That They Might Live*, ed. Michael Downey, New York: Crossroad, 1991, p. 87).

So, we—even if the smallest parish in the Kansas plains—do belong to something more. We belong to a larger family, to a chain and linkage of authority and fellow pilgrims. We are not our own source (the basic sin of pride); we are joined, connected, inextricably bonded to all those who have lived before us, are with us now, and will come after us in every earthly and heavenly realm. They supply what we cannot. They utter prayers we cannot groan. We're a large, encompassing brotherhood and sisterhood beyond time and space (which necessarily makes it impossible to practice racism or sexism of any kind. Or it should). So, each parish is connected and that notion should be cherished.

Second, my personal opinion is that the modern church architecture, which is so anxious to focus (correctly) solely on the altar, does us a disservice by omitting statues, murals, and stained-glass windows of the saints. I'd rather worship in a church replete with saints and other "clouds of witnesses"—even poorly executed ones—than an antiseptic, sterile building that tells me I'm all alone.

Third, I give three tiny cheers for the hierarchy. Not the media and often actual hierarchy of ineptitude, fumbling, and regressiveness, not the hierarchy I have criticized, but the hierarchy as such. The parish priest—yes, even a bumbling one—is a living symbol of the bishop and therefore of all those other worldwide bishops, including the bishop of Rome, that reminds us of our connectedness, past, present, and future. A hierarchical church is pretty good and not a bad design. Abuses of power, corruption, and scandal have sullied it, and the maddening habit (policy) of appointing people from administration or ivy tower universities and seminaries or of a conservative bent, and avoiding like the plague the prophets, drives me wild and flies in the face of the wise words of the popes cited above. We've *got* to get back to having more say concerning our leaders,

and the secrecy of those three names for potential future bishops that every current bishop sends to Rome is intolerable without widespread consensus. But, aside from such frustrations, the hierarchy reminds us of our catholicity.

Besides, in a cynical mood, I can reflect that, although Catholics get regularly ridiculed for having a hierarchy, they are reveling in freedom compared to others who protest no hierarchy but would not make a move without consulting the latest directive from Geraldo, Donahue, Calvin Klein, and the current Rappers as how to think, dress, and speak. I've known ministers and rabbis (not to mention politicians and university presidents) who out-pope the pope on a daily basis with their infallible pronouncements and intolerant postures. Everyone has a hierarchy. It's a matter of which one you want.

The Catholic Parish

I guess all I'm sharing in this final chapter is that, even if we follow every suggestion in this manual, even if we do so with great success, we are still doing these things as church, as a people whose lives, liturgy, and sacraments are fundamentally and irradicably communal, both horizontally and vertically. We exist for others and the parish is a sign (sacrament) of that. Whatever face of Christ we wear, from the middle-class, all white suburban parish or the multifaced visage of the inner city, we are a part of something larger. We are not engaged in making *this* parish a success. We are engaged in being church, being Christ, of pointing to the Kingdom. We are part of the mighty chorus, the Communion of Saints, the Mystical Body of Christ.

A manual such as this tries to help a

parish community come alive. It suggests some attitudes and ideas that engage people, draws on their talents and helps them sense that they are the church wherever they are. We just have to keep reminding them that, although located in this time and place, they are cosmic actors and bearers of grace which, as Karl Rahner reminds us, occurs when people laugh, cry, stand up for what is right, hope against hope, accept responsibility, refuse to be embittered by the stupidities of life, and live in opposition to selfishness and despair. A parish is a good place to celebrate all of this.

Resources

Why Be Catholic? by William O'Malley, S.J. (New York: Crossroad, 1993). Grab this one. ACTA Publications produces a lot of material for helping parishes: 4848 N. Clark St., Chicago, IL 60640.

A burglar stalked the neighborhood watching for homes left unguarded by people leaving for vacation. He watched this particular family load suitcases into their car and drive away. Being a seasoned burglar, he waited till dark and then approached the front door and rang the bell. Good. No answer.

The burglar deftly picked the lock and let himself it. He called out in the darkness: "Is anybody home?" He was absolutely stunned to hear a voice reply, "I see you—and Jesus sees you too." Terrified, the burglar called out, "Who's there?" But again, the voice came back, "I see you and Jesus sees you too."

The burglar switched on his flashlight and aimed it in the direction of the voice. He broke into a smile, instantly relieved, when his light revealed a caged parrot reciting the refrain, "I see you and Jesus sees you too." He chuckled to himself, found the wall switch, switched off his flashlight and put on the room lights.

Then he saw it. Beneath the parrot's cage was the biggest Doberman pinscher he had ever seen in his life. Then the parrot looked at the dog and said, "Attack, Jesus, attack!"

To all who have read this manual and who hopefully have been fired and inspired, my advice is to face the parish—and "attack!"

Ministry to others and for others really begins at the intersection between God and his people revealed in their stories and conversations. But if, on the contrary, ministry is seen as *serving* others, then disdain is not far behind. You serve and they do not respond. "No one turns out for anything," you complain. The people must be—are—indifferent and apathetic. How can you love such an uncooperative and unappreciative people? And all that you do for them!

But if you leave this "serving" concept of people behind, and instead seek to enter into their conversations and stories, then you will be one with them. It will not be you and them, but we. We see this most dramatically in that well-known story of Damien. We remember that frightening moment when he put his foot into the hot water after a futile day's evangelizing and felt nothing, the unmistakable sign of leprosy. That Sunday he got in the pulpit and did not begin with his customary "You lepers" but with "*We* lepers. . . ." From that point on, his unsuccessful ministry is electric, fruitful beyond his wildest dreams. He has now entered their conversation. *He* is their story and once more a word has been made flesh, however leprous, and dwelt among people.

—William J. Bausch, *Storytelling: Faith and Imagination* (Mystic, Conn.: Twenty-Third Publications, 1984).

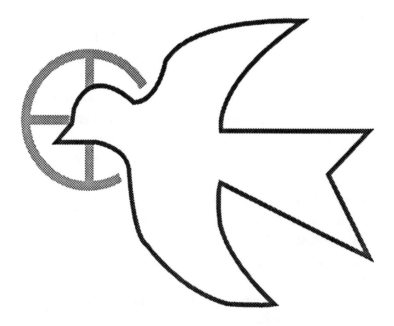

Parish Papers

Documents
Fliers
Ceremonies
Letters

Documents

Called and Gifted
The American Catholic Laity

Reflections of the American Bishops Commemorating the Fifteenth Anniversary of the Issuance of the *Decree on the Apostolate of the Laity*

November 13, 1980
National Conference of Catholic Bishops

(Reprinted with permission)

Introduction

Among the most enduring contributions of the Second Vatican Council is its description of the Church as the People of God.

> This was to be the new People of God. For, those who believe in Christ, who are reborn not from a perishable but from an imperishable seed through the Word of the living God (cf. I Pt 1:23), not from the flesh but from water and the Holy Spirit (cf. Jn 3:5-6), are finally established as "a chosen race, a royal priesthood, a holy nation, a purchased people. . . . You who in times past were not a people, but are now the people of God" (I Pt 2:9-10), (*Lumen Gentium*, 9).

This image, drawing on a rich biblical and historical tradition, gives marvelous expression to the role of the Church as the sign of the Kingdom of God. It was this kingdom which Jesus came to announce and to inaugurate by his life, death, and resurrection. "After John's arrest, Jesus appeared in Galilee proclaiming the good news of God. 'This is the time of fulfillment. The reign of God is at hand. Reform your lives and believe in the gospel' "(Mk 1:14-16).

Jesus established the Church to bear witness to God's kingdom especially by the way his followers would live as the People of God. "This is my commandment: love one another as I have loved you" (Jn 15:12).

The image of the People of God has many dimensions; its meaning is best grasped through a variety of experiences. Each sheds light on the whole and enables us to appreciate and live it more deeply.

At the present time the light shed on the meaning of the People of God by the laity is especially noteworthy and exciting. In an exercise of our charism of "bringing forth from the treasury of Revelation new things and old" (*Lumen Gentium*, 25), we bishops praise the Lord for what is happening among the laity and proclaim as well as we can what we have been experiencing and learning from them.

While focusing on the laity, we wish to address the whole Church. We affirm the vision of the Second Vatican Council and the importance it gives to the laity. We look forward to what is still to come under the guidance of the Holy Spirit, making the Church more and more the perfect image of Christ. We also acknowledge that these continuing developments may require new concepts, new terminology, new attitudes, and new practices. In prayerful dialogue with all our sisters and brothers we are prepared to make those changes which will aid in building the kingdom.

The Call to Adulthood

As the *Decree on the Apostolate of the Laity* of Vatican II says:

> Indeed, everyone should painstakingly ready himself or herself personally for the apostolate, especially as an adult. For the advance of age brings with it better self-knowledge, thus enabling each person to evaluate more accurately the talents with which God has enriched each soul and to exercise more effectively those charismatic gifts which the Holy Spirit has bestowed on all for the good of others (30).

One of the chief characteristics of lay men and women today is their growing sense of being adult members of the Church. Adulthood implies knowledge, experience and awareness, freedom and responsibility, and mutuality in relationships. It is true, however, that the experience of lay persons "as Church members" has not always reflected this understanding of adulthood. Now, thanks to the impetus of the Second Vatican Council, lay women and men feel themselves called to exercise the same mature interdependence and practical self-direction which characterize them in other areas of life.

We note the response of many lay persons to different opportunities for faith development. There is the "coming to faith in Jesus" and a strengthening of commitment to him and his mission which we commonly call evangelizaton. There is also the adult catechesis movement which allows persons to grow and deepen their faith, and there are those who in faith are seeking greater understanding through theological reflection. These and other adult lay persons have taken responsibility in their parish or diocese by serving in leadership positions on committees and boards.

Adult Christian living is also noticeable, though not always as publicized, in the daily struggle to live out Christian values in family, neighborhood, school, government, and work. This is a hopeful sign because the laity are uniquely present in and to the world and so bear a privileged position to build the Kingdom of God there. "You are the light of the world. . . .Your light must shine before all so that they may see goodness in your acts and give praise to your heavenly Father" (Mt 5:14-16).

The adult character of the People of God flows from baptism and confirmation which are the foundation of the Christian life and ministry. They signify initiation into a community of believers who, according to their state of life, respond to God's call to holiness and accept responsibility for the ministry of the Church.

The Call to Holiness

> Thus it is evident to everyone that all the faithful of Christ of whatever rank or status are called to the fullness of the Christian life and to the perfection of charity. By this holiness a more human way of life is promoted even in this earthly society (*Lumen Gentium*, 40).

The Second Vatican Council clearly proclaimed the universal call to holiness. Not only are lay people included in God's call to holiness, but theirs is a unique call requiring a unique response which itself is a gift of the Holy Spirit. It is characteristic that lay men and women hear the call to holiness in the very web of their existence (*Lumen Gentium*, 31), in and through the events of the world, the pluralism of modern living, the complex decisions and conflicting values they must struggle with, the richness and fragility of sexual relationships, the delicate balance between activity and still-ness, presence and privacy, love and loss.

The response of lay people to this call promises to contribute still more to the spiritual heritage of the Church. Already the laity's hunger for God's word is everywhere evident. Increasingly, lay men and women are seeking spiritual formation and direction in deep ways of prayer. This has helped to spur several renewal movements.

These developments present a challenge to the parish because, for the most part, the spiritual needs of lay people must be met in the parish. The parish must be a home where they can come together with their leaders for mutual spir-itual enrichment, much as in the early Church: "They devoted themselves to the apostles' instruction and the communal life, to the breaking of bread and the prayers" (Acts 2:42).

We call special attention to the effect this should have on liturgy. The quality of worship depends in great mea-sure on the spiritual life of all present. As lay women and men cultivate their own proper response to God's call to holiness, this should come to expression in the communal worship of the Church.

Simultaneously, as lay persons assume their roles in liturgical celebration according to the gifts of the Spirit bestowed on them for that purpose, the ordained celebrant will be more clearly seen as the one who presides over the community, bringing together the diverse talents of the community as a gift to the Father.

Whatever else the growing spiritual life of the commu-nity entails, it certainly means more intense sharing among the whole People of God of the gifts of the Spirit. And this we wish to reinforce.

The Call to Ministry

From the reception of these charisms or gifts, including those which are less dramatic, there arise for each believer the right and duty to use them in the Church and the world for the good of humankind and for the upbuilding of the Church (*Decree on the Apostolate of the Laity*, 3).

Baptism and confirmation empower all believers to share in some form of ministry. Although the specific form of participation in ministry varies according to the gifts of the Holy Spirit, all who share in this work are united with one another. "Just as each of us has one body with many members, and not all the members have the same function, so too we, though many, are one body in Christ and individually mem-bers of one another. We have gifts that differ according to the favor bestowed on each of us" (Rom 12:4-6).

This unity in the ministry should be especially evident in the relationships between laity and clergy as lay men and women respond to the call of the Spirit in their lives. The clergy help to call forth, identify, coordinate, and affirm the diverse gifts bestowed by the Spirit. We applaud this solidar-ity between laity and clergy as their most effective ministry and witness to the world.

Christian Service Ministry in the World

The laity, by their vocation, seek the Kingdom of God by engaging in temporal affairs, and by ordering them accord-ing to the plan of God (*Lumen Gentium*, 31).

Christian service in the world is represented in a preemi-nent way by the laity. It is sometimes called the "ministry of the laity" and balances the concept of ministry found in the ecclesial ministerial services. Because of lay persons, Chris-tian service or ministry broadly understood includes civic and public activity, response to the imperatives of peace and justice, and resolution of social, political, and economic con-flicts, especially as they influence the poor, oppressed, and minorities.

The whole Church faces unprecedented situations in the contemporary world, and lay people are at the cutting edge of these new challenges. It is they who engage directly in the task of relating Christian values and practices to complex questions such as those of business ethics, political choice, economic security, quality of life, cultural development, and family planning.

Really new situations, especially in the realm of social justice, call for creative responses. We know that the Spirit moves among all the People of God, prompting them accord-ing to their particular gifts and offices, to discern anew the signs of the times and to interpret them boldly in light of the Gospel. Lay women and men are in a unique position to offer this service.

Just as by divine institution bishops, priests, and deacons have been given through ordination authority to exercise leadership as servants of God's people, so through baptism and confirmation lay men and women have been given rights and responsibilities to participate in the mission of the Church. In those areas of life in which they are uniquely present and within which they have special competency be-cause of their particular talents, education, and experience, they are an extension of the Church's redeeming presence in the world. Recognition of lay rights and responsibilities should not create a divisiveness between clergy and laity but should express the full range of the influence of the People of God. We see this and affirm it.

Ministry in the Church

As sharers in the role of Christ the Priest, the Prophet, and the King, the laity have an active part to play in the life and activity of the Church (*Decree on the Apostolate of the Laity*, 10).

Since the Second Vatican Council new opportunities have developed for lay men and women to serve in the Church. We acknowledge gratefully the continuing and increasing contributions of volunteers and part time work-ers who serve on parish and diocesan councils, boards of education, and financial, liturgical, and ecumenical com-mittees, as well as those who exercise roles such as special minister of the Eucharist, catechist, and pastoral assistant.

We are grateful, too, for the large numbers of lay people who have volunteered and are serving in the missions.

Growing numbers of lay women and men are also preparing themselves professionally to work in the Church. In this regard religious sisters and brothers have shown the way with their initiative and creativity.

Ecclesial ministers, i.e. lay persons who have prepared for professional ministry in the Church, represent a new development. We welcome this as a gift to the Church. There are also persons who serve the Church by the witness of their lives and their self-sacrificing service and empowerment of the poor in works such as administration, housing, job development, and education. All these lay ministers are undertaking roles which are not yet clearly spelled out and which are already demanding sacrifices and risks of them and their families. As lay persons increasingly engage in ecclesial ministry, we recognize and accept the responsibility of working out practical difficulties such as the availability of positions, the number of qualified applicants, procedures for hiring, just wages, and benefits.

Special mention must be made of women who in the past have not always been allowed to take their proper role in the Church's ministry. We see the need for an increased role for women in ministries of the Church to the extent possible. We recognize the tensions and misunderstandings which arise on this question, but we wish to face these as part of a sincere attempt to become true communities of faith.

The combination of all these responses to the challenges of our time proclaims the interrelated oneness of ministry as a gift of the Spirit, and we rejoice in this.

The Call to Community

For from the wedlock of Christians there comes the family, in which new citizens of human society are born. By the grace of the Holy Spirit received in baptism these are made children of God, thus perpetuating the People of God through the centuries. The family is, so to speak, the domestic Church (*Lumen Gentium*, 11).

Most lay persons have a primary identification with family. This influences their expectations of and contributions to the Church as the People of God. The family, as a way of life, is often taken as a model for the Church. In most families life is interdependent. Ideally, strengths and weaknesses are blended so that a growthful atmosphere is maintained.

And yet we must frankly admit that failure occurs, that in many families the ideal is not reached. For example, divorce and neglect are realities. The parish has a vital contribution to make to all families struggling to be faith communities, for the parish can serve as a model and resource for families.

Because lay women and men do experience intimacy, support, acceptance, and availability in family life, they seek the same in their Christian communities. This is leading to a review of parish size, organization, priorities, and identity. It has already led to intentional communities, basic Christian communities, and some revitalized parish communities.

It is likely that this family characteristic of the laity will continue to influence and shape the community life of Christians. If it does, this should enable the clergy to give the kind of overall leadership which their office requires. Such trends are welcome in the Church.

Conclusion

The Church is to be a sign of God's kingdom in the world. The authenticity of that sign depends on all the people: laity, religious, deacons, priests, and bishops. Unless we truly live as the People of God, we will not be much of a sign to ourselves or the world.

We are convinced that the laity are making an indispensable contribution to the experience of the People of God and that the full import of their contribution is still in a beginning form in the post-Vatican II Church. We have spoken in order to listen. It is not our intention rigidly to define or control, to sketch misleading dreams, or bestow false praise. We bishops wish simply to take our place and exercise our role among the people of God. We now await the next word.

Prepared by the Secretariat for the Laity, National Conference of Catholic Bishops.

Publication No. 727-8
Office for Publishing and Promotion Services
United States Catholic Conference
Washington, D.C.

ISBN 1-55586-727-8

Census Taker _____

Name   Phone

St. Mary's Parish
Colts Neck, N.J.

Perhaps it's best to start off with the sensitive issue of locating your status in the parish. Two reasons for this, especially for anyone in "D" category, are (1) there are so many families that wish to join us from outside the parish boundaries that we could make room for if we knew for sure that some families in the parish no longer wished to be identified with it; (2) it might give us the chance, if so desired, to dialogue and renew ourselves with those who may have drifted for some reason or other.

So, please check off one of the categories below. If you check the first three, then proceed to fill out the Census Form on the other side.

___ A. I (we) am a registered parishioner and desire to continue as such. We attend church worship every weekend.

___ B. I (we) am a registered parishioner and desire to continue as such even though I (we) do not attend church worship every weekend.

___ C. I (we) am a registered parishioner, but no longer go to church at all. I (we) wish, however, to continue to remain on the parish files and mailing list.

If you wish, would you explain why you no longer attend church? _____
_____
_____

___ D. I (we) am a registered parishioner, but do not bother with church any more. I (we) wish to be removed from the parish register, files and mailing list.

If you wish, would you explain why? _____
_____

Name_____Address_____

___ E. I (we) am not registered in the parish and never have been. However, I would like to register here and now with this census form.

NOTE: "E" does not automatically register you. Fill out the other side, but acceptance of the form will be determined by the pastor.

Detach here and give to your census taker in a sealed envelope.

Census Taker_____ Today's Date_____

St. Mary's Parish Census
Colts Neck, N.J.

Full Name_____ Phone No._____

Mailing Address_____

Occupation_____ Birth Date_____
(month, day, year)

Status:

___ Single   ___ Married (if wife, insert Maiden name here)

___ Widowed   ___ Separated   ___ Divorced & Single   ___ Divorced & Remarried

___ Religion   ___ Baptized   ___ First Communion   ___ Confirmed

Attend Mass: ___ Regularly   ___ Occasionally   ___ Never

If Married:

Was your marriage witnessed by a Catholic priest?   ___ Yes ___ No

Husband's (or wife's maiden) Name_____

Occupation _____ Birth Date_____

___ Religion   ___ Baptized   ___ First Communion   ___ Confirmed

Attend Mass: ___ Regularly   ___ Occasionally   ___ Never

Children 18 & Under Including Those Away From School. Over 18 Fill Out Own Form.

Name	Birth date	Rel.	Baptized	1st Comm.	Conf.	School	Grade

Other parishioners, relatives, boarders living with you. (Indicate with note whether any of these is disabled, a shut-in, or ill.)

Name	Birth date	Rel.	Baptized	1st Comm.	Conf.	Relationship

St. Mary Church
COLTS NECK · NEW JERSEY

SECTION I

This questionnaire is anonymous (no names please) so that you can respond as honestly as you can. Put a check mark next to the one (and only one) statement that best reflects how you feel. You'll notice that there are three sets of the same statements marked Person A, Person B and Person C. This is so that at least three people in your house can also express their opinion if they care to. Your census taker will pick up this questionnaire also—unless you prefer to mail it in.

1. I find most meaning in attending Mass at:

Person A	Person B	Person C
___ St. Mary's	___ St. Mary's	___ St. Mary's
___ another local church	___ another local church	___ another local church
___ a local chapel or college campus	___ a local chapel or college campus	___ a local chapel or college campus
___ a church in another	___ town a church in another town	___ a church in another town

2. At Mass I most prefer:

Person A	Person B	Person C
___ no music	___ no music	___ no music
___ only organ music	___ only organ music	___ only organ music
___ the choir singing	___ the choir singing	___ the choir singing
___ folk music	___ folk music	___ folk music
___ congregational singing	___ congregational singing	___ congregational singing

3. I would most prefer to learn about my faith by:

Person A	Person B	Person C
___ reading more about it	___ reading more about it	___ reading more about it
___ through a sermon	___ through a sermon	___ through a sermon
___ attending parish lectures	___ attending parish lectures	___ attending parish lectures
___ discussion groups	___ discussion groups	___ discussion groups

4. The last time I talked with my parish priest in person or over the phone was:

Person A	Person B	Person C
___ in the past 2 days	___ in the past 2 days	___ in the past 2 days

___ in the past week ___ in the past week ___ in the past week

___ in the past month ___ in the past month ___ in the past month

___ in the past 6 months ___ in the past 6 months ___ in the past 6 months

___ in the past 5 or more years ___ in the past 5 or more years ___ in the past 5 or more years

___ never ___ never ___ never

5. The last time I went to Communion was:

Person A **Person B** **Person C**

___ in the past week ___ in the past week ___ in the past week

___ in the past month ___ in the past month ___ in the past month

___ in the past 6 months ___ in the past 6 months ___ in the past 6 months

___ in the past 12 months ___ in the past 12 months ___ in the past 12 months

___ in the past 5 years ___ in the past 5 years ___ in the past 5 years

___ more than 5 years ago ___ more than 5 years ago ___ more than 5 years ago

6. The last time I went to confession (private or communal—circle one) was:

Person A **Person B** **Person C**

___ in the past week ___ in the past week ___ in the past week

___ in the past month ___ in the past month ___ in the past month

___ in the past 6 months ___ in the past 6 months ___ in the past 6 months

___ in the past 12 months ___ in the past 12 months ___ in the past 12 months

___ in the past 5 years ___ in the past 5 years ___ in the past 5 years

___ more than 5 years ago ___ more than 5 years ago ___ more than 5 years ago

7. Being a Roman Catholic in today's times is:

Person A **Person B** **Person C**

___ extremely difficult ___ extremely difficult ___ extremely difficult

___ very difficult ___ very difficult ___ very difficult

___ difficult but worth it ___ difficult but worth it ___ difficult but worth it

___ easy ___ easy ___ easy

___ very easy ___ very easy ___ very easy

8. My feeling about St. Mary's Parish is:

Person A	Person B	Person C
___ very good	___ very good	___ very good
___ good	___ good	___ good
___ fair	___ fair	___ fair
___ poor	___ poor	___ poor
___ indifferent	___ indifferent	___ indifferent

9. The sermons given by Father Mokrzyciki at St. Mary's are generally:

Person A	Person B	Person C
___ very good	___ very good	___ very good
___ good	___ good	___ good
___ fair	___ fair	___ fair
___ poor	___ poor	___ poor
___ indifferent	___ indifferent	___ indifferent

10. The sermons given by Father Williams at St. Mary's are generally:

Person A	Person B	Person C
___ very good	___ very good	___ very good
___ good	___ good	___ good
___ fair	___ fair	___ fair
___ poor	___ poor	___ poor
___ indifferent	___ indifferent	___ indifferent

11. The sermons give by Father Bausch at St. Mary's are generally:

Person A	Person B	Person C
___ very good	___ very good	___ very good
___ good	___ good	___ good
___ fair	___ fair	___ fair
___ poor	___ poor	___ poor
___ indifferent	___ indifferent	___ indifferent

12. The music at Mass (cantors, organists, congregational singing) is generally:

Person A	Person B	Person C
___ very good	___ very good	___ very good
___ good	___ good	___ good
___ fair	___ fair	___ fair
___ poor	___ poor	___ poor
___indifferent	___ indifferent	___ indifferent

13. The lectors are generally:

Person A	Person B	Person C
___ very good	___ very good	___ very good
___ good	___ good	___ good
___ fair	___ fair	___ fair
___ poor	___ poor	___ poor
___indifferent	___ indifferent	___ indifferent

14. The parish CCD program is generally:

Person A	Person B	Person C
___ very good	___ very good	___ very good
___ good	___ good	___ good
___ fair	___ fair	___ fair
___ poor	___ poor	___ poor
___indifferent	___ indifferent	___ indifferent

15. The banners, flowers, decorations for special feasts and occasions are generally:

Person A	Person B	Person C
___ very good	___ very good	___ very good
___ good	___ good	___ good
___ fair	___ fair	___ fair
___ poor	___ poor	___ poor
___ indifferent	___ indifferent	___ indifferent

16. The Parish Organizations (the Rosary Guild and Men's Guild) are generally:

Person A	Person B	Person C
__ very good	__ very good	__ very good
__ good	__ good	__ good
__ fair	__ fair	__ fair
__ poor	__ poor	__ poor
__ indifferent	__ indifferent	__ indifferent

17. I believe in:

a) A Personal God	__ yes	__ no	__ unsure
b) Jesus as divine Son of God	__ yes	__ no	__ unsure
c) Heaven	__ yes	__ no	__ unsure
d) Sacraments as occasions of union with God	__ yes	__ no	__ unsure
e) God's assistance is available:	__ yes	__ no	__ unsure
f) Jesus' resurrection	__ yes	__ no	__ unsure
g) Existence of hell	__ yes	__ no	__ unsure
h) Our redemption through Christ	__ yes	__ no	__ unsure
i) the Church as a community of believers	__ yes	__ no	__ unsure

18. I have thoughts of agreement or disagreement with the following:

a) responsibility to share with those who have less	__ agree	__ disagree
b) responsibility to oppose injustice	__ agree	__ disagree
c) moral convictions affect work	__ agree	__ disagree
d) Church rules are no longer clear	__ agree	__ disagree
e) Confused about Church's teachings	__ agree	__ disagree
f) Church's rules are too inflexible	__ agree	__ disagree

And now, if you will, just a few fill-ins (where they apply). Other household members can copy these statements on another piece of paper and attach them to this if they wish.

19. Something I've always wanted to say to the pastor is this: _____

_____

_____

_____

20. What do you think of the pastor? _____
_____
_____
_____

21. What do you think of the Associate Pastor? (Sister Claire)?_____
_____
_____
_____

22. If you marked any of the preceding pages as only fair, poor, or indifferent, can you give suggestions for improvement? (Identify area) _____
_____
_____
_____

23. I think the parish should:_____
_____
_____
_____

24. I think the biggest problem we the people have to face today is:_____
_____
_____
_____

25. Something we never hear preached from the pulpit—and we should—is:_____
_____
_____
_____

26. Given the rising cost of construction and the cost of energy, do you think we should reconsider the erection of a parish Center?   ___ yes   ___ no

27. Any other comments?_____
_____
_____
_____

SECTION II

A Stewardship of Time, Talent and Treasure

Dear Friends,

We have a small and intimate community here at St. Mary's. We celebrate and share many things. Interaction seems to be quite high and we have enough events and activities to keep Madison Square Garden on the move.

Although so many people, as you well know, are involved in parish activities we feel that we've come to the point of formalizing certain areas and of reaching out to even more people. To this end we are proposing a Program of Stewardship for your TIME, TALENT, and TREASURE.

The reason for this is that we must recognize that we are essentially a missionary parish. We have no school, no nursing homes, no hospitals, no institutions to take care of. Instead (again, as you well know) we do much service for others. Many outsiders come to worship with us, many take part in our activities, many support us, many offer their services. And many take ideas away to bring back to their own parishes.

In short, both physically, because of our location and loveliness of building and ground, and spiritually, because of our worship and liturgy, we are a kind of center of hope and inspiration for many people.

Therefore, as a missionary parish, we are bound to grow ourselves and increase our outreach as Jesus would have us do. We have in fact several operating committees, but we now want to formalize them and we want to establish a board of advisors, a Parish Assembly. All of this comes under our general program of TIME, TALENT and TREASURE.

So, look over the attached carefully. Think and pray about it—and then make your move by checking off the appropriate boxes.

Sincerely yours in the Lord,

Father Bausch
Sister Claire
Ralph Imholte

Family Name_____ Phone_____

T I M E

The following are descriptions of the various committees and sub-confraternities. All of them fall under the category of TIME, the first step of our stewardship Program.

As for TIME, the committee heads will be in office for two years, but the Confraternities are but one year terms, from September to June. Such confraternities are open to individuals, couples or whole families.

The only obligations are to fulfill the needs for which the confraternity exists, to receive a brief formation session and to report to the Parish Assembly whenever it shall meet.

The term "confraternity" has been chosen as a vague term to distinguish it from a club or a parish organization. The confraternity is strictly a voluntary gift of your TIME without any other commitments.

Select any of those interesting to you by checking off box and indicate name of interested member of household.

I. The Christian Gospel Concerns Committee

This already exists. It has been dealing with charitable needs, the Spanish apostolate in Keyport and many other areas of genuine kindness. We are looking for more members here. However, under this General Concerns Committee are listed the following confraternities.

1. The Samaritans. As its name suggests, this confraternity deals with the sick and would cover such areas as:

   a) visiting the sick at home or in the hospitals
   b) sending them cards
   c) providing them with tapes and cassettes
   d) bringing them Holy Communion
   e) assisting in the homes
   f) baby sitting to cover doctor's appointments
   g) doing cancer wrappings (in connection with the Catholic Daughters)
   h) visiting the nursing homes in the area
   i) assisting in our Communal anointings of the sick

   ☐ I would be interested in working in this area

Name_____ Phone _____

2. The Theos Confraternity

This is a sensitive apostolate which deals with families that have suffered death. Members would be affiliated with the national Theos Confraternity in Washington and be given some insights and approaches. This confraternity covers all of the spiritual, legal, emotional aspects of dealing with survivors. It is a tender and needed confraternity.

☐ I would be interested in working in this area

Name_____ Phone _____

3. The Lazarus Confraternity

This deals with death itself. As you know we have instituted a funeral policy here to make funerals less expensive and at the same time, more Christians. Members of this Lazarus confraternity would assist in the funeral arrangements, especially those held in the church and parish hall. They would assist in arrangements with the undertaker, be called first in the case of a death, provide refreshments for guests, represent the parish community at the Mass of Christian burial, be present for prayers the evening before and in general assist in the whole Christian program of the funeral.

☐ I would be interested in working in this area

Name_____ Phone _____

4. The Anna Confraternity

This deals with the elderly. Mostly assisting and arranging for Senior Citizens days of recollection, anointings, transportation and issues of help and housing for senior citizens.

☐ I would be interested in working in this area

Name_____ Phone_____

5. Other Areas of justice must be explored from questions of housing, farm workers to all those things the bishops urge us to.

☐ I would be interested in working in this area

Name_____ Phone_____

II. The Gospel Proclamation Committee

This is all about Christian Education in all of its forms. We need people to give TIME to these activities.

1. The CCD Program

We have a large CCD program and we always need both CCD teachers and teacher helpers (another adult in the classroom). Training is given. We also need secretaries, people to assist with special programs, liturgies, activities.

☐ I would be interested in working in this area

Name_____ Phone_____

2. The Jerome Confraternity

Named after St. Jerome, the great biblical scholar. This year we are going to have home Bible programs: a study of the Bible, a reading of the Bible, a better formation of faith. We need leaders who will conduct these various home meetings.

☐ I would be willing to have such a group in my home

☐ I would be willing to head such a group in another home

Name _____ Phone_____

3. Adult Education

We always have lectures by Father Bausch, Sister Claire and outsiders. We need someone to give TIME to head the program, arrange the calendar, provide speakers and seek out needed topics.

☐ I would be interested in working in this area

Name_____Phone_____

III. The Liturgy and Spiritual Life Committee

This committee deals with all aspects of the liturgy: cantoring, lectoring, organ playing, singers of the choir and various folk groups. We have committed people heading the various areas, but we need more people to give their TIME.

We also need people to work out liturgies for the various seasons of the year.

And yes, we need your TIME, once a year to clean the church. Sign up through the Rosary Guild with your friends. It takes exactly an hour and fifteen minutes with about six or seven persons. Giving your TIME generously makes it possible to come only once in the entire year.

☐ I would be interested in working in this area

Name_____ Phone_____

1. Prayer Groups

This is an important area: we all need to learn how to pray better together as well as privately. Therefore we are having home programs whereby interested people, whether adults or young people, can meet for prayer discussion and shared prayer. Guide booklets will be provided.

☐ I would be interested in joining a Prayer Group

Name_____ Phone_____

☐ I would be interested in hosting a Prayer Group in my home.

Name_____ Phone_____

2. The Serra Club

This is a family orientated diocesan vocation program of men dedicated to raising the consciousness of people concerning the need for vocations to the priesthood and religious life. There is a Monmouth County Region under the direction of Judge Patrick McCann. Men would have regular meetings to attend and also be willing to go out and speak to small groups on vocations.

☐ I would be interested in joining the area Serra Club.

Name_____ Phone_____

3. Retreats

One of the most important needs of modern man and woman and youth is the opportunity to get away in prayer, in solitude and in relaxation. Time is needed just to rethink what life is all about, where we're going, what we make of ourselves and how we stand with God. About seventy adults last year went away to the Franciscan Christ House in north Jersey and found it delightful. And there are many other places just like this. If you would be interested in getting away for a day's retreat or a weekend, sign your name below. This includes young people as well.

☐ I would like to get away for a day's retreat

Name_____ Phone_____

☐ I would like to get away for a weekend retreat.

Name_____ Phone_____

IV. The Christian Family Life Committee

This deals, of course, with the most needful area of promoting and supporting family life. Giving your TIME to these areas is essential.

1. The Pre-Cana

This is open to married couples who are willing to be trained to share with engaged couples a better vision of marriage than they have received from the Mass Media. It is valuable and rewarding work.

☐ I would be interested in working in this area

Name_____ Phone_____

2. CFM

This is for couples willing to conduct home programs which use a format to discuss building family life on spiritual and scriptural foundations. A great ice-breaker, a great help.

☐ I would be willing to have such a group in my home

☐ I would be willing to head a group in another home

Name_____ Phone_____

3. The Marriage Enrichment Program

An exciting new program that offers joy and insight into marriages. Details of this new program will be available later.

☐ I would be interested in working in this area

Name_____ Phone_____

4. Lectures

Someone is needed to give his/her TIME to arrange for lectures that cover topics that parents most want to hear today, to know about, to handle.

☐ I would be interested in working in this area

Name_____ Phone_____

V. Christian Social Life

We have had dances, picnics, trips, pet and children blessings, etc. Won't you give your TIME for one year to expand and promote such activities that bring us together on a very human plane?

☐ I would be interested in working in this area

Name_____ Phone_____

VI. The Neighborhood Confraternity

Our parish is fairly wide spread and not always too well defined. Still, we do have certain close-knit neighborhoods. So we need some person to be a kind of "neighborhood captain" to arrange neighborhood meetings, home Masses, home discussion groups, retreats, etc.— and just to keep us informed of the problems of a given area.

☐ I would be interested in working in this area

Name_____ Phone_____

All these thins are under the heading of "TIME." Can you give your parish time? Just for a year? Can you make an investment of yourself just for a year? Time is all we ask.

T A L E N T

There's something anyone can do to enrich another, to enrich our parish, our community. Some talents are extended ones (for example, CCD teachings), others are just needed for the occasion (for example, drama or a banner). Again, we ask your service of TALENT. What can you do? What can you share? Here are some suggested areas. Beside each that you check, write the name of the family member so talented.

___ drama _____

___ tutoring _____

___ CCD teacher _____

___ CCD helper _____

___ variety shows _____

___ Band _____

___ sing _____

___ arts and crafts (specify) _____

___ flower arrangement _____

___ needlepoint _____

___ banners _____

___ gardening _____

___ youth work _____

___ play musical instrument (specify) _____

___ physical therapy _____

___ teach the retarded or children with disabilities _____

___ lecture _____

___ write _____

___ librarian _____

___ nurse _____

___ nurse's aide _____

___ sew _____

___ other _____

___ other _____

Date_____

_____
(Name of individual or family)

voluntarily wishes to enter into a preliminary

Covenant

with the community of St. Mary's,
Colts Neck, New Jersey

These days, journeying with a particular faith-community is largely voluntary. There is no compulsion to choose this way of life or this parish. Rightly or wrongly people do not attach any kind of mortal sin in missing Mass. Unbaptized infants are considered as going to heaven. There must be a reason, then, why freely and without such compulsions you are seeking to join this community. We presume that you are accordingly motivated by a desire both to give and to receive from this community; that is any relationship, you are bonding yourself freely in the give and take of our common life.

Therefore, you are ready to enter into a covenant with us—that most solemn contract of mutuality, concern and shared responsibility. There is no requirement to be perfect or without flaw or sin; only the promise to be faithful. Accordingly, this Covenant states as follows:

I/we promise to walk faithfully with our fellow parishioners of St. Mary's to worship with them regularly and to make some commitment of Christian service, however temporary, as described in the Parish Booklet.

My/our Christian service is_____

Signed_____

Pastor/Associate_____

Parish Council President/delegate_____

Witness_____

In due time you and/or your family, along with other families, will be welcomed publicly and joyously into the community at one of the weekend Masses.

Explanation

1. A single name or the family name will go on the blank line.

2. Discuss and pray over the Covenant with your family. When you're ready, call the office (780-2666) and one of the staff will visit you.

3. The one obvious fact today is that current culture no longer supports a religious way of life, much less a Catholic way. This means that now you deliberately and willingly have to make a personal choice: do I want to travel with this people or not? to give, contribute, be faithful with and to them? Do I and my family intend to be a genuine and full part of this faith-community?

4. Worshipping regularly with the community means just that: every week end (or most) celebrating with the community, joining in the prayer, the sorrows, the boredoms, the highs, the sins, the reconciliations. It is most powerfully in our common prayer together at Mass that we are most community, most publicly supportive and witnessing.

5. The commitment opportunities are to be found all throughout our Parish Booklet which you have received in this packet, especially the list in back. If you need more information, call the name and number listed or the parish office.

6. It is possible, of course, that at this time, in all honesty and integrity you cannot sign this Covenant. We understand and will be ready when you can. We are willing to do all we can to support you in coming to a decision. Just keep the form until such a time you can sign it—and meanwhile call us at any time you want any further discussion or help.

7. Meanwhile, let us all pray for one another. To be a Christian i the Catholic tradition, to be openly counter culture is difficult. It is not easy to follow Jesus and his Gospel in such an unsettled time. That is precisely why we need each other, precisely why we have to openly support one another, why we have to pledge faithfulness.

SAINT MARY'S PARISH

"A Christian Community in the Roman Catholic Tradition"

Last Name _____

Mailing Address _____
(Street)   (Town)   (Zip)

Phone _____ Date _____

Married by a Catholic Priest? Yes _____ No _____

Husband's Occupation _____

Wife's Occupation _____

First Name	Age	Rel.	Bap.	F. Com.	Conf.
Husband					
Wife					

(Full Maiden Name)

Please fill in information only on those living at home:

Children	Age	Rel.	Bap.	F. Com.	Conf.	School	Grade

Please list any other relatives or boarders living with you and their relationship
_____
_____
_____
_____

Today's date _____

FAMILY PICTURE HERE

+ *Memento* +

Name of the Deceased_____

Date of Death_____ Date of Burial_____

Place of the Mass of Christian Burial_____

Celebrant_____

Readers_____ _____

Gift Bearers_____ _____

_____ _____

Pall Bearers _____ _____

_____ _____

Funeral Director _____

Notes _____

_____

_____

_____

[You may take the booklet home if you wish.]

Suggested Living Will

Copies to: _____

_____

In the event of a terminal illness and/or any condition where I am diagnosed as brain dead, I instruct you as follows:

1. At a certain moment, a doctor will determine that my brain has ceased to function and that for all intents and purposes, my life has stopped. When that happens, do not attempt to instill artificial life into my body by the use of a machine or other extraordinary means. Do not call this my "death bed." Call it my "Bed of Life," and let my body be taken from it to help others lead fuller lives.

2. Give my sight to a person who has never seen a sunrise, a baby's face, or love in the eyes of another.

3. Give my heart to a person whose own heart has caused nothing but endless days of pain.

4. Give my blood to a person who has been pulled from a wreckage of a car, so that she might live to see grandchildren at play.

5. Give my kidneys to one who depends on a machine to exist from week to week.

6. Take my bones, every muscle, every fiber in my body and find a way to make a crippled person walk.

7. Explore every corner of my brain. Take my cells, if necessary, and let them grow so that someday a speechless person will shout at the crack of a bat and a deaf person will hear the sound of rain against the windows.

8. Give my soul to God.

9. If you must bury something, let it be my faults, my weaknesses, and all my prejudices against my fellow humans.

10. If by chance you wish to remember me, do it with a kind deed or word to someone who needs you. If you do all this that I ask, I will live forever.

Dated: _____

Signed: _____

Instructions for My Funeral

Believers may not fear death but, like many others, put off thinking about it. A funeral is often handled in a rush and in a manner which does not reflect the wishes of the deceased (because survivors often don't know them). The following directives have been distributed in some parishes to enable Christians to have some say in their own funerals and over their own bodies. Far from being morbid, this approach is both a courtesy and a responsibility. You are invited to fill out these forms and request the parish, mortuary, and the relatives to keep them on file.

Information for the church

Funeral instructions for (Name) _____

To assist those responsible for my funeral arrangements, I wish the following:

1. At my death I want (Mortuary) _____ to be contacted.

2. I have [ ] or have not [ ] consulted with the funeral director of the above named mortuary regarding the following:

Selection of casket [ ] or vault [ ]

Selection of cemetery plot [ ] or crypt [ ]

Other specific directions not covered above _____

_____

_____

3. I wish the following:

a) Morning Mass and burial [ ]

b) Evening Mass and burial [ ]

c) Evening Rosary with morning Mass and burial [ ]

d) Evening Prayer or wake service with morning Mass and burial [ ]

e) Graveside service only [ ]

f) Memorial service [ ]

g) Other [ ]

4. I want these services conducted at:

[ ] church _____

[ ] the funeral home_____

[ ] other _____

5. I wish the following person to conduct my funeral service:

   1st choice: _____

   2nd choice: _____

6. I wish the following person to give my eulogy:

   1st choice: _____

   2nd choice _____

7. I do [ ] or [ ] do not wish to have an open casket.

   Other specific directions not covered above.

8. I would prefer, that instead of sending flowers, my friends make memorial gifts to:_____

_____

9. I make the following suggestions of material which I would like to have used in my service:

Scripture passages to be read: _____

_____

Favorite Appropriate Poem or Article _____

_____

Prayers _____

_____

Music _____

_____

Other _____

_____

Instructions to Mortuary   Date _____

1. My Name _____
2, Address _____
3. Date of birth _____ Place of birth _____
4. Race _____ Citizen of what country_____
5. Single _____ Married _____ Widowed _____ Divorced_____

6. Name of Spouse _____ Occupation of Spouse_____

   Phone _____

   Relationship _____

   Address _____

8. Name of birthplace of father _____

_____

10. Last occupation: _____ how long? _____

   Kind of business _____

11. Last Employing Co. or Firm _____

   Social Security No. _____

12. Resided in country of _____ since_____ in State_____

   since _____

13. If Veteran: Rank & Branch of Service _____

   Name of War _____

   Date & Place Entered Service & Discharge _____

   Service No. _____ _____

   I would want an American Flag for my family [ ] yes   [ ] no

Final Disposition: Burial [ ]   Cremation [ ]   Donation [ ]

A. I leave this to my next of kin: _____

B. I have made arrangements regarding my cremated remains or interment as

   follows: _____

_____

Designate location of burial plot, cemetery, mausoleum, columbarium or other instructions_____

_____

This authorizes release of my remains to (name mortuary) _____

_____

Witness _____ Signature _____

Make copies available to: Mortuary of choice; Executor of Will; Next of Kin

Information for Survivors   Key Persons to Be Notified

1 Church _____Phone Number_____

2. Doctor _____ Phone Number _____

3. Funeral Home _____ Phone Number _____

4. Executor of Will _____ Phone Number _____

Relatives and Friends to be Notified - Names, addresses, phone numbers, relationship:

1. _____

2. _____

3. _____

4. _____

Insurance Policies: Company   Policy No.   Amount   Agent

1. _____

2. _____

3. _____

Veterans Records:

Identification Number _____

VA Office to Notify _____

Location of Discharge papers _____

Social Security Number _____

Pension Benefits from employer -- who should be notified _____

_____

Location of Will _____

Location of Safe Deposit Box _____

Attorney: names, address, phone number _____

_____

Bank Accounts: Name of bank, type of account (Stocks & Bonds): _____

_____

_____

Outstanding Loans and Credit Obligations _____

Biographical Information:

Date baptized: _____Date Confirmed:_____

Location of baptismal papers_____

Confirmation papers_____

For Married Persons: place and date of marriage_____

Pursuant to the Uniform Anatomical Gift Act, I hereby give, effective upon my death:

A. _____ Any needed organ or parts

B. _____ Parts of organs listed_____

My signature _____

Date _____

Witnessed by: _____

Witnessed by: _____

To Whom It May Concern:

This letter is not a request -- it is an order. I have tried to live with dignity and I want to die the same way. If my fate is such that I should become old and afflicted with an irrevocable illness and unable to make a rational decision, you are hereby instructed to give the physician orders that he /she must not attempt to prolong my life by using extraordinary means; by which I mean:

1. _____ 2. _____

3. _____ 4. _____

I have made this decision so as to relieve you of the responsibility of making it.

      With appreciation and love,

      Signature _____

      Witnessed by _____

      Date _____

Pilgrimage of Faith: The Beginning and the End

We offer you the names of those who, during the past year, have either begun or completed their pilgrimage of faith on Earth at St. Mary's Parish. Please remember them all in your prayers as we begin this New Year of grace.

Saint Mary's Parish
"A Christian Community in the Roman Catholic Tradition"

NEW CHRISTIANS
(in order of appearance)

Meghan Colleen Fitzpatrick
Victoria Marie Gobat
Bryce Edward Walsh
Christopher Thomas Curro
Brian Stewart Duggan
Alfonso Vincent Kealy
Brendan Scott Trimboli
Philip Andrew Carroll
Wesley Steven Castello
Catherine Alanna Woods
Ryan Paul Nix
Tierney Katherine Purce
Justin Matthew Lardiere
Courtney Elizabeth Skehn
Colby Connolly Ann Bartis
Ashley Ruth Beard
David Michael Gallello
Thomas Alden Gassert
Erin Marie Kelly
Alex Manuel DeAlmeida
Morgan Joy Dispoto
Allison Beth Mechanic
Kristyn Lauren Soria
Gayle Michele Smithson
Aaron Francis Lay
Colleen Michelle Tufaro

DIED IN THE LORD
(in order of their death)

Mary Ellen DelMaster
Geraldine Owen
John J. Elgonitis
Alex Ruskavich
Raymond Fazewski
Joseph Twardus
Anna Piazza
Joseph DelMaster
John Dmyterko
Albert Bertrand
Frederick Dorando
Marie Burke
Martin McCann
Kathryn Reeve
Adele Schubert
Joseph Trost
Laura Servidio

Whole Wheat Altar Bread

Five Loaves
5 1/3 cups unsifted whole wheat flour
3 Tablespoons baking powder
1 1/2 teaspoons salt
1 3/4 cups warm water
3 Tablespoons vegetable oil
2/3 cups honey

One Loaf
1 cup unsifted whole wheat flour
1/2 Tablespoon baking powder
1/4 teaspoon salt
1/3 cup warm water
1/2 Tablespoon vegetable oil
1/8 cup honey

(vegetable oil and honey already mixed)

Method

1. Pour flour mixture into bowl
2. Add warm water
3. Add honey/oil mixture
4. Stir all ingredients for 2 to 3 minutes
5. Grease the outside **bottom** of a 9-inch cake pan (turn pan upside down)
6. Put dough in center of pan and pat out to the edge.
7. Score with a knife as per diagram
8. Bake at 350 for 10 minutes; brush lightly with vegetable oil and continue baking for another 5 minutes. Do not overbake.

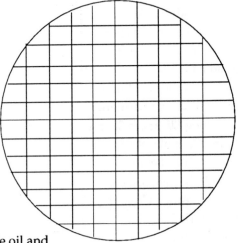

Family Banner

1. The background material: any heavy sturdy material that holds shape, such as felt or heavy cotton.

2. Design: felt or any material easy to cut out. Embroidery, needlepoint, quilting are all beautiful. Any design you like, perhaps a host and chalice, flowers, etc. Be sure to have the child's name (first name only is okay if you wish) and you might add the date of the First Communion.

3. dowel: 12 inches

4. Size: keep it to a 12" width as wider banners cause difficulty for people leaving and entering the pews.

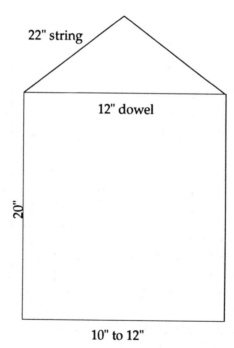

22" string

12" dowel

20"

10" to 12"

HANDBOOK
OF
HELPFUL AND HOPEFUL
INFORMATION

FOR _____ AND _____

WHO ON _____

WILL

CELEBRATE

THEIR MARRIAGE

IN THE LORD

AT

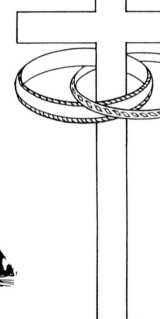

St. Mary's Parish, Colts Neck, N. J.

An important note, Your wedding date is TENTATIVE. It is only after the usual testing and interviewing that a firm date will be given and you should not make final plans until that time. Special circumstances such as under age, pregnancy, immaturity, unpreparedness and the like — all these may demand a temporary postponement of the wedding.

WELCOME!

Because we believe wholeheartedly in marriage and because we want **your** marriage to be as successful and rewarding as possible, we the People of St. Mary's parish, your friends and neighbors, offer you with affection this little booklet of

MARRIAGE PREPARATION

As you shall discover, there are a lot of people in your parish family anxious to share with you the wisdom, experience and joy of being married in the Lord.

So, turn the pages and let's begin together the adventure of getting ready for a lifetime of committed love.

THE SACRAMENT OF MATRIMONY

You may be familiar with that title. In our tradition marriage is a sacrament. That means, as you may recall, that it's an outward sign, given to us by Jesus, of inner grace. A visible sign of something invisible.

And *that* in turn simply means that many things in life are simply signs that point to something deeper. Your wedding ring is not love, but it's a sign of love: it's a circle to show that it has no beginning and no end...just like your love.

So with marriage. The union of man and woman as husband and wife is a sign. Of what? Of the way God loves us.

But you have to understand what that really means. It means that this is the one sacrament that grows as it goes along. That as husband and wife grow together, love, argue, forgive, reconcile, work through disappointments and trials together and emerge as united lovers, they become a living and effective sign that says to the world: *this is the way God is*. God loves us through thick and thin, for better, for worse, in sickness and in health, till death...and beyond. Marriage is a sign...a sacrament...of that.

You see, the pilgrimage union of husband and wife is powerful evidence of the union of God with us. The forgiving, reconciling, deepening love of husband and wife announces that this is the way God loves us. This husband-wife growing togetherness, this marriage union, is truly a living sign of God's action, of grace. It's a sacrament.

And that's what you're about to celebrate. And it takes faith. You are about to undertake a special commitment not only to each other but to society. "This is the way we love" you are saying, "and it's but a shadow of the way God loves us all."

FIRST —

JUST FOR THE RECORD ...

Before we begin, we need some basic information for here and the tear-off section to the right.

Bride's name _____

Address _____

Phone _____ Age _____

Groom's name _____

Address _____

Phone _____ Age _____

Date of wedding_____ Time _____

_____ Nuptial Mass _____ Ceremony

Sponsor Couple _____

Clergyman's Record

Bride _____

Address _____

Phone _____

Groom _____

Address _____

Phone _____

Date _____ Time _____

_____Nuptial Mass _____Ceremony

Sponsor Couple _____

Notes

_____

_____

_____

Office Record

Bride _____

Address _____

Phone _____

Groom _____

Address _____

Phone _____

Date _____ Time _____

_____ Nuptial Mass _____Ceremony

Sponsor Couple _____

Notes

_____

_____

_____

SOME TAKEN FOR GRANTED BASICS

1. You must both be at least 18 years old to marry according to New Jersey State Law.

2. You must be free to marry. That is to say, you must not have been married before (unless widowed). If one of you has been married previously, whether you are Catholic or not, you must possess a Catholic Church Annulment. (Sometimes people think that if you're Protestant or Jewish you can get divorced and remarried. Not so. Protestants and Jews and all human beings are held to a faithful and enduring marriage. If they divorce they may not, according to the Catholic view, remarry without an annulment.)

3. In due time you will need, of course, such things as a blood test and civil marriage license — which you obtain at our local Town Hall — and certain Church certificates. We'll give you a check list later.

4. Since you are approaching the Catholic Church to celebrate the Sacrament of Matrimony, we presume that your faith is alive and well. Shakey maybe and unsure at times, but basic enough to bring you here in complete honesty and integrity to publicly celebrate your marriage in the Lord before us all. Marrying *"in church"* just to please one's family or because you want the aura of a *"church"* wedding, is not enough. Faith and practice and some commitment to community life and worship are both desirable and just plain honest. Where faith and/or practice is weak or non-existent for a long time — well, we will have to have a lot of dialogue on the subject and try to discern the wisdom of a church wedding. Please read the next page for a statement of our policy.

Policy on Nuptial Mass

The celebration of one's marriage within the Nuptial Mass tells the world that the couple value faith, the sacrament and the special blessing of the Lord in the Holy Communion at their wedding. It says that the Mass is quite important to them as demonstrated by their devotion to it.

For, after all, the couples' values, what they consider important, like everything else in life, is measured by deeds.

If, for example, they value one another, they see each other frequently. Long absences without cause, seeing each other once or twice a year, contradicts mere *words* of affection. To neglect one's parents for years and then to go to them when a need arises is to tell the world loudly and clearly that parents are not important except in a pinch. (Not very flattering!)

So with the Nuptial Mass. The assumptions are that a couple requests it because (1) Mass is important to them (2) the Eucharist is important to them. *And* those importances are, or course, obvious and easily proven because they have been faithful. At least most times, at least frequently.

So, that brings us to our policy concerning the celebration of a Nuptial Mass. That policy is that we offer the lovely and meaningful **marriage ceremony** rather than the Mass for those who have not demonstrated their devotion to Mass and the Eucharist because they have not been to Mass for five years or more. We offer the ceremony especially in cases where church going has not been a part of the person's formative years.

It's a fair offer because the ceremony is not only a real and meaningful celebration of the sacrament of matrimony in church but it is also a lovely beginning of marriage and, hopefully, a fresh invitation that in their new life together, the couple will reaffirm their faith and reunite themselves as a married couple to a faith community.

Life is a process and married life even more so. The ceremony is our gift to those who wish to return to the values and spirit they know they will need in their life together.

Much peace and blessing from St. Mary's Faith Community.

NOW — OUR SEVEN-STEP PROGRAM or
HOW DO WE LOVE YOU? LET US COUNT THE WAYS:

STEP I

The Initial Contact. This is your first call to the parish to see the priest or deacon to start the whole process moving. This is a call that should be made anywhere from eight months to a year ahead of the wedding date. To call later than this is to risk someone else getting your date and time. In this initial contact we will give you the basic details and general procedures and also tentatively pencil in your date so you can have it reserved. (Note that at this point it is tentative).

STEP II

At that initial meeting you will be asked to contact Ralph Imholte, our deacon and counselor, immediately for a series of interviews, oral and written. Call him at 780-7343 and he will set up a time mutually convenient. By the way, we request that after your first meeting, each partner donate five dollars each for subsequent sessions to help defray the cost of overhead and materials.

STEP III

This is really nice. Twice a year we have in the parish a public Betrothal Ceremony for all of our engaged couples. Ask the priest or deacon for this year's dates and pick out the one more convenient. The Betrothal Ceremony is a simple promise of commitment and preparation before the assembled community at Mass. This gives the community not only a chance to know who among them is getting married, but also it gives them the chance to pray deeply for you.

STEP IV

This is an easy step because here you don't do anything but just receive in the mail, during your courtship, little flyers, thought provokers and just plain funny things to move you along the way.

STEP V

This step involves a choice of two delightful and joyous experiences: The Pre-Cana Conferences or the Engaged Encounter Weekend. Take your pick. We admit that we are prejudiced towards the Weekend Encounter simply because it gives you more undisturbed time together to experience the depth and beauty of each other. But both are good. Ask your priest or deacon for the brochure which contains all the places, times and dates for the entire year. Advice: Go early and call early since they tend to get filled up quickly! Go, learn, enjoy!

STEP VI

After all the Steps are completed and you have received a certificate from the Pre-Cana or Engaged Encounter Weekend, call your priest or deacon to meet with him to take care of the final legal and liturgical details. Here we're down the home stretch, nearing the day of mutual promise which will take a lifetime to unfold.

STEP VII

About six months to a year after your marriage we would like you to call us again and, if you're settled anywhere near Colts Neck, to come back for a visit. We'd like to see how you're doing. So, leave us your name and address where we might reach you. If you know it now, write it in:

Name _____

Address _____

> Husbands, love your wives, as Christ loved the church and gave himself up for her . . . He who loves his wife loves himself for no one ever hates his own flesh but nourishes and cherishes it as Christ does the church . . .
>
> St. Paul

ON THE PRACTICAL SIDE,

HERE IS A CHECK OFF LIST FOR YOU

_____ Baptismal Certificate (Bride)

_____ Baptismal Certificate (Groom)

_____ First Communion (Bride)

_____ First Communion (Groom)

_____ Confirmation (Bride)

_____ Confirmation (Groom)

_____ Pre-Cana or Engaged Encounter Certificate

_____ Blood Test

_____ Marriage License

_____ Counselling Follow Up Completed (where applicable)

_____ Letter of freedom. This means that, if you're from another parish, you have to contact your pastor or one of the priests and ask for a *"Letter of Freedom"* ...which is a legal term and standard form which says, that as far as your current parish knows, you are legally free to contract marriage.

About that Baptismal Font...yes, it's right smack in the center aisle, blocking the bridal procession. But it has to stay in place and may not be moved. Two reasons. (1) the practical one is that it's made of cast iron and therefore is very heavy and will crack if moved too often (2) the theological reason is that it stands there in a direct line between the Bible and the Altar to remind us that this is the way Christians travel spiritually: they encounter the word of God and if they believe, they are baptized. Upon baptism they are admitted to the Eucharist. For the couple about to be married, going to and returning from the sanctuary and passing the font is a sign that the sacrament of marriage is a further development of their basic baptismal faith journey.

Rehearsal Time: _____

One of the most beautiful and moving love stories that I have ever heard is a true story. It's the story of Thomas Moore, the 19th century Irish poet. Shortly after his marriage, he was called away on business. It was some time before he returned home, and when he did, he found waiting for him at the front door of the house, not his beautiful bride, but the family doctor.

"Your wife is upstairs," said the doctor, "but she has asked that you do not come up." Then Thomas Moore learned the terrible truth: His wife had contracted smallpox. The disease had left her once flawless skin pocked and scarred. She had taken one look at her reflection in the mirror and had commanded that the shutters be drawn and that her husband never see her again.

Moore would not listen. He ran upstairs and threw open the door of his wife's room. It was black as night inside. Not a sound came from the darkness. Groping along the wall, Moore felt for the gas jets.

A startled cry came from a black corner of the room. "No! Don't light the lamps!"

Moore hesitated, swayed by the pleading in the voice.

"Go!" she begged. "Please go! This is the greatest gift I can give you now."

Moore did go. He went down to his study where he sat up most of the night, prayerfully writing. Not a poem this time, but a song. He had never written a song before, but now it seemed more in keeping with his mood than simply poetry. He not only wrote the words, he wrote the music too. The next morning as soon as the sun was up he returned to his wife's room. He felt his way to a chair and sat down. "Are you awake?" he asked.

"I am," came a voice from the far side of the room. "But you must not ask to see me. You must not press me, Thomas."

"I will sing to you, then" he answered. And so, for the first time, Thomas Moore sang to his wife the song that still lives today:

"Believe me, if all those endearing young charms,
Which I gaze on so fondly today,
Were to change by tomorrow and flee from my arms,
Like fairy gifts fading away.
Thou wouldst be adored, as this moment thou art,
Let they loveliness fade as it will —"

He heard a movement from the dark corner where his wife in her loneliness, waiting. He continued:

"Let thy loveliness fade as it will,
And 'round the dear ruin each wish of my heart
Would entwine itself verdantly still."

The song ended. As his voice trailed off on the last note, Moore heard his bride rise. She crossed the room to the window, reached up and slowly drew open the shutters.

WEDDING WITHIN MASS

Processional _____

First Reading _____ Reader _____

Responsorial Psalm

Second Reading _____ Reader _____

Gospel _____& Homily _____

Marriage Ritual plus any options after it: _____

_____

Prayers of the Faithful: Readers _____

Offertory Hymn _____

Offertory Gift Bearers _____

Sign of Peace

Communion Hymns _____

Options _____

Dismissal and Recessional _____

Notes: _____

_____

OUTSIDE OF MASS

Processional _____

First Reading _____ Reader _____

Responsorial Psalm _____

Second Reading (optional)_____ Reader _____

Gospel _____ and Homily _____

Music/options after homily _____

Marriage Ritual

Nuptial Blessing

Dismissal and Recessional _____

Notes _____

_____

SAINT MARY'S PARISH

"A Christian Community in the Roman Catholic Tradition"

WILLIAM J. BAUSCH
Pastor

STELLA POTVIN, O.P.
Associate Pastor

SUSANNE THIBAULT
Spiritual Director

RALPH IMHOLTE
Permanent Deacon
and Maintenance Coordinator

RICHARD HAMBLETON
Permanent Deacon

LUCILLE CASTRO
Director Religious Education

MARTHA ANNE CICERO
PATRICIA STEED
Secretaries

JOE GEORGE
Coordinator
Parish Spiritual Center

JO ANN MOLLER
Librarian

WALTER ZIMMERER II
MARIE CURRAN
Trustees

JOHN CARLUCCI
Diocesan Pastoral
Council Delegate

CARL BARAN
Alternate Delegate

MADELINE TIBBITT
Delegate At Large

JANE SIPOS
President
Parish Assembly

LYNN GEORGE
Cultural Affairs

KATHLEEN MOGENSEN
Social Concerns Director

A Memo to Brides and Grooms

Just a concern that we wish to raise.

Can Christians justify spending hundreds, perhaps thousands, of dollars on a single day's celebration (caterers, photographers, gowns, etc.) in view of the large numbers of people today who are unemployed, homeless, hungry?

Is this consistent with the Gospel and your own personal values?

Anyway, a suggestion: If you spend a lot, donate a lot to charity.
To our parish unemployment fund,
To Mother Theresa's Soup Kitchen in Newark.
To whatever good work you feel will represent the concern and kindness you would like to see in your own marriage.

St. Mary's Social Concerns

Highway 34 & Phalanx Road, P.O. Box H, Colts Neck, N.J. 07722-0076 (908) 780-2666

On Living Together Before Marriage
A Parish Policy

1. What is St. Mary's policy on living together before marriage?

Our policy, shared in our annual parish booklet, is that we ask the couple to separate before we will witness their marriage. We feel that their position is not the best one, sociologically, morally, and pastorally (which means, not a good example for others).

2. Why? You're behind the times. Everyone (at least the ones we know) does it.

We have two reasons for disapproving living together before marriage: 1) There's an enormously practical reason: Couples who live together before marriage have a higher divorce rate than those who don't. 2) With marriages so fragile today, why would anyone add one more handicap? It's as simple as that.

We didn't make that up. The social scientists and their various polls tell us that. Here is a sample:

Trial Marriages No Guarantee of Marital Success

Some of your patients may consider living with their lover, believing that a "trial marriage" will allow them to work out differences before making a legal commitment, thus leading to a stronger marriage. Warn them that it ain't necessarily so. A new study shows that couples who cohabit before marriage are actually more likely to separate and divorce than those who head straight for the altar.

The study, by researchers at the University of Wisconsin, found that 38% of couples who had lived together beforehand separated within 10 years of their wedding, compared with 27% of those who had not cohabited before marriage.

Another article in the *New York Times* (June 9, 1989) reported: Researchers who expected the widespread practice of "trial marriages" to usher in an era of increased marital stability have been surprised by new studies showing that those Americans who lived together before marriage separate and divorce in significantly greater numbers than couples who go directly to the altar. . . . The fragility of the post-cohabitation marriage was the most surprising result of the research on American households and the fluctuating patterns of family life. . . .

Another study is Andrew Greeley's study of marriage entitled *Faithful Attraction* (1991). It's full of tables and survey material, but the conclusion is the same: Living together, for some reason, produces more divorce and not a more stable marriage. "Try before you buy" doesn't seem to work. Only 12%-25% of cohabiting couples eventually marry.

Other recent studies show that couples who never lived together before marriage "had higher marital adjustment scores after one year of marriage," while, on the other hand, those who *did* live together before marriage "scored significantly lower in both perceived quality of marital communication and marital satisfaction."

And this, for what it's worth: A recent study at the University of New Hampshire shows that violence among unmarried couples who live together is more than *twice* as common as among married couples.

All in all, living together before marriage has little to recommend it from a simple human point of view. Our position is that we want marriages to work. We want the least amount of obstacles from the beginning. You can't blame us for that, any more than you can blame us for being skeptical about the couple who declare that, of course, they'll be different.

3. You said there were other reasons, reasons you called moral. What are they?

The moral reasons concern commitment. It's easy and non-committal to simply move in together without a public display of commitment. Yes, yes, couples say, they're committed—but no one knows that but themselves and anyone else they try to convince. The fact is, there is no public ceremony, no courageous act of putting themselves boldly on the line in front of the whole world in a public display, no go-for-broke sign.

To begin a family unit, to live as married but not married, is basically not to honor one another with the public act of committed love that each deserves. To announce to the whole world that this is it; we're bonded to one another for better or worse, richer or poorer, in good health or bad health until death—that's a bold and heroic proclamation. That's the least each partner can give to the other. In addition, each other's families and the community as well deserve that pledge. If you can't do this, you have to ask yourself why. What fear is present? What confidence is lacking? These are moral issues. You're fiddling with love.

4. Anything else?

Yes. At this point we usually ask the live-in couple a question: *Why get married?* What's the advantage? You can get common law legal protection rights or write palimony contracts and then have some friends over to celebrate. So, what does getting married mean? And what does getting married in church add?

You see, the couple has to be honest here—very honest. Here are more good questions that demand honesty if their relationship is to go anywhere:

If a cohabiting couple tell us they now want to get married because their parents feel bad or are embarrassed because of their living together, we respond that they're already unhappy that they're living together. The couple didn't consider their feelings then, so why bring them up now? And they should not claim, "I've always wanted a church wedding!" because that puts the sentiment in the same category as, "I always wanted a white gown or a horse-drawn carriage!" There's no faith in that. More questions:

- Why do live-in couples who are acting as married want to get married?
- Why did they choose to live together in the first place? Fear of permanent commitment? Escape from home? Testing the relationship? Convenience? The need for companionship? Financial reasons?
- What have they learned from living together?
- What is causing them to want to get married at this time?

•Was there a previous reluctance or hesitation to marry? If so, what was it?

•What prompts them to marry in the Catholic church?

•What does marriage as a sacrament and sacred union mean to them?

•What does the ceremony add that's presumably missing? What difference does it make?

•Why don't they stay as is and send out announcements?

Live-in couples should answer these questions as truthfully as they can and discuss their responses with each other and with the priest or deacon.

5. You spoke of a pastoral issue. What is that?

The pastoral issue is the issue of witnessing. All the live-in couple's friends and family know they're living together. And here they are, walking publicly up the church aisle. What is the message to the people, to the teens, to the young? A recent poll (*Newsweek*, 1991) showed that 50% of the respondents saw no reason to get married. And, of course, they are right. Absolutely right.

Celebrities have babies without being married. Ordinary people live together all the time. Woody Allen and Mia Farrell were a famous live-in couple. It's all quite open. No big deal. Everybody accepts it. Everybody does it. Contracts, lawsuits, day care centers—all provide for domestic arrangements. So, again, what's the big deal?

But that's the world. That's not the religious covenant of man and woman envisaged by the Bible, by our tradition. Living together gives poor witness, goes along with the culture and announces that this couple will not be countercultural as Jesus demands. Living together gives a casual message about profound human relationships, a casualness that is already too prevalent. We don't want to bless that, to encourage it. In short, to use an old word, there's the issue of scandal, especially to the young and vulnerable.

6. Can you explain that further?

All right, let's try. Let's suppose that there is a mature couple really in love and seriously committed and they move in together. So what? They're adults.

Granted. But look at the context of society today. We have easy divorce, common live-ins, unmarried people having babies in record numbers (one out of every four babies born in America is born out of wedlock). Family life has fallen on hard times, and with the breakdown of the family many social ills, from crime in the streets to conscienceless children, have followed. Male-female relationships are fragile and shallow; sex is quick and casual. Our point is that living together without marriage is part of that context, part of the general disrespect for marriage and family life. It simply confirms the widespread indifference to public commitment and so becomes part of the problem. To that degree it gives scandal to the young. It teaches a lesson to the teen and pre-teen. All *they* know is that this couple have lived together (just like on TV) and here they are, getting married in church. The message to them is that living together without marriage doesn't matter. *But it does matter statistically, spiritually, and culturally to society.* The example of people they know and admire may be potent in the lives of observers and onlookers. A faith couple, it seems, would want to give a better example.

7. Some couples have said that at least they were honest in saying they were living together and their friends told them they were crazy for admitting it. They should just lie—as their friends did.

The answer to this is 1) to begin one's marriage on a lie is not wise, and 2) keep an eye on these friends and see if they keep the divorce statistics alive.

8. But then, the ones who tell the truth get penalized!

Of course! Who ever said otherwise? The kid who will not go to the school picnic if he admits to smoking in the bathroom will get "rewarded" if he lies and penalized if he tells the truth. What would you advise him? Every virtue is persecuted. People *will* do better by lying and cheating and often will get penalized if they are truthful and honest. Heroes and heroines are made here. What do you suggest? What do your choices say about your character?

9. O.K. What do you ask such live-in couples to do?

We ask that such couples separate. We ask that they do this for two reasons: First, as a gesture to the public, to the young, that they have rethought their position and want to enter a mutual life together in God's grace through a real and actual sacramental celebration of marriage.

The second reason is most tender and most sincere. We ask couples to separate as a *gift* to one another. To use the time spiritually to prepare for this great lifelong journey. To practice that separation they will come to know so often in married life through travel or sickness. To give each other space to grow and get ready for marriage without the presence and pressure of one another. To learn to give each other one of married life's most precious and sought after virtues: trust. Trusting each other out of each other's sight. Trusting each other's fidelity. (Remember: to give permission for sex outside of marriage by living together is to implicitly continue that permission after the ceremony. Premarital and extramarital sex are highly correlated.) Trust that you can grow and be whole in yourself. You don't marry to complete yourself. You complete yourself first and give that in marriage. And that takes time.

10. An honest question: Do we ever envisage an exception?

Our answer is a careful yes. We say this because we realize that for some there may be a real dilemma of economics, living quarters, distance. We understand that. It simply may not be practical, emotionally or financially, for an engaged couple in some instances to maintain separate dwellings without a great deal of tension and hardship. In these rare instances, what do we suggest? We suggest that the couple approach us and we will have a quiet but public wedding (known to take place by family and friends) and then celebrate the more open event on the regularly planned day. The first is a genuine wedding and will be recorded as such. The second is the big wedding for the larger public celebration.

The advantages are these: 1) The couple can live as committed husband and wife and come to terms with the hardships that led to this decision. 2) Think of the striking counterculture example it gives to the family, to friends, to the young! What a statement it makes against the more immature, media-approved, and casual "Let's move in together." 3) Think of what such a couple can say to their children: "Yes, dear, we just didn't want to live together without being married. That's not what our faith called for. That's not what *we* are about. So we had our sacramental wedding quietly with just a few people present and then later we had a big church celebration afterward at the time we had originally planned."

As we say, a nice countercultural Christian witness that maintains the value and the practicality—and gives an indication of the values by which such a couple hope to live.

11. Any last words?

No. There you are. Our reasons. We will dialogue with any couple on this issue. We might wind up adopting the approach of other bishops and permitting a small wedding ceremony, not a Nuptial Mass, or come to an understanding. Or be open to unusual circumstances.

In any case, nothing is closed yet. We want to challenge gently, to talk; and these pages are the content of our dialogue.

Talk we will and pray we will—and love we will.

See the article, "Cohabitation: A Perplexing Pastoral Problem," by Mitch Finley in *America*, July 31, 1993. See also the policy of the Galveston-Houston diocese: *The Diocesan Policy for Cohabiting Couples Seeking a Church Marriage* and that of the Diocese of St. Cloud, Minnesota. See also the fine article,"Chastity as Shared Strength: An Open Letter to Students," by Mary Barth Fourqurean in *America*, November 6, 1993. Finally, see the pamphlet, *Living Together and the Christian Commitment* by James Healy (Allen, Tex.: Tabor Publishing Co., 1993).

There is one final follow-up. If, you recall, we send the couple flyers (see page 71, Step IV) during their engagement, we are careful to get their new address as a married couple. Then, for three years, we send them timely articles concerning the first years of marriage. You can do this either by freelancing it, for example, sending them articles yourself from various magazines such as *Church* or *Marriage*, or subscribing for them to a professional source such as the bimonthly newsletter *Foundations: A Newsletter for Newly Married Couples* (National Association of Catholic Family Life Ministers, P.O. Box 1632, Portland, ME 04104-1632). This newsletter subscription runs for three years.

Moppet Mass

Once a month the five o'clock Mass on Saturday evening is devoted to a children's Mass celebration. These delightful liturgies mean maximum participation by the small fry of our parish. The Moppet Choir sings, the children do the readings, sometimes act out the gospel, and, when they do not, they always come up and sit with Father in the sanctuary for a story. They bring up Father's vestments. (Note: I process in wearing my street clothes and, after the homily, during the Creed, the children bring up my vestments. The public vesting becomes a visual aid for them.) They bring up the Offertory gifts, read original Prayers of the Faithful, and act as ushers and take up the collection. All are invited to the parish hall for refreshments and balloons afterwards.

Such a celebration necessarily requires the involvement of many adults to prepare and direct the children along with the teachers and parents.

The Moppet Mass coordinators inspire, direct, guide, and support the host couple. This year they are Elaine Baran, Cathleen Brown, and Joan Vitale. Specifically they :

1. Call the host couple to remind them this is their month!
2. Make contact with the children who will participate according to grade level assignments.
3. Direct and rehearse the children before Mass.
4. Assist the host couple in selecting a theme, and, in general, make themselves available for consultation.

Elaine Baran:	31 Wannamassa Point Road, Wanamassa	774-3658
Cathleen Brown:	Green Hill Road, Colts Neck	780-1321
Joan Vitale:	13 Ann Street, Colts Neck	946-3840

The Moppet Mass Host Couple

The Moppet Mass host couple is responsible for these duties:

1. With the help of the Moppet Mass coordinators, they select a theme for the Mass.
2. The decorate the church and parish hall according to the theme selected. Couples are urged to be creative!
3. They sit in the front pews with the children who are doing the readings and the Prayers of the Faithful. They alert the children as to when they are to move to the lectern.
4. They hold the microphone for the very small children and see that there is a stool for them to stand on so they can reach the microphone (and be seen!).
5. They contact Elaine Baran or Joan Vitale, the choir directors, in regard to the chosen theme.
6. They direct the blowing up of the balloons with helium.
7. They touch base with the Refreshment Committee. They may also want to coordinate the Mass theme with them.
8. The host couple should send out a reminder to the parents of the children who are participating. Forms are available from the Religious Education office.

Example of the form:

Dear Parents,
This is a reminder that your child, _____, has been chosen to be _____ at the 5:00 P.M. Moppet Mass on Saturday, _____.

Please:
1. Have your child in church by 4:30.
2. Remind your child to report to the host couple, _____ , who will also be wearing name tags. Thank you for your cooperation.

Note: While the children will practice in the religious education classes, they should also come early to church to rehearse just before Mass.

Moppet Mass Host Couples

Sept. 28:	Steve and Elaine Carroll,	23 Bernice Dr., Freehold	780-3454
Oct. 26:	Bob and Linda Meyers,	Green Hill Rd., Colts Neck	431-5648
Nov. 23:	Rudy and Anna May Schellenerger,	84 Gallopping Hill Rd., Colts Neck	542-0253
Jan. 25:	Ron and Barbara Willis,	44 Carriage Hill Rd., Colts Neck	431-0973
Feb, 22:	Tom and Christine Hitchock,	18 Darien Ct., Colts Neck	431-5187
Mar. 22:	Harry and Kathryn Neu,	15 Westminster Dr., Colts Neck	946-2969
Apr. 26:	Children's Liturgy Coordinators		

Suggested Themes

September:	Year of the family, beginnings
October:	Good and evil, fall, election
November:	Thanksgiving, Harvest time
January:	Snow, New Year, winte, goals
February:	Love, patriotism
March:	Spring, Lent
April:	Easter, new life, creation

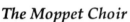

The Moppet Choir

Children who like to sing are encouraged to join the Moppet Choir, which sings at all the children's liturgies including Christmas, First Communion, and other special occasions. The Moppet Choir is under the direction of Elaine Baran and Susan Hermann and is for grades K-4. They practice on Saturday mornings from 10:00 to 11:00.

Decorating the Church

The host couple may decorate the church in any way they wish in keeping with the chosen theme. (Note: Often the church itself is already seasonally decorated and that's sufficient.) Cut-outs appropriate to the theme or season may be put on the back wall with masking tape. A few balloons may be attached to the altar and lecterns.

Be creative. One year the theme was "Creation" and FOA Schwartz was contacted to loan us huge stuffed animals which, along with potted plants, transformed the sanctuary into a Garden of Eden! (Note: Pretty pricey. Contact K-Mart.)

Balloons

Balloons, string, and helium are supplied by the parish. It is best to blow the balloons up in early afternoon, but not so early that they begin to droop. Ask friends to help you. (Note: Balloons are stamped: "St. Mary's Community. Alive and Loving!" Also, being ecologically sensitive, we urge care in disposing of them.

The Children

When the Moppet Mass coordinators have the names of the children participating, they call the Moppet Mass host couple who will make name tags for all these children with their assignments listed; for example: "David Smith: first reading." This year the assignments by class will be as follows:

First Grade:	will carry the vestments to the altar
Second Grade:	will bring up the offertory gifts
Third Grade:	will write and read original petitions
Fourth Grade:	will dramatize Gospel readings (if this is to happen)
Fifth Grade:	will assist with the decorations
Sixth Grade:	will practice and read the first reading, psalm, and second reading. *(Note: We often go to the lower grades for this.)*

Mass Planning Check List

1. Date: _____

2. Theme: _____

3. Songs: Processional_____

   Offertory_____

   Communion _____

   Recessional _____

   Other Music _____

4. Readers: First Reading _____

   Psalm _____

   Second Reading _____

5. Prayers of the Faithful:

   _____

   _____

   _____

   _____

   _____

6. Vesting Procession:

Chasuble_____

Alb _____ Stole _____

7. Offertory Procession:

_____   _____

_____   _____

8. Ushers:

_____   _____

_____   _____

9. PLANNING

Excerpt from the Parish Booklet

Saint Mary's Parish

Saint Mary's Parish

Saint Mary's Parish

1 — Staff reflection; exposition

2 — Mass with Children; Pre-Cana; Cancer support group

3 — Compassion Sunday; Singles' Journey; High Mass; preschool;
youth group

4 — AA; Al-anon; Martha/Mary Board; Dr. Noone's course; play
group

5 — R.E. ; GA; Samaritans; Girl Scout leaders; Bereavement series

6 — Dance; Fellow Pilgrims' ATG; evangelization video; infant massage; quilting; dancersize

7 — Women and finance seminar; MOPITS; quilting; Scripture
Study

8 — Prayer group

9 — Seekers Group; wedding;
liturgy of the word

10 — 9:00, Dialogue Sunday;
liturgy of the word; Singles'
journey; preschool; Jr. High

11 — Columbus Day; AA; Al-
anon; Dr. Noone's course;
play group; Koinonia Core
group; dancersize

12 — R.E.; GA; Girl Scout
leaders; spiritual reading;
Bereavement series

13 — Dance; Fellow Pilgrims;
Martha/Mary installation; ATG;
Healing Mass

14 — Newcomers; Women
and finances seminar; The
Dot Boese series, "Modern
Myths in Classical Literature"

15 — Prayer group

16 — Wedding; women and work seminar; ATG; 5:00, lay homilist;
Koinonia facilitators

17 — Senior Citizens day of recollection; Singles' journey; family
ed; youth group; Young Adult meeting

18 — AA; Al-anon; Parents' first Eucharist meeting; play group;
mini-retreat

19 — R.E. ; GA; Holy Spirits; Parish Assembly; Parents' first
Eucharist meeting; Bereavement series

20 — Dance; Fellow Pilgrims; prebaptism; ATG; quilting outreach;
evangelization video; dancersize

21 — Embroidery Guild; women and finances; quilting outreach

22 — Prayer group

23 — Wedding; liturgy of the word; Seekers group

24 — Liturgy of the word; Singles' journey; preschool; youth
group;Jr. High; Music Ministry Day of Recollection

25 — AA; Al-anon; Parents' first penance meeting

26 — R.E. ; GA; Fr. Venard; staff meeting; Parents' first penance
meeting; spiritual reading; Bereavement series

27 — Dance; Fellow Pilgrims; Women's away retreat; ATG; infant
massage; dancersize

28 — MOPITS; Scripture Study

29 — Prayer group; Kids' halloween party

30 — Christian conscience seminar; fall clothing drive; liturgy of
the word; ATG

31 — Singles' journey'; food/agape; liturgy of the word

October

Toll-Free Hotlines
(Check with your diocese for specifically Catholic hotlines.)

AIDS: 800-342-AIDS

Alzheimer's Association: 800-621-0379

American Council of the Blind: 800-424-8666

American Kidney Fund: 800-638-8299

Cancer Information Services: 800-4-CANCER

Child Find: 800-426-5678

Domestic Violence: 800-572-7233

Healthline for the Homeless: 800-528-1000

Heartlife: 800-241-6993

Lifeline Systems (for elderly and handicapped): 800-451-0525

National Child Abuse Hotline: 800-422-4453

National Institute on Drug Abuse: 800-638-2045

National Runaway Switchboard: 800-621-4000

Senior Citizens Hotline: 800-792-8820

The Living Bank (organs, bones, etc., donations): 800-528-2971

Gang Peace: 617-442-1919

The Council on Urban Peace and Justice: 614-345-7559

Lifeline Crisis Pregnancy Hotline: 800-852-LOVE

Birthright: 800-848-LOVE

V.D. or S.T.D. Hotline: 800-227-8922

National Cocaine Hotline: 800-COC-AINE

Suicide Hotline: .... 800-call INFOLINE

Stewardship: Time & Talent

NAME_____ ADDRESS_____ PHONE_____

Availability: Daytime_____ Evenings____ Weekends_____

In recognition and in appreciation of God's gifts to me, I would like to offer my services in the following area/s:

____Adult Education
____Altar Servers
____Altar Care
____Arts and Crafts
____Baby Sitting
____Bible Study
____Bingo Worker
____Carpentry
____Census
____Choir
____Clerical Work
____Driving
____Electrical Work
____Eucharistic Minister
____Evangelization
____Family Concerns
____Finance
____Flower Committee
____Folk Group
____Handicapped
____Home Visiting Committee
____Hospital Visits
____Instrumentalist
____Interfaith Committee
____Landscaping
____Lawn Care
____Lector
____Liturgy Committee
____Marriage Encounter
____Media-Communications
____Minority Concerns

____Newspaper
____Nursing Home Visits
____Painting
____Parish Council
____Plumbing
____Pre-Cana
____Prayer Groups
____Printing
____Retreats-Men
____Retreats-Women
____Retreats-Youth
____Retreats-Young Adult
____Senior Citizens
____Separated and Divorced Ministry
____Social Actions
____Social Activities
____Telephone
____Transportation
____Trips
____Typing
____Usher
____Vocations
____Wake Attendance
____Welcoming Committee
____Women's Interests
____Young Adult Ministry (18-30)
____Youth Ministry
Religious Education
____teacher
____substitute teacher
____classroom side
____tutor
____other_____

Signature_____

Religious Education and Parents

It is important that each parent be involved in our Religious Education Program to assure its continued success. Below are some areas in which you could serve. Please check at least one area. For more information call the Religious Education Office, 294 - 8841.

Name _____ Phone_____

[ ] Teacher: Grade _____ Day _____ Time_____
[ ] Catechist for Children's Liturgy of Word (twice a month) during:
_____ 5:00 p.m. _____ 9:00 _____ 10:30 _____ 12 noon
[ ] Coordinator for Catechists for Children's Liturgy of the Word (i.e. call the catechists, check the time, materials, etc.). Specify Mass time: _____
[ ] Substitute teacher. Grades _____
[ ] One-to-one teacher for a child who needs to be moved from class.
[ ] Host for First Communion meetings (set up refreshments, clean up). A Parent of a 2nd grader.
[ ] Host for the First Communion celebration itself.
[ ] Host for First Penance meeting (4th grade parent)
[ ] Host for the First Penance Celebration
[ ] Host for Moppet Mass (2 or 3 families handle each occasion)
[ ] Host for special happenings: ___Halloween party _____ 6th Grade Seder
___ Thanksgiving Eve Family Mass _____ Sunday "Fun Fair"
[ ] Help with 7th and 8th grade activities (dance, retreats etc.)
[ ] Assist with Children's choir
[ ] Grade level coordinator for "Adopt-A-Family":Grade _____
[ ] Holy Childhood liaison (distribute coin boxes, count money,send certificates)
[ ] Represent St. Mary's at the International Peace Fair at Brookdale Community College
[ ] Clerical assistance

___My family would like to participate as altar servers during a Sunday 10:30 Mass
___ I would like to know more about such participation.

Do you have any ideas, traditional or novel for the Religious Education Program?
_____
_____

Liturgy Assignments

THE MONTH OF _____

First Week	Second Week	Third Week	Fourth Week	Fifth Week
Monday	*Monday*	*Monday*	*Monday*	*Monday*
Cantor_____	Cantor_____	Cantor_____	Cantor_____	Cantor_____
Lector_____	Lector_____	Lector_____	Lector_____	Lector _____
Gifts _____	Gifts_____	Gifts _____	Gifts_____	Gifts _____
Tuesday	*Tuesday*	*Tuesday*	*Tuesday*	*Tuesday*
Cantor _____	Cantor _____	Cantor_____	Cantor_____	Cantor _____
Lector_____	Lector _____	Lector _____	Lector _____	Lector_____
Gifts _____	Gifts _____	Gifts _____	Gifts _____	Gifts _____
Wed	*Wed*	*Wed*	*Wed*	*Wed*
Cantor _____	Cantor _____	Cantor _____	Cantor _____	Cantor _____
Lector _____	Lector _____	Lector _____	Lector _____	Lector _____
Gifts _____	Gifts _____	Gifts _____	Gifts _____	Gifts_____
Thursday	*Thursday*	*Thursday*	*Thursday*	*Thursday*
Divine Office	Divine Office	Divine Office	Divine Office	Divine Office
Leader _____	Leader _____	Leader _____	Leader _____	Leader _____
Cantor _____	Cantor _____	Cantor _____	Cantor _____	Cantor _____
Friday	*Friday*	*Friday*	*Friday*	*Friday*
Cantor_____	Cantor_____	Cantor _____	Cantor _____	Cantor _____
Lector _____	Lector _____	Lector _____	Lector _____	Lector _____
Gifts _____	Gifts _____	Gifts _____	Gifts _____	Gifts _____

Fliers

Tree of Love

On
December 1st
there will be a
CHRISTMAS TREE
in the Spiritual Center
foyer.It is not a regular tree, but a
TREE OF LOVE
Decorated not
with colored balls
and garland, but with
the NEEDS of the adults and
children. Printed on paper ornaments
these needs decorate our tree. To give this
tree meaning we ask that everyone come over and
help undecorate the tree by taking an ornament and
fulfilling the need. After purchasing
the gift requested, place
it under the tree wrapped
and with the paper ornament
attached. It is very important that
the ornament be attached so that we know where
to deliver the gift. Please return all gifts
before December 16th. With everyone's help, this will
truly be Saint Mary's TREE OF LOVE. Call 462 - 7967 or
946 - 3474 for more information. Help spread the Chrismas
message of Joy, Peace and Love.

Introducing . . .

"THE AFTER MASS MINI CLASS"

After all Sunday Masses : Self-served coffee, juice, donuts, danish in the parish hall *while* you watch a half hour video on a timely topic. Then stay around and discuss or go home. **Starts January 21st.**

Great for rounding out your Sunday mornings while you're at church anyway plus a quick breakfast, only a half hour of your time and a neat outlet for interest and discussion as a family. A good family and friends Lenten Project. The topics:

Cults (28 minutes) - *January 21st*

Communication Within the Family (28 minutes) - *January 28th*

Interfaith Marriages (28 minutes) - *February 4th*

Saving Sex for Marriage (16 minutes) - *February 11th*

Chemical Dependency (28 minutes) - *February 18th*

One Parent Family (28 minutes) - *February 25th*

Alcoholism, Part I (28 minutes) - *March 4th*

Alcoholism Part II (28 minutes) - *March 11th*

Boys and Babies (28 minutes) - *March 18th*

Martrydom and Beyond (30 minutes) [Archbishop Oscar Romero] - *Mar. 25*

Taize: That Little Springtime (26 minutes) [Ecumenical Community] - *Ap. 1st*

Persons, Places and Practices in the Catholic Church (20 minutes) - *Ap. 8th*

+ Remember; Parish Mission from February 3rd to 7th +

Come to the

Cracker Barrel

with Father Bausch

on Sunday afternoon, JANUARY 21st in the Parish Hall from 2:00 to 4:00

What is a "Cracker Barrel"? It's a combination Town Meeting, pot-bellied stove exchange and news conference wherein you can ask whatever you want about:

- ☐ the Church in general or the parish in particular
- ☐ parish policies and problems
- ☐ future trends, personally and collectively
- ☐ the priest shortage and its effects
- ☐ peeves and praise
- ☐ my dealings with the Holy Office, diocese, etc.
- ☐ whatever you want to ask or voice at a town meeting

It will be candid, honest, entertaining

Liquid refreshments will be served plus pretzels, cookies and shelled peanuts . (You *must* throw the shells on the floor.)

"Honored Parishioners"

March 6

12 Noon

Mass for Retirees

You and your loved ones are invited
to a Celebration of Mass
on March 6, 12:00

A small reception will
follow in the Parish Hall
for our honored guests
and their families

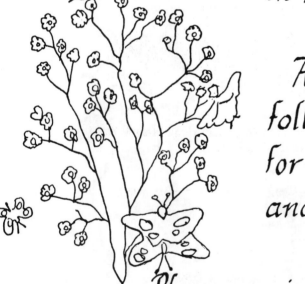

Please register ~Call Spiritual Center
10~1 p.m.   780~7343

Two-Part Lecture Series on _____

Fundamentalism and You

October 18 and 25 in the Parish Spiritual Center. Given by Father

Bausch. $5.00 each session. From 8:00 p.m. to 10:00 p.m.

Covers: the issues, the problems (political alliance, literalism, anti-Catholicism),the virtues (certainty, community, caring), the Seven Beliefs of Fundamentalism, the Basic argument (Church vs. Bible), how to deal with it. Suggested readings, flyers.

Preregistration desired, so fill out form below and mail in/ hand in to St. Mary's, Box H, Colts Neck, N.J. 07722 or call 780 - 7343. Limited to 75 people.

Dear Father,

Yes, register me for ☐ session 1   ☐ session 2   ☐ both sessions.

My check is enclosed ($ 5.00 each session; make out to "St. Mary's Church")

Name _____ Phone _____

Address _____

SAINT MARY'S PARISH

"A Christian Community in the Roman Catholic Tradition"

HOME AND HEARTH WEEK

March is here and with it comes our "Home and Hearth" week once again. Hard to believe that it's been three years since we started this.

Again, we invite and encourage our parish family to accept and believe that staying home evenings for one week, doing something you like with family members, friends or just being alone, is a refreshing and enriching experience. Which is why we have called off all meetings and activities at the parish this special week, so you can stay home.

The only time we really have is the present moment, so gift yourself with the beauty within and around you this week. Take time for yourself, yourselves. Here are some suggestions you might follow or you can "do your own thing".

<u>A Parent's Pledge </u>(Mom or Dad)

"The greatest gift I ever received," said a young successful attorney, "was a gift I got one Christmas when my dad gave me a small box. Inside was a note saying,'Son, this year I will give you 365 hours, an hour every day after dinner. It's yours. We'll talk about what you want to talk about, we'll go where you want to go, play what you want to play. They will be your hours.'"

"My dad not only kept his promise of that gift," said the attorney, "but every year he renewed it -- and it's the greatest gift I ever had in my life. I am the result of his time." What a a truly loving gift to a child. Try it!

Great mountains of happiness grow out of little hills of kindness. Send that Thank You note you've been putting off because "there's no time." Make extra videos of family gatherings and send them to Grandma and Grandpa , aunts and uncles.

Make those phone calls you've been putting off. Bake. Ply your hobby. Play cards around the table with the family. Turn off the TV. Invite friends over. Write those letters to friends and neighbors who have moved away. Take a good book and your dog to the beach or park and enjoy. Invite someone to dinner and make it special, using your best China and Crystal, complete with flowers and candles. Make one evening a special family dinner, each person choosing a favorite dish and then preparing it. Buy construction paper and make "Hug Coupons" to send or give: "Good for one hug, redeemable from any participating human being." In short, take this week to slow down, relax, enjoy those around you.

SAINT MARY'S

Blessing of the Pets

Saturday
Sept. 29th
2 P.M.

St. Francis
Garden

A Christmas Musical

THE GREAT [LATE] POTENTATE

presented by
Children of St. Mary's Church
Phalanx Road & Rte 34
Colts Neck, N.J.

December 11 and 12 — 8:00 p.m.
December 13 — 2:00 p.m.

Adults — $3.00
Children — $1.00
(under 12)

St. Mary's Spiritual Center (780-7343)

* Tickets available at Spiritual Center from
10 a.m. to 1 p.m. or at the door.

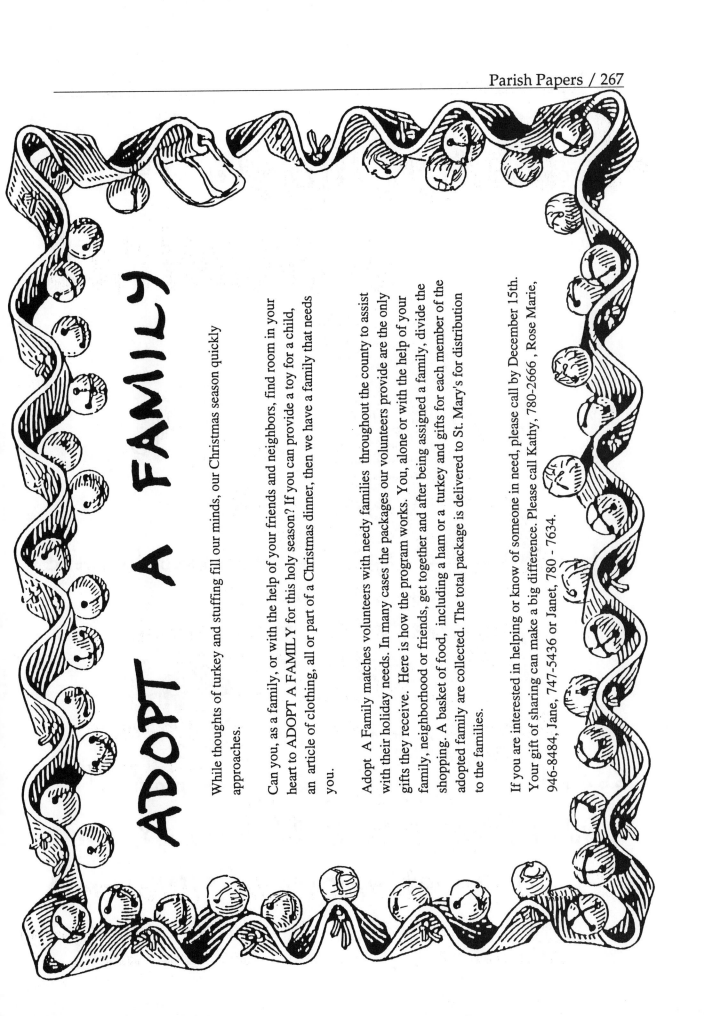

ADOPT A FAMILY

While thoughts of turkey and stuffing fill our minds, our Christmas season quickly approaches.

Can you, as a family, or with the help of your friends and neighbors, find room in your heart to ADOPT A FAMILY for this holy season? If you can provide a toy for a child, an article of clothing, all or part of a Christmas dinner, then we have a family that needs you.

Adopt A Family matches volunteers with needy families throughout the county to assist with their holiday needs. In many cases the packages our volunteers provide are the only gifts they receive. Here is how the program works. You, alone or with the help of your family, neighborhood or friends, get together and after being assigned a family, divide the shopping. A basket of food, including a ham or a turkey and gifts for each member of the adopted family are collected. The total package is delivered to St. Mary's for distribution to the families.

If you are interested in helping or know of someone in need, please call by December 15th. Your gift of sharing can make a big difference. Please call Kathy, 780-2666 , Rose Marie, 946-8484, Jane, 747-5436 or Janet, 780 - 7634.

Coming Friday, November 8th!
at 6:30 P.M.
St. Mary's Famous

enjoy

fruit coctail, salad, spaghetti and meatballs, bread
Soda, wine, beer
dessert, coffee, tea
and then —

Pinocchio!

Good friends — good food — good movie!!

Adults, $6.00   children under 8, $3.00
Tickets at Spiritual Center

BOO! KIDS, COME

to the

JACK O'LANTERN
CELEBRATION

GHOST STORIES

GAMES

Bobbing for apples

Sunday October 27
2-4 P.M. Parish Hall

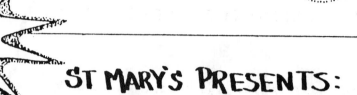

ST MARY'S PRESENTS:

AN ORIENTATION ON SPIRITUAL DIRECTION

AFTER ALL MASSES NOV 3 and 4, 1990

Sister Susanne will meet with you to discuss:

* **WHAT IS SPIRITUAL DIRECTION?**
* **WHAT HAPPENS IN A SPIRITUAL DIRECTION MEETING?**
* **WHY AND WHEN DOES A PERSON USUALLY SEEK SPIRITUAL DIRECTION?**

IF YOU HAVE WONDERED ABOUT THESE AND RELATED QUESTIONS - THEN PLAN TO ATTEND ONE OF THE ORIENTATION MEETINGS - WHICH WILL BE REPEATED AFTER EACH OF THE WEEKEND MASSES HERE AT ST. MARY'S SAT. EVE NOV 3 AND SUN, A.M. NOV. 4 IN THE SPIRITUALITY CENTER WITH SISTER SUSANNE FOR MORE INFO. CALL 780-4332

COME AND SEE !!

If you or someone you know feels distanced from the Church,

bring your concerns to:

ST. MARY'S ALIENATED CATHOLICS DAY

2 P.M. FEBRUARY 25, 1990

ST. MARY'S SPIRITUAL CENTER

RT. 34 & Phalanx Rd.,

Colts Neck, N.J.

The Church needs you!

God loves you!

. DIVORCE

. REMARRIAGE

. LITURGICAL CHANGES

. NEW CHURCH PRACTICES

Our meeting is

FRIENDLY and INFORMAL

PLEASE COME!

HALLELUJAH

Monday, November 19
Sister Ann Theresa Nagy
Ecumenism: Into the 21st Century

Friday, November 30–
Saturday, December 1st
Colts Neck Blood Drive
St. Mary's Church Hall

Sunday, January 20 at 12 noon
Celebration of Christian Unity Week

Saturday, February 9
Ecumenical Retreat
The Barracks from 10 AM–4 PM

Monday, April 15
Ecumenical Speakers Panel
Christian Family Lifestyles

PRAISE GOD ALL YOU PEOPLES!
—— Ps 117 ——

Your Ecumenical Committee invites you to come—
"See how these Christians love one another!"

Colts Neck Ecumenical Committee
St. Mary's Church
Highway 34 & Phalanx Rd.

Questions?
Call Celia Eldred
431-9278

Joan Henderson
431-2784

St. Mary's *Variety Show* is Here !

All Aboard the St. Mary's Local !!

St. Mary's Presents *'A Musical Journey Through the U.S.A. "*

Join us on a train
ride as we sing
& dance our way
across the U.S. A.

St. Mary's Railroad

St. Mary's Railroad

St. Mary's Railroad

Presents
A Journey Through the U.S.A.
Departure: 8:00 P.M.
Good for: Friday, April 19, 1991

FARE: $6.00

Round Trip Passage
Good for Coach Only

St. Mary's Church
Colts Neck, N.J.

Punch
Here

Travel North, East, South, West
with Whistle Stops in between

Tours: Friday, April 19 at 8:00 p.m. Saturday, April 20 at 8:00
p.m and Sunday, April 21 at 2:00 p.m. Tickets, $6.00 person.

Ticket Information: Dot Groll, 431 -3477 or Joe George, 780 - 7343

Get your train reservations early. Limited Seating on this train.
So cut off form below and mail in or hand in early.

Yes, I want a reservation for this train ride!

Name _____Phone_____

Number of tickets _____ Amount enclosed at $6.00 per ticket_____

Day you're coming aboard: _____ Friday eve _____ Sat. Eve. _____ Sunday afternoon

That's Entertainment !

What is? *Why, the evening of Saturday, March 2nd from 7:30 to 9:30 at St. Mary's Sp. Center*

The Ed Stivender Show! You haven't laughed so hard--especially if you're Catholic --if you haven't heard Ed Stivender do his famous "The Kingdom of God is Like a Party". He's a stand-up comic, gentle and reverent but <u>very</u> funny as he tells stories from the scriptures with a comic twist. You must see this! Ed's played all over the country with great acclaim.

After Ed, we'll have an intermission --which you'll need to recover. We'll have refreshments of wine and cheese, soda and snacks.

Then--we're back to chuckle down with a short but engaging video followed by a number by St. Mary's Dancers and we finish up with a grand Sing-A-Long with Eileeen Connair. What an Evening !

The cost for all of this? A meager $7.00 per person. Call this number for reservations (which are limited) : 780 - 7343 and ask for Joe George.

Or , fill out this form and mail as soon as possible to St. Mary's:

Dear Father,

☐ Yes, I want to go to *"That's Entertainment"* on Saturday evening, March 2nd . Reserve for me _____ places. Enclosed is my check for $_____ (at $7.00 per person). Make checks payable to "St. Mary's Church"

Name _____ Phone _____

SAINT·MARY'S·JANUARY·SPIRITUALITY·PROGRAMS

ON-GOING PROGRAMS

A. Weekly Scripture sharing on Sunday Readings

Every Monday 10:30 a.m. in the Spiritual Center

We Gather to share our faith as we reflect on scripture active in our lives.

B. Spiritual Reading
First and third Tuesdays
10:00 a.m. - Spiritual Center

We begin again - January 7th

Our next selection.

PAYING ATTENTION TO GOD by William A. Barry, S.J.

Cost of book $6.00

A WINTER SPIRITUALITY SERIES FOR PERSONAL GROWTH

SEASONS OF OUR LIVES

This four-week program will explore four movements in our spiritual growth.

Tuesdays - 8-9 P.M. spiritual center

Jan. 14th - "Spring-Breaking Through"

Jan. 21st - "Summer - Opening-up"

Jan. 28th "Autumn - Bearing fruit"

Feb. 4th - "Winter - Growing within"

FOR MORE INFORMATION · CALL SR. SUSANNE · 780-4332

Join the CROP
Walk for the
Hungry...
and help make a difference.

April 28, 1991

10K (6.2 mile) walk, Sponsor Sheets are Available!
for more information, contact Linda Bingler
(431-9332)

SAINT·MARY'S·FEBRUARY·SPIRITUALITY·PROGRAMS·

a rediscovery of life
by Anthony de Mello, S.J.

This video recording of a Tony de Mello teleconference involves over forty university and college campuses. Father Tony de Mello is at his relaxed best as he challenges his audience to understand a basic paradox: the less you need, the more you will enjoy life.

A SPIRITUALITY WORKSHOP

WHEN: Saturday - Feb. 15th 10-4 p.m.

WHERE: St. Mary's Spiritual Center
        Colts Neck, N.J.

FACILITATED BY: Sr. Susanne, M.S.B.T.

FEE: $10 - Lunch included

To Pre-Register
Call Sr. Susanne 780-4332

B. WOMEN'S DAY OF RECOLLECTION

WHEN: Monday - February 10, 1992
        10:00 a.m. - 3:00 p.m.

WHERE: St. Joseph By The Sea
        Retreat House
        Montoloking, N.J.

WHAT: Bringing Your Life To Scripture

PRESENTED BY: Sr. Susanne, M.S.B.T.

Fee: $15.00 - Make checks payable to
              St. Joseph By The Sea

Pre-Registration Required-

Call: Sr. Susanne - 780-4332

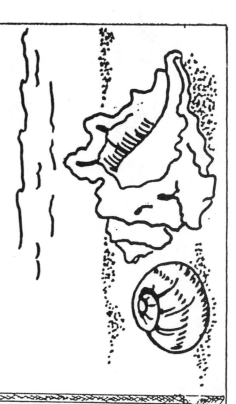

CALLING ALL STITCHERS!

During the month of February we would like to offer quilting classes to produce baby quilts for the Afflicted Babies Connection. This is a tri-state organization which makes quilts and distributes them to babies who are sick or in need of a warm covering. Kathy Mogensen will see that they get to the right places.

We will begin with the Log Cabin quilt using the strip quilting method. It's simple, fast, and fun! You could learn the skill, make a quilt for a sick or dying baby, and then later make a quilt for your own family.

Please bring your own sewing machines. We can teach those without sewing machines a hand sewing method, so don't stay away. Materials for the baby quilts will be provided. If you have any scrap cotton fabric you would like to use or can share with us, please bring it with you.

We plan to meet on Wednesday afternoons, February 5, 12, and 19 from 10:00–2:00 and on Saturday afternoons, February 1 and 15 from 1:00–4:45 in the basement of the Parish House. *Welcome!*

Anyone who is interested in meeting and stitching with us can call Sister Pat at 780-2512 or Suzanne Thomas at 842-7699

THANKSGIVING

THE SAMARITANS WILL BE HAVING A THANKSGIVING DAY COLLECTION FOR LOCAL NEEDY FAMILIES AND WE NEED YOUR HELP! SINCE LAST YEAR'S DRIVE WAS SO SUCCESSFUL, WE WILL ONCE AGAIN BE DISTRIBUTING SHOPPING LISTS.

SHOPPING BAGS WILL BE ON THE ALTAR NOVEMBER 15th THROUGH NOVEMBER 22nd. A FOOD LIST WILL BE ATTACHED; THE LISTS ARE NOT MEANT TO TELL YOU WHAT TO GIVE BUT RATHER HELP US OBTAIN A NUMBER OF NEEDED ITEMS WHICH WE WOULD NOT OTHERWISE RECEIVE. PLEASE PLACE YOUR CONTRIBUTIONS OF FOOD AND/OR MONETARY DONATIONS TO BUY TURKEYS IN THESE BAGS. IF YOU WISH TO DONATE FROZEN TURKEYS, PLEASE BRING THEM TO THE SPIRITUAL CENTER AND PLACE THEM IN THE FREEZER NO LATER THAN NOVEMBER 22nd; WE NEED OVER 200 TURKEYS.

ALL CONTRIBUTIONS WILL BE GREATLY APPRECIATED BY THE FAMILIES WHO WILL RECEIVE OUR HELP. MANY THANKS FOR YOUR GENEROSITY!! ANY QUESTIONS, PLEASE CALL MARILYN AT 544-8652 OR KATHY AT 780-2666.

Fall Freezer Meal Drive

It's time once again to fill our church freezers with prepared meals for the homebound. Next weekend, October 24 and 25, you are invited to take home a container to fill with a home cooked meal. Label the container as to contents, number of portions, and any special defrosting and/or cooking instructions. Return the meal to the freezer in the Spiritual Center kitchen.

These meals are so appreciated by those who get them, especially during the cold winter months . . . and we always are able to provide so many because of your generous help.

Any questions, please call:

Gail Hempstead 946-7241

Fall Clothing Drive

WHEN: Saturday, Oct. 31st 4 to 6 PM
Sunday, Nov. 1st After all masses

WHERE: Please bring clothing to the <u>Sharing Shed.</u>

NEEDED: Fall and winter clothing, infant through adult sizes.

INFANTS -- All clothing in sizes "newborn" thru 24mos.
Also blankets, crib sheets, bibs, etc.
CHILDREN -- All clothing in toddler thru teen sizes including PJs, socks
and shoes(must be in excellent condition).
ADULTS: ---- Mens and Womens casual clothing, nightwear, work boots
and sneakers, maternity clothing, especially "large" sizes.

MISC: Sets of sheets and blankets (please label sizes), bath and kitchen towels.

NOT NEEDED: Summer clothing of any kind. Pocketbooks, belts, high-heeled shoes, and
mens dress shoes.

NOTE: Please remember poor people need to feel good about themselves. No
stained, ripped, or out-of-date clothing. All items should be clean and in
excellent condition. Please presort clothes and separate into children's,
men's, and women's and label sizes -- especially suits and shoes. This helps
tremendously with the job of processing the clothing so we can get it to
those who need it quickly.

If you can donate any time after one of the masses or during the week,
please call Dot at 431-3477, or Maureen at 431-3175.

Thank you for your help with this project!

A DAY OF RECOLLECTION FOR SENIOR CITIZENS

ENJOY A PLEASANT DAY WHICH INCLUDES MASS, DINNER, ENTERTAINMENT, AND A GUEST SPEAKER.

DATE: SUNDAY, OCTOBER 18, 1992

TIME: 2 TO 7 P.M.

PLACE: ST. MARY'S PARISH, COLTS NECK

SEATING IS LIMITED TO 150, SO PLEASE MAKE YOUR RESERVATION **EARLY** . PLEASE CALL OR WRITE BY OCTOBER 6 WITH YOU NAME , ADDRESS, & TELEPHONE TO :

MRS. EILEEN AYALA
35 RIMWOOD LANE
COLTS NECK, NJ 07722
(908) - 530-1905

NAME: _____

ADDRESS: _____

TELEPHONE: _____

Charismatic Healing Service

The Lion of Judah Prayer Group
invites all to come
and celebrate!

May 5, 1993 at 8 pm
St. Mary's Church
Route 34 and Phalanx Road ✤ Colts Neck, NJ

✤ ✤ ✤ ✤ ✤ ✤ ✤ ✤

Celebrant:

Padre Pio Mandato

✤ ✤ ✤ ✤ ✤ ✤ ✤ ✤

Please publicize this Healing Mass and invite your friends
to join you.

For further information contact Dick Hambleton at (908) 536-3874

Music Ministry:
Dick and Maria Incremona, Holy Cross R.C. Church, Rumson, NJ

The Samaritans

COME MEET WITH US

"what you do for the least of my brothers you do unto me." The code of the church, and the code of the Samaritans. So - in the Twilight of a cool and lovely autumn we invite all of you Men and Women of the parish to meet with us, the Samaritans, October 6, 7:30 p.m. in the Spiritual Center.

This will be the one and only meeting of the year and will give all of you the opportunity to learn about the various programs and what they entail, in order to help others who need food and support.

We need the participation of the men and women of the parish in order to continue the programs that have been so successful. Can you give an hour or two of your time?

FALL & SPRING CLOTHING DRIVES

THANKSGIVING BASKETS   **LUNCH BREAK**
VISITING THE SICK   **ADOPT A FAMILY**
TREE OF LOVE   **SENIOR CITIZENS LUNCHEON**
MASS OF ANOINTING   **AGAPE**
SHARING SHED   **FREEZER MEALS**

If you would like someone to come with, Call Judy J. - 409-6817 or Dolores C. - 946-9620.

Are you a grandparent?

To celebrate the blessedness of being a grandparent, grandparents will be recognized at all the Masses on the weekend of 2-3 November. There will be a mini breakfast after the 10:30 Mass.

Some ideas for families who wish to celebrate this special day!

- Invite a grandparent to dinner. Have them share their "early" years stories.

- Do something different with your grandparents - like flying a kite together.

- Write a letter to your grandparent and give it to them that weekend or send it so they receive it that weekend.

- Adopt grandparents for the day if yours are far away.

Grandparents lucky to get second chance

We have so many days to honor everyone; I thought a reminder to all grandparents would be appropriate:

I wonder how many grandparents realize what a wonderful thing it is to be given a second chance — a second chance to do many of the things we were unable to do with our own children.

As grandparents, we all have a second chance. We have more time to show our love and our affection, and in turn we receive much of the same.

If you're not a grandparent, you have no inkling of the feeling you get when a little face looks up at you with a twinkle in his eyes and says "Grandpa, I love you."

To all my children, and seven grandchildren, we say, "Thank you, with love."

EDDIE and MILLIE GRANT,
Atlantic Highlands

Abury Park Press

Join the Caravan to:

The Great Christmas Show at

Radio City Music Hall

When?...............Tuesday, December 26th

Schedule?..........Leave St. Mary's parking lot promptly at 9:00 a.m. We
should be home around 5:00 p.m. So bring your lunch
with you (or buy in in N.Y.) We'll have time to visit
Rockerfeller Center and St. Patrick's cathedral.

Cost?...................A low $35.00 per person. This includes the ticket for the
show and the bus fare.

Tickets?............No tickets. Just fill in the form below and mail in with your
check **no later than December 12th**. First sent, first
reserved.

Dear Father:

Yes, (we) I wish to go to the Radio City Music Hall Great Christmas Show on Tuesday,
December 26th. The bus leaves at 9:00 a.m.

Name of the one in charge _____

Phone No. _____ How many going ? _____ Amount enclosed in

_____ (at $35.00 per person: make checks to "St. Mary's Church. ")

Ceremonies

Communal Confession for Advent

A sample, composed by Grace Collins

(Lights in the church are soft and low; meditative tape or record playing while people arrive.)

Cantor:	Opening Song: *Hosea*, #262, "Glory and Praise," Vol. 3

Father Bausch: Opening Prayer:
Loving God, we gather in this time of Advent. We pray this night to know your will. We pray to be able to hear your voice, your call, to feel your touch and respond to your invitation to us.

Our days are filled with tasks and agenda. Enable us to let your love warm our scurrying and worrying and running about.

We come together as people who have sinned; who have hurried so much through our days as to ignore your presence. This night, forgive us, heal us, and slow us down. Help us to be brought together in love of you.

May our time together now help us to see more clearly how you call us in our everyday lives. We ask this through Christ our Lord. Amen.

Lector I: First Reading: Jeremiah 22:13–17

Cantor: Responsorial Psalm:
Spirit, come transform us.
Come, be our breath, be our hope. (Gregory Norbert, 1988)

All: Spirit, come, transform us.
Come, be our breath, be our hope.

Cantor: Deep in the womb of your presence, O God,
Draw us to share others' burdens, healing and loving with truth.

All: Spirit, come, transform us.
Come, be our breath, be our hope.

Cantor: Open our lives to each other, show us that we are all one. You are the grace that sustains us, comforting spirit of God.

All: Spirit, come, transform us.
Come, be our breath, be our hope.

Cantor:	Light for our summers of wholeness, fire for our winters of pain, Nurturing friend, you invite us to freedom, healing and joy.
All:	Spirit, come, transform us. Come, be our breath, be our hope. Spirit, come, transform us. Come, be our breath, be our hope.
Father Bausch:	Gospel: Matthew 3:1–6
Father Bausch:	Homily

(Quiet reflection: soft instrumental music)

The Challenge of Conscience

Father Bausch:	You are invited to relax and close your eyes and meditate in solitude as the narrator suggests a challenge of conscience. Let us realize first that our God is present, calling us, wanting us close, forgiving us for the times we were distant and uncaring and aloof. Let us know of God's healing power and warmth of touch. Let us know that there is no sin in us, no hurt in us, no wound so deep that God's loving touch and presence cannot cure it.
Narrator I:	Let us reflect upon what we earn and own and the spirit in which we share. Help us to understand the true meaning of justice and sacrifice. *(pause)*
Narrator II:	Let us remember our own life's weaknesses when we project attitudes or words of racism and prejudice and cast stones at our neighbors, having difficulty in seeing our God in them. Help our vision, Lord. *(pause)*
Narrator I:	Let us ask forgiveness for the times when it was easier to be distant and remain wrapped up in ourselves. We have contained you in weekend Masses and only the rules and laws that make it easy to be your followers. We ask forgiveness for not challenging ourselves with your love. *(pause)*
Narrator II:	Let us remember our sisters and brothers and those who have been entrusted to us to love and care for, who are too difficult for us. We are at times impatient and irritable and judgmental. We make excuses for not loving them or we decide what love should look like. We ask forgiveness for not loving. *(pause)*
Narrator I:	Let us seek forgiveness and healing for the many types of abuse that we

may have allowed to exist or have inflicted on family members or others in our social or professional lives, whether it be verbal, emotional, sexual, or physical abuse. Help us to heal those broken and abused lives. *(pause)*

Narrator II: Let us reflect on how we have allowed our stress from our workplace or classroom to project anger and self-righteousness on our family members. Lord, we ask your forgiveness. *(pause)*

Narrator I: Let us reflect upon excuses for not praying, for not being a true follower. We pretend that the Gospel is too difficult for real life; turning the other cheek, forgiving the most hardened sinner, giving our shirt for the love of another. We make excuses about why that doesn't or shouldn't work. We need to be reminded day after day that you call us to perfect love. Help us, Lord, to love more perfectly. *(pause)*

Narrator II: Let us remember times when vengeance was present in our lives and spirits. Let us remember that vengeance turns victims into sinners. God reminds us that the justice of this world is the unjust of God's world. Lord, we seek the strength to forgive. *(pause)*

Narrator I: Let us believe in ourselves. You created us to build the Kingdom: to heal, preach, love, and give life. We too often think that these commandments are for someone else. We doubt that we are disciples. We think that we are only husband, wife, son, daughter, worker, student, or parishioner. We diminish our importance. You, Lord, have created us for excellence—for sainthood— for peacemaking and Kingdom building. Give us vision, Lord. Give us courage. Give us life. *(pause)*

Father Bausch: At this time we invite you to come forward to be anointed with Holy Oil. As you do so, offer a silent prayer of repentance and sorrow. (This is our individual "sign"; it could be any of those mentioned in the text, page 65, in the Holy Hours on the Tuesdays of Lent.)

[The Celebrant and other ministers anoint the foreheads. People come up as they do for Communion. Background music is playing. We always make some gesture, some movement that underscores solidarity. Here, for example, the use of the baptismal, covenanted oil that made us all one in baptism and now one in repentance.]

Father Bausch *(when all is done)*:
Let us stand and pray the prayer Our Father taught us: Our Father....
(It is our long standing custom always to join hands at the Our Father).

Father Bausch *(the penance):*

Plan a time of prayer for tomorrow and make it definite in length and place. Promise to repair any damage and make amends for what you have done to others.

(Absolution is given. All are invited back to the parish hall for coffee and fellowship.)

Cantor:

Our closing song is "Every Valley," #14, *Glory and Praise,* Vol. I.

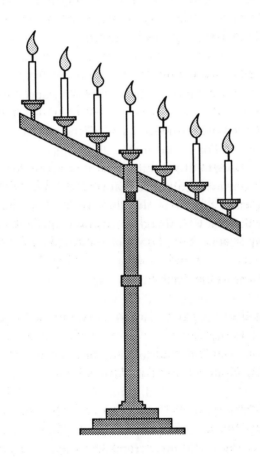

A Prayer Service for Those Who Have Lost a Child
Through Stillbirth or Miscarriage

(There may be the usual opening and closing hymn, scripture reading, etc., perhaps followed by Benediction. Here is a simple suggested prayer and reflection to flesh out any gathering.)

Let Us Pray

Father, we reaffirm our conviction that your love for us is never interrupted. We do not understand the situation in which we find ourselves, but our faith in you and in the deeply personal love you have for us continues unabated. Please deepen that faith that this experience may touch our lives and bring us closer to you. We ask this through Christ Our Lord.

Meditation

We are puzzled and questioning about our God. We looked for so much from Him and now our hopes are dashed and deferred. We come together to be reassured by God, to realize that He has not been absent. That nothing has been subtracted from His love. There is no simple answer to the questions we have in mind. God is a mystery and when we walk in faith there is always darkness.

In the Book of Wisdom the wise man tells us "God did not make death, nor does He rejoice in the destruction of the living. For He fashioned all things that they might have being." What we are told is that there is more to life and living that is apparent to us. We are overwhelmed by the finality of death, by the awful absence that it brings. But God is not limited to one form of life. Once He communicates life He is always faithful to it and never ceases to bring it to perfection. The very brief life that we mourn is very much in the mind and love of God. While we are denied the consolations of that life, we can know that it is flourishing in the presence of God.

Perhaps we are disturbed by the inability to baptize and feel that the child is doomed to live without the vision of God. Not so. St. Paul, with deep insight into the saving will of God, reminds us that God wants all people to be saved and to come to know the truth. All, at any time or place in their lives, at any age.

God is not limited to the sacraments. He has other ways of doing things and His will to save every human being is not thwarted by the inability to baptize. Your child is saved. Your child is with God. Jesus has already embraced his little brother and sister.

Things have not developed as we had hoped. On the face of it, God has disappointed us. But we must remember that "God choose us in Christ before the world began to be holy and blameless in His sight, to be full of love." There is no moment in our lives that God is absent any more than He was absent on Calvary. In every experience He is trying to bring us to holiness and perfection. He is not only always present to us, but that presence is always loving—even in our loss and sorrow.

Compassion Sunday

(Directions for the Celebrant)

The people will bring up a basket of petitions right after the homily. Go down and receive them.

Take them and put into fire bucket. Then, say aloud this prayer. (Note: you might read aloud one or two petitions before you put them into the bucket.)

Almighty God, we bless + these heartfelt petitions that have hung on our Wailing Wall.

They are Cries of the Heart and we ask you to heed them and to heed our own needs as well.

As we touch the fire to them and they wind their way before your throne of mercy, have pity on those who wrote them. Listen to all of our cries, for you have made us and we are your own.

O Lord, have mercy, have mercy. Hear us as we make our plea through Christ Our Lord. Amen.

Here light the petitions in the bucket and return to your chair for the "Prayers of the Faithful." Skip the Creed. All now proceeds as normal.

Letters

SAINT MARY'S PARISH

"A Christian Community in the Roman Catholic Tradition"

A reminder of

St. Mary's Social Concern's Fund

On the occasion of a holiday, a birthday, anniversary, wedding, or any significant occasion, why not give a gift that keeps on giving in your name?

That gift is a check in any amount made out to "St. Mary's Social Concerns Fund" and that money will never be used for the parish—even for administrative costs—but solely for the use of the poor and needy. A card will be sent in your name or you can send it yourself. If you want to see that card, a sample is on the next page. Just fold twice and you can see what it is like.

Since we started this fund and its card, we have provided for many, many people: their rent, heat, gas, electric, car repairs, housing, drug and alcohol rehabilitation, job placements, counseling, medicine, court fines, and aid for emergencies of all kinds. And the demands on his fund have grown greatly with the very real hard financial times for many.

In addition, from this fund we aid Martin House, the Interfaith Neighbors for Housing, Birthright, Manna House, Discovery House, Endeavor House, Lunch Break, Emmanuel Cancer Foundation, Aslan Youth Project, Project Paul, Asbury Park Mercy Center, and many others.

Truly, the demands on our charity are daily and you can help by giving the Social Concerns Card in your name for any occasion, joyous or sad.

Much peace and gratitude,

Father Bausch

Highway 34 & Phalanx Road, P.O. Box H, Colts Neck, N.J. 07722-0076 (908) 780-2666

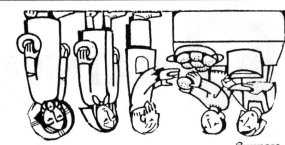

Partial List of Social Concerns Causes:

Endeavor House	clothing
shut-ins	food baskets
Birthright	Interfaith Neighbors
Discovery House	Emmanual Cancer
Mercy Center	Martin House
medicine	counseling
placements	car repairs
rehab	utilities
heating	rent

Colts Neck, N.J.

St. Mary's Social Concerns Fund

*What good is it, my brothers, if a man
claims to have faith but has no deeds? Suppose
a brother or sister is without clothes and daily
food. If one of you says to him, "Go, I wish you
well; keep warm and well fed," but does
nothing about his physical needs, what good
is it? In the same way, faith by itself, if it is
not accompanied by action, is dead.*
-- James 2: 14 -17

A Donation to

St.Mary's Social Concerns Fund

has been made on behalf of

_____

so that many people may continue to

receive the assistance they need.This

donation has been made by

_____

SAINT MARY'S PARISH

"A Christian Community in the Roman Catholic Tradition"

WILLIAM J. BAUSCH
Pastor

STELLA POTVIN, O.P.
Associate Pastor

SUSANNE THIBAULT
Spiritual Director

RALPH IMHOLTE
Permanent Deacon
and Maintenance Coordinator

RICHARD HAMBLETON
Permanent Deacon

LUCILLE CASTRO
Director Religious Education

MARTHA ANNE CICERO
PATRICIA STEED
Secretaries

JOE GEORGE
Coordinator
Parish Spiritual Center

JO ANN MOLLER
Librarian

WALTER ZIMMERER II
MARIE CURRAN
Trustees

JOHN CARLUCCI
Diocesan Pastoral
Council Delegate

CARL BARAN
Alternate Delegate

MADELINE TIBBITT
Delegate At Large

JANE SIPOS
President
Parish Assembly

LYNN GEORGE
Cultural Affairs

KATHLEEN MOGENSEN
Social Concerns Director

An Invitation to Engaged Couples

Dear Engaged Couples,

At St. Mary's, we are having a special liturgy to honor you, your finance, and your upcoming marriage.

This is an invitation to attend that liturgy.

What will happen is uncomplicated, simple, and lovely. The plan is to have you come, along with other engaged couples, to the 10:30 Mass on Sunday, April 29, to receive a special public prayer and blessing for a successful and grace-filled marriage. You remain in your pews and stand there when we call out your names. You openly pledge your love, and then we extend you a blessing and give you a gift of remembrance. And that's all.

In other words, it's a kind of public Betrothal Ceremony where we have the entire congregation acknowledge you and pray for you.

We have a place of honor reserved for you. Please call the parish at 780-7343 to let us know if you are coming. Or, you may prefer to fill out the form below and hand it it or mail it in to the parish office.

Your engagement and marriage are important to us. Let us honor and pray for you.

Sincerely yours,

Father Bausch
Deacon Ralph Imholte

- -

[ ] Yes, we will attend the Betrothal Ceremony at the 10:30 Sunday
     Mass on April 29.

[ ] Regrets

Names

Highway 34 & Phalanx Road, P.O. Box H, Colts Neck, N.J. 07722-0076 (908) 780-2666

An Invitation to R.C.I.A.

SAINT MARY'S PARISH

"A Christian Community in the Roman Catholic Tradition"

WILLIAM J. BAUSCH
PASTOR

RICHARD HAMBLETON
PERMANENT DEACON
PASTORAL ASSOCIATE

SUSANNE THIBAULT. M.S.B.T.
SPIRITUAL DIRECTOR

RALPH IMHOLTE
PERMANENT DEACON
AND MAINTENANCE COORDINATOR

LUCILLE CASTRO
DIRECTOR RELIGIOUS EDUCATION

MARTHA ANNE CICERO
OFFICE MANAGER

PATRICIA STEED
SECRETARY

SHARON STURCHIO
PROGRAM COORDINATOR

JOE GEORGE
COORDINATOR
PARISH SPIRITUAL CENTER

KATHLEEN MOGENSEN
SOCIAL CONCERNS DIRECTOR

JO ANN MOLLER
LIBRARIAN

JUNE ZERINGUE
YOUTH MINISTER

WALTER ZIMMERER II
MARIE CURRAN
TRUSTEES

JOHN CARLUCCI
DIOCESAN PASTORAL
COUNCIL DELEGATE

CARL BARAN
ALTERNATE DELEGATE

MADELINE TIBBITT
DELEGATE AT LARGE

GEORGE TOWNE
PRESIDENT
PARISH ASSEMBLY

JOYCE DONADO
LOLA GAUTHIER
JEAN KELLY
CULTURAL AFFAIRS

August 3, 1993

Dear Parishioners and friends,

Although the Easter season is several weeks behind us, it is always important for us to realize the significance of this feast in the Church's year of grace. The mystery of Jesus' life, death and resurrection is played out time and again as we experience the joys, sorrows and renewed life in our own individual journeys - experiences which reveal the presence of Jesus in new ways. It is that recognition of the belief in Jesus which empowers us to continue his work " to all nations until the end of time."

This past year the "work" of Jesus has been evident in the completion of the initiation of six new members into our parish family. With their sponsors and catechists, they progressed through the various stages of formation. They came into the Church because they experienced the presence of God in their families and in our parish community. Since their acceptance, they have been praying and reflecting on their role in the Church and their particular witness to the world.

There are people in our community and perhaps in your own neighborhood who are not fully membered in a Church or faith community but who are searching nevertheless for a deeper experience of God. Perhaps you know one or more who might welcome an invitation to "come and see" what the Holy Spirit may be saying through the Roman Catholic Church. Perhaps it is someone in your own family or a co-worker.

Please know that it is not our intention to draw anyone from active membership in another church or faith community. We enjoy a very amicable relationship with the other congregations in Colts Neck and support their good work. Our interest is in those

Highway 34 & Phalanx Road, P.O. Box H, Colts Neck, N.J. 07722 - 0076   (908) 780-2666

-2-

who feel part of no faith community or for whatever
reason would like to know more about the Roman Catholic
Church. This invitation is also open to Catholics
who are curious about the Rite of CHristian Initiation
of Adults (RCIA) into full Communion with the Roman
Catholic Church.

If you are a bit shy about extending an invitation
to a relative or friend, you may wish to forward their
name to me so that I might extend a personal invitation.

A return slip is attached for your convenience.

Sincerely yours in Christ,

Deacon Dick Hambleton
Pastoral Associate

_____I am interested in the Rite of Christian Initiation
of Adults (RCIA) and would welcome an invitation to
an information session.

Name   Address   Phone

_____I believe the following person/s might welcome
a personal invitation to an information session.

Name   Address   Phone

Return to:

Deacon Dick Hambleton
St. Mary's Parish
P.O. Box H
Colts Neck, New Jersey 07722

SAINT MARY'S PARISH

"A Christian Community in the Roman Catholic Tradition"

Hostess

May, 1994

Dear Andrea,

I'm always slightly embarrassed to write a letter like this, but let me ask you a favor.

As you know, for over twenty years I have invited parishioners to dinner on Saturday evenings. This has proven to be a wonderful way to get to know people and to extend hospitality. Since I set the table and do the cooking (no one's died yet) I am necessarily in the kitchen most of the time before dinner.

Which is why, professional bachelor that I am, I have always had a hostess. Which is why I am writing this letter to *you*, inviting you to be such hostess for a limited time.

What's involved? Simply coming to the Parish House at 6:30 (guests arrive at 7:00), greet the guests when them come, make them feel at home and offer them a drink. Period. Plus help to clean up afterwards.

The dates I have for you are four Saturdays of March: March 4, 11, 18 & 25.

I'm slightly embarrassed, as I said, because I know you have other things to do and that you're a far better cook than I am. But if you assist me I and the guests would be most grateful. I promise a lovely evening.

You may, of course, not be available and I understand that. Thanks for reading this to begin with. Whatever your answer, would you call the parish office (780 -2666) within the week and let us know it?

Sincerely yours,

Fr. Bausch

Highway 34 & Phalanx Road, P.O. Box H, Colts Neck, N.J. 07722 - 0076 (908) 780-2666

SAINT MARY'S PARISH

"A Christian Community in the Roman Catholic Tradition"

Food Carriers

Dear Friends,

As you know, on the last Sunday of each month we have a food collection for the poor. That food, placed in the sanctuary at the beginning of each Mass, is picked up at end of the 10:30 Mass by volunteers who, after receiving a blessing, carry the goods down the center aisle with the priest and then on up to our Sharing Shed to be put on the shelves.

I am writing to ask if you and your family would be one of those carriers on the date listed below? It's a one time effort, but a good and witnessing one and a true source of charity for many needy people.

I can appreciate it if you're unable to do this or wish to take another date, but if you could all of us would be most grateful. Please call us within the week (780-2666) and let us know. Many thanks for considering this , for being a part of St. Mary's.

Sincerely yours,

Father Bausch

Highway 34 & Phalanx Road, P.O. Box H, Colts Neck, N.J. 07722 - 0076   (908) 780-2666

Your month is checked off for the 10:30 Mass on:

[ ] September 25   [ ] October 30   [ ] November 27   [ ] December 18

[ ] January 29'95   [ ] February 26   [ ] March 26   [ ] April 30   [ ] May 28

[ ] June 25   [ ] July 30   [ ] August 27

SAINT MARY'S PARISH

"A Christian Community in the Roman Catholic Tradition"

Dear Friend,

Many times you have seen the notice in our parish bulletin that the **"Martin House Helpers"** were meeting on a Saturday at St. Mary's to go to Trenton or Asbury Park to work. What do they do and who are they? These Martin House Helpers assist Father Brian McCormack to rebuild houses in the inner city which the diocese has bought cheaply. They work with the poor people (not instead of them) and reclaim houses which are then rented to the poor at a reasonable cost. These people are strictly held to accountability in keeping the houses in order and in helping others to build their house. That's it and that's a lot.

Who are these Martin House Helpers? They are people like yourself, parishioners like yourself. They are men and women, skilled and unskilled, who do anything from carpentry and plumbing to hammering nails and cleaning up.

We as a parish are committed to going to work in the inner city on five Saturdays a year. This year those dates are: September 21, November 23, January 25, March 21 and June 13.

Would *you* be interested to give just one Saturday this year to this Christian work? Would your teen age son or daughter, your spouse be interested? It's a good chance for a good deed and it's a good chance for you and your family to bear witness, to realize how the "other half" (really, the other nine-tenths) of the world lives and struggles. It's a chance to put yourself and your faith on the line. Just one day. Just one Saturday of your choice.

If you are interested in one or more of these dates, please call John Steed, 946 - 4324. He's in charge and will be glad to give you more details.

Thanks for reading this letter. We're proud to have you as a parishioner. And whether your schedule permits you to help or not, be assured of our gratitude for all that you are to the parish and to the community.

Sincerely yours in Christ,

Jn. Bausch

Father Bausch

SAINT MARY'S PARISH

"A Christian Community in the Roman Catholic Tradition"

Dear Friend,

Our youth are an important part of our parish and in fact help out in many ways. For example, some this year have promised to help sort and bag food and clothing for the poor. Others are delivering baskets to needy families during the holidays. Others help rebuild houses with the poor through our Project Martin House. Others teach in our Bible Vacation School.

We would like to extend such opportunities to you -- this time, to ask you to give of your time <u>just for one month</u> in assisting at our weekend Masses. What we offer is four tasks that contribute to our weekend worship and we have checked off one which we ask you to do .

You will, of course, get some training. I know you might not be able to do this or be available, but if you would we would be pleased and the whole community would get a chance to see young people like yourself in role that contributes to us all. Thanks for considering this. Here's the tasks and the one I've checked off is what I ask you do to for the month of

_____ at the _____ Mass

☐ Eucharistic Minister

☐ Lector

☐ Usher

☐ Acolyte (Mass server)

Thanks for reading this. You're important to us and we're glad you're part of our parish family. Have a great summer and give my best to your family.

Your friend in Christ,

Father Bausch

Father Bausch

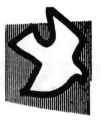

SAINT MARY'S PARISH

"A Christian Community in the Roman Catholic Tradition"
To Singles

WILLIAM J. BAUSCH
Pastor

STELLA POTVIN, O.P.
Associate Pastor

SUSANNE THIBAULT
Spiritual Director

RALPH IMHOLTE
Permanent Deacon
and Maintenance Coordinator

RICHARD HAMBLETON
Permanent Deacon

LUCILLE CASTRO
Director Religious Education

MARTHA ANNE CICERO
PATRICIA STEED
Secretaries

JOE GEORGE
Coordinator
Parish Spiritual Center

JO ANN MOLLER
Librarian

WALTER ZIMMERER II
MARIE CURRAN
Trustees

JOHN CARLUCCI
Diocesan Pastoral
Council Delegate

CARL BARAN
Alternate Delegate

MADELINE TIBBITT
Delegate At Large

JANE SIPOS
President
Parish Assembly

LYNN GEORGE
Cultural Affairs

KATHLEEN MOGENSEN
Social Concerns Director

Those who are single (and statistically they are society's fastest-growing segment) by choice or circumstance, especially the widowed and divorced, often have a deep sense of being cut of from the community. They frequently feel alienated, out of step.

The parish faith community of St. Mary's can do something. We provide for the meeting and healing of the Singles' Journey group, which meets every Sunday. But we also offer a deeper symbol of acceptance; namely, we invite the people from this group to serve as a temporary (3 months) Eucharistic Minister, or Usher at our parish worship.

Rationale

1. We make this offer to the Singles who come to St. Mary's for the Singles' Journey group, many of whom are outside the parish.
2. We are mindful that the divorced, the widowed, the gay or lesbian Catholic are hurting and feel cut off from the larger community, from the church.
3. We realize that such people need a public symbol that they belong, are wanted; that our faith community has room and indeed is in need of them.
4. Therefore, the invitation of a brief term at serving at our public liturgy in a public and recognized capacity is our gesture of acceptance, our embrace of recognition and healing.
5. We ask them to recognize that the short-term (3 months) service is not a restriction, but an expansiveness, a reach out, a symbol, and is offered wholeheartedly. (Those who are or become members may, of course, enter the regular program.)
6. We will give them training.
7. There are three criteria:
    a. Such singles must be Catholic.
    b. They must be reconciled or at least journeying toward reunion with the church if they have left.
    c. They must be striving to life a life in accordance with Christ and his church.

- -

Yes, I wish to serve as   [ ] Eucharistic Minister   [ ] Usher   [ ] Lector

Name_____Phone_____

Highway 34 & Phalanx Road, P.O. Box H, Colts Neck, N.J. 07722-0076   (908) 780-2666

SAINT MARY'S PARISH

"A Christian Community in the Roman Catholic Tradition"

Agape

Dear Friends,

As you know, it has long been our parish custom to have an Agape or mini-breakfast after all the Sunday Masses on the last Sunday of the month.

To make such a community affair easy and comfortable, the hands of many people are needed. Hence this letter. We need your help.

Would you and the other families whose names we have listed take care of the Mass written in below? It's easy. Let me tell you first what "helping" is not. It does not mean that (1) you have to order the buns, coffee and cider. We do that. (2) It does not mean that you have to set up the fix the tables. We do that.

What helping *does* mean is that after Mass (1) you refill the coffee and milk containers and check the buns and (2) you serve the people (pouring coffee and cider for them). Period. The people at the last Mass tidy up a bit but that's all.

I realize that the time and date listed here may not be convenient and either you may wish to change to another date or cancel altogether because of the conflict. But if you could help, all of us would be most grateful.

Please call the parish office (780-2666) within a week to let us know.

Many thanks for considering this, for being a part of St. Mary's.

Sincerely yours,

Father Bausch

Date _____ Mass time _____ People working with you:

_____

Highway 34 & Phalanx Road, P.O. Box H, Colts Neck, N.J. 07722 - 0076   (908) 780-2666

SAINT MARY'S PARISH

"A Christian Community in the Roman Catholic Tradition"

Thanksgiving Food Packers

May, 1994

Dear Friends,

St. Mary's has a long tradition of helping people in many ways through counseling, financial assistance, food collections, clothing drives, and the like.

One of the more open generosities of our people is the way they donate large quantities of food at holiday time, especially at Thanksgiving. It is this holiday I'd like to ask you about.

People do in fact give such large quantities of food that it is a challenge to sort and bag it all. But many hands make light work -- a work we do in our parish hall on the Sunday before Thanksgiving, this year, November 20th.

I am asking if you and your family would be free to give a hour of your time after your usual Mass by coming back to the parish hall and helping sort and bag the food so the needy can have it in time for Thanksgiving.

I know that this request might be an imposition and you may not even be available, but if you could give that one hour, many families will be grateful and you would have added to the spirit of the parish and the spirit of the gospel.

Please call the parish office this week (780-2666) and let us know if you and your family are free to give an hour on Sunday, November 20th and what Mass you expect to attend. Thanks very much for your attention. Have a relaxing and restful summer.

Sincerely yours,

Fr. Bausch

Father Bausch

SAINT MARY'S PARISH

"A Christian Community in the Roman Catholic Tradition"

Food Deliverers

Dear Friends,

As you know, our parish has a long tradition of helping many people through counseling, financial assistance, clothing drives, food collections, frozen meals and the like.

One of our consistent generosities is that monthly food collection when people come and lay food and paper goods in the sanctuary before Mass on the last Sunday of the month. We do have people to carry such goods to the Sharing Shed, but from there we need help.

We need help in getting much needed food and clothing to the poor. We can take care of Lunch Break, Paul's Place and the Freehold center, but we need help in getting such things to the Sisters of Mercy Mercy Center in Asbury Park which caters to the poor elderly on fixed incomes.

So -- I am asking you *for one time only* if you would haul food to the Mercy Center, about 20 minutes away, anytime during the week I have checked off between 9:00 a.m. and 4:00 p.m.? (See the other side of this paper).

You can contact Kathy Mogensen (780-2666) and she'll supply directions and any other information you need.

I realize that you may not be able to do so or want to take another month, but if you could help, many people would benefit from your kindness. Please call the parish office within the week (780-2666) and let us know.

Thanks for considering this and for being a part of St. Mary's.

Sincerely yours,

Father Bausch

Can you help anytime during the week of :

[ ] September 25, 1994   [ ] October 30, 1994   [ ] November 27, 1994

[ ] December 18, 1994   [ ] January 29, 1995   [ ] February 26, 1995

[ ] March 26, 1995   [ ] April 30, 1995   [ ] May 28, 1995

[ ] June 25, 1995   [ ] July 30, 1995   [ ] August 27, 1995

General Resources

In the course of this manual I have listed many resources that are helpful to the parish. Let me list a few more here. Some are modest in cost, others more expensive. Several parishes may want to share such resources or pass them on when they're through. This list, along with those in the text, is hardly exhaustive, but it contains samples of what is available.

Publishing Services, United States Catholic Conference, 3211 Fourth Street, N.E., Washington, D.C. 20017. These publications are excellent. The people who produce them are savvy and right on the mark. Anything from this source is quality. Send for their catalogue.

National Association of Church Personnel Administrators, 100 East Eight Street, Cincinnati, OH 45202. Offers a host of resources on practical administrative matters.

Princeton Research Center, P.O. Box 389, Princeton, NJ 08542. Ongoing surveys from Gallup on religious matters.

Liturgy Training Publications, 1800 North Hermitage Avenue, Chicago, IL 60622. Just what it says. Fine work.

Leadership. P.O. Box 11681, Des Moines, IA 50340. A Protestant magazine offers good ideas and topics for all.

Origins. Catholic News Service. 3211 Fourth Street, N.E., Washington, D.C. 20017. Documentations that keep you up to date.

Catholic Trends. A four-page newsletter from the above service.

Crux, 3 Enterprise Drive, Albany, NY 12204. Newsletter.

Church, a superior magazine from the National Pastoral Life Center. In depth articles. 229 Elizabeth Street, New York, NY 10012. Check, too, their "Do & Don't" pamphlets to be given to cantors, songleaders, eucharistic ministers, lectors, etc. Bulk prices.

Today's Parish. Twenty-Third Publications, P.O. Box 180, Mystic, CT 06355. A monthly magazine for parish staff on pastoral and liturgical matters. Practical and solid.

Index

Note: This index covers pages 1–186, not the Parish Papers.

Other Books by Bill Bausch...

While You Were Gone
A Handbook for Returning Catholics*
*And Those Thinking About It
Bausch's tone is informative and non-threatening as he welcomes Catholics returning to the church after an absence, as well as those new to the Catholic faith.

ISBN: 0-89622-575-5, 112 pp, $5.95

More Telling Stories, Compelling Stories
Bausch captures the essence of the lectionary readings and makes them relevant to the Christian assembly today.

ISBN: 0-89622-534-8, 176 pp, $9.95

Telling Stories, Compelling Stories
35 Stories of People of Grace
Bausch illuminates the Gospels with examples of people from the past and present living fully as Christians.

ISBN: 0-89622-456-2, 192 pp, $9.95

Timely Homilies
The Wit and Wisdom of an Ordinary Pastor
Bausch demonstrates his driving commitment to helping people live God's Word in today's world.

ISBN: 0-89622-426-0, 176 pp, $9.95

Storytelling
Imagination and Faith
Bausch taps a treasured wellspring of stories from the masters of antiquity to anonymous authors of more recent days.

ISBN: 0-89622-199-7, 232 pp, $7.95

Pilgrim Church
A Popular History of Catholic Christianity
General readers will enjoy this concise and comprehensive study of the history of Catholicism.

ISBN: 0-89622-395-7, 480 pp, $12.95

A New Look at the Sacraments
Traces the history and development of the seven sacraments from a pastoral perspective.

ISBN: 0-89622-174-1, 306 pp, $7.95

Available at religious bookstores or from

TWENTY-THIRD PUBLICATIONS
P.O. Box 180 • Mystic, CT 06355

1-800-321-0411